Dynamic Security

Community, Culture and Change series

A Culture of Enquiry
Research Evidence and the Therapeutic Community
Edited by Jan Lees, Nick Manning, Diana Menzies and Nicola Morant
ISBN-13: 9 781 85302 857 1   ISBN-10: 1 85302 857 6

Dangerous and Severe – Process, Programme and Person
Grendon's Work
Mark Morris
ISBN-13: 9 781 84310 226 7   ISBN-10: 1 84310 226 9

Thinking About Institutions
Milieux and Madness
R.D. Hinshelwood
Foreword by Nick Manning
ISBN-13: 9 781 85302 954 7   ISBN-10: 1 85302 954 8

of related interest

Constructive Work with Offenders
Edited by Kevin Gorman, Marilyn Gregory, Michelle Hayles and Nigel Parton
ISBN-13: 9 781 84310 345 5   ISBN-10: 1 84310 345 1

Reparation and Victim-focused Social Work
Edited by Brian Williams
ISBN-13: 9 781 84310 023 2   ISBN-10: 1 84310 023 1
Research Highlights in Social Work 42

Children Who Commit Acts of Serious Interpersonal Violence
Messages for Best Practice
Edited by Ann Hagell and Renuka Jeyarajah-Dent
ISBN-13: 978 1 84310 384 4   ISBN-10: 1 84310 384 2

Finding a Different Kind of Normal
Misadventures with Asperger Syndrome
Jeanette Purkis
Foreword by Donna Williams
ISBN-13: 9 781 84310 416 2   ISBN-10: 1 84310 416 4

Dynamic Security

The Democratic Therapeutic Community in Prison

Edited by Michael Parker

Foreword by Professor John Gunn

Jessica Kingsley Publishers
London and Philadelphia

First published in 2007
by Jessica Kingsley Publishers
116 Pentonville Road
London N1 9JB, UK
and
400 Market Street, Suite 400
Philadelphia, PA 19106, USA

www.jkp.com

Library of Congress Cataloging in Publication Data
A CIP catalog record for this book is available from the Library of Congress

British Library Cataloguing in Publication Data
A CIP catalogue record for this book is available from the British Library

ISBN-13: 978 1 84310 385 1
ISBN-10: 1 84310 385 0

Printed and bound in Great Britain by
Athenaeum Press, Gateshead, Tyne and Wear

Contents

Method and Practice

Psychodynamic Aspects: Inside Forensic Therapy

Managing the Therapeutic Community

Audit and Experience

Foreword

This important book should be read by anyone who has an interest in crime, the prevention of crime, or in prisons. It could also usefully be read by those who are interested in the social origins of crime. It should be required reading for both politicians who purport to take an interest in crime and those in government who are responsible for the allocation of research funds and who at the moment shamefully neglect matters crucial to the public wellbeing such as criminology, psychology and psychiatry.

Murray *et al.* in Chapter 1 give an overview of the external factors leading to crime with useful references to some of the research behind current social theories of crime. Ormsby rightly draws attention to the poor mental health of prisoners, their high suicide rates, and the strong association between drug dependency and crime. The social factors and the psychiatric factors behind crime have been known for many years, for example in repeated surveys in my old department (Gunn *et al.* 1978; Gunn *et al.* 1991). We pointed out, on more than one occasion, these excesses and the need for at least one-third of the prison population to have active psychiatric treatment and for well over 1000 prisoners to be transferred to hospital beds in the National Health Service (NHS). Very little has been done to tackle either the social problems outlined or the psychiatric factors, even though recently the NHS has taken over responsibility for prison healthcare.

One very important counterbalance to this gloomy picture has been the development of therapeutic communities (TCs) within British prisons. As the three chapters of this book outlining the history of the TC in prison indicate, this development has hardly been an overkill. Grendon prison opened in July 1962 and as far as I know remained the only TC in British prisons until the opening of a second TC at Wormwood Scrubs prison, which was introduced by Dr Max Glatt in the early 1970s as a means of helping prisoners dependent on drugs and alcohol. He said 'I felt frustrated because the little that could be attempted during individual or group sessions once or twice weekly seemed to become lost during the 24 hours a day in a custodial nontherapeutic atmosphere' (Glatt 1974, p.56).

The difficulty of sustaining and indeed increasing the number of therapeutic environments in prisons is well described here. This points to serious attitudinal problems in our society. TCs tend to be more expensive than ordinary prison environments and the public mantra 'why should we spend more than the minimum on these people who have committed crimes' reigns supreme. Those of us who have worked and published in this field have not succeeded in persuading journalists, politicians, or the general public that enlightened self-interest requires some investment and that total hostility to our offender population may be more expensive, especially in emotional and physical damage.

Our detailed study of Grendon prison (Gunn *et al.* 1978) showed, with a reasonable matched control design, that the TC made significant changes in prisoners' attitudes and mental state. The problem we were faced with, in our discussions behind the scenes within the Home Office, when trying to convince officials to keep Grendon and indeed develop other such prisons, was the constant cry that the prison doesn't reduce reconviction rates. We pointed out that reconviction rates are not a good measure of the efficacy of a closed prison environment, if anything reconviction rates are a measure of after-care services. This cut little or no ice and prisoners were discharged from Grendon straight back to the criminogenic environments they had come from. Grendon prison officers often went beyond their call of duty to assist ex-Grendon prisoners who had run into trouble following discharge and who telephoned the only supportive friend they knew.

Matters have improved since then and Miller tells us in Chapter 9 that a whole new philosophy of after-care was developed in 2001 (i.e. 39 years after the development of the TC model). The arrangements he describes seem eminently sensible and likely to work. The sixty four thousand dollar question remains: 'do they work?' Here we are back to the earlier point that research, plenteous and sophisticated, is required. We need to know the crude overall success rates but we also need to examine in some detail the individual failures that will inevitably occur, to devise adjustments that will reduce the number of failures. This will require money, it will require scientific personnel, and it will require a proactive policy on the part of government.

It is difficult to unravel the complexities of Treasury figures, but by searching the Internet for British research budgets I have discovered figures that suggest that the British Government spends between £2.1 billion and £2.4 billion on defence research, and just over £2.2 billion on 'science' research. In the 2003–2004 science budget the Medical Research Council (MRC) was allocated £415 million, and the Education and Social Science Research Council (ESRC) was allocated just under £100 million. £67 million was spent on research and £26 million on postgraduate training. The Department of Health has allocated overall some £650 million in 2005–2006 for policy research programmes and NHS research and development (R&D). The NHS R&D programme, which aims to identify NHS needs for research and to commission research to meet those needs, is only £100 million. My best guess from the 2003–2004 Home Office accounts is that just under £30 million are spent on research development and statistics.

These figures are approximate but they give some idea of Government priorities. The £2-plus billion spent on defence research is only just a little less than the rest of the science budget put together. The sums of money allocated to mental health research, and particularly to forensic psychiatry research by HM Government are minuscule. Similarly, the small Home Office budget can only allocate a small amount of money to crime prevention and to the treatment of offenders. It is pretty clear that we take external defence seriously; it would be an enormous step forward in public security, health, and happiness if we took internal defence (i.e. defence against crime) as seriously. Of course, we will be told that terrorism is now a big priority but this is partly external defence and overall is a small part of the total crime problem.

To end where I began, I hope that this book will be read by a wide audience that includes politicians with purse-strings as well as those of us who are interested in the reduction of crime by scientific and therapeutic means.

John Gunn, Emeritus Professor of Forensic Psychiatry
King's College London and Royal College of Psychiatrists

References

Glatt, M. (1974) Letter to the British Medical Journal. *British Medical Journal*, ii, 56.

Gunn, J., Maden, T. and Swinton, M. (1991) Treatment needs of prisoners with psychiatric disorders. *British Medical Journal, August 10, 303*, 338–341.

Gunn, J., Robertson, G., Dell, S. and Way, C. (1978) *Psychiatric Aspects of Imprisonment.* London and New York: Academic Press.

Acknowledgements

I would like to acknowledge the help and learning I have been fortunate to gain from staff members and residents at the Henderson Hospital, Greenwoods Therapeutic Community and Grendon's A-Wing therapeutic community (TC) in the past. They have taught me how TCs might work and pointed out to me some of my many mistakes. Particular thanks are due to Dr Stuart Whitely for his steady interest, support and kindness to me during my years working in TCs. Also to David Jones at Grendon for providing inspiration to begin the process of trying to write about the work we do in prison democratic TCs. Thanks must go to Gill for her patience and understanding in tolerating my spending the time necessary to collect chapters together into this book and particularly to Rex Haigh and Jan Lees for including this volume in their series on TCs. For patiently waiting for the book to be completed, thanks must go to Jessica Kingsley. Most recently thanks are due to Brian Ritchie, Governor of Send Prison, which now hosts the women's TC, and to the staff of Send, who had the community suddenly thrust upon them, for their remarkable patience and foresight in understanding some of the inevitable early difficulties of starting a new community.

Introduction

This volume of chapters focuses on the combination of activities that are needed to run a democratic therapeutic community (TC) in prison. This combination includes management of the communities; assessing need and risk of re-offending; conducting targeted and focused therapy work within therapy groups; the provision of clinical supervision for the therapy work undertaken all contained together within the setting of a predictable and suitable structure and timetable in which offending behaviour-focussed work can be combined effectively with attention to the emotional life of the Community. It may be important to add that such work can, by its nature, be felt to be intrusive into the mental and emotional life of offenders and of staff, and so must be conducted with the greatest respect, compassion and decency. There are major exclusions from this volume and there is no attempt made to include research into TC effectiveness. This has been ably drawn together by John Shine (2000) into a volume dealing with research conducted at Grendon's TCs. Other prison TCs have not yet reached the point of completing and publishing research. Essential additions to the overall integrity of TC work such as the contributions made by education, psychodrama, art therapy, work, faith activities, music therapy and probation work in through-care are also excluded for reasons of space but have been described elsewhere (Cordess and Cox 2002; Welldon and Van Velsen 1997). The specific skills of Programmes such as Enhanced Thinking Skills and the Sex Offender Treatment Programme can also be integral to the multi-disciplinary nature of TC work and are also described more fully elsewhere (McGuire 1995; Marshall *et al.* 1999; McGuire 2002).

The book begins with a section of three chapters looking at the theory of criminality. Chapter 1, Social Factors and Crime, by Joseph Murray,

Leonidas Cheliotis and Shadd Maruna from the Institute of Criminology at Cambridge, makes wide reference to research and criminology theory, but particularly to the Cambridge Study, a longitudinal research project, still ongoing, conducted by Cambridge University's Department of Criminology. This study has helped clarify key factors which, if present, indicate an increased likelihood of offending and represent criminogenic risk factors. It identifies: poor parental child rearing, parental conflict, broken homes, family poverty, larger-sized families, and criminal parents as factors that tend to predict boys' as well as girls'delinquency. The overall experience of socialization seems more important than isolated incidents of difficulty or abuse, and, parental disharmony and harsh or inconsistent discipline appear to be particularly important factors in the generation of delinquency. In a clear and accessible review Chapter 2 – Psychiatric Factors in Criminality, by Jim Ormsby, points out that risk factors for psychiatric disorder may be shared risk factors for criminality. Also that amphetamines, cannabis and cocaine can cause psychotic illness and are psychotogenic, in contrast to opioids, which do not appear to share this property. Substance misuse stands out in this chapter as a clear criminogenic risk factor and heightened risk is also associated with the immediate post-release period from prison. More broadly, the prison population has far higher rates of mental illness generally and particularly in the diagnostic groups neurosis (76 per cent of women and 59 per cent of men) and personality disorder (78 per cent of men and 50 per cent of women). There is a strong argument from Jo Day in Chapter 3, Psychological Theories of Criminality, for a number of genetic factors pre-disposing individuals towards criminal behaviour but the social learning model is found to be most convincing, in which attitudes and behaviour modelled become learned and develop into established and patterned behaviour traits that tend to repeat over time: how else could we have arrived at the concept offence-paralleling behaviour? This phenomenon describes offending behaviour that repeats in a problematic way over time and across different social settings and among different sets of people, and it is these patterns that are identified and targeted for work in therapy.

Tim Newell, long associated with prison TC work and restorative justice in the community, describes in Chapter 4, The Historical Development of the UK Democratic Therapeutic Community. He describes the early beginnings of therapy in prison in the 1930s at Wormwood Scrubs, when psychiatrists believed something needed to be done about particular problematic groups of prisoners: those who were diagnosed psychopathic; those who were more than usually vulnerable, and those with adjustment problems who were difficult to manage in prison. From these discussions the plan for Grendon was developed, including provision for women and young offenders within the same broad remit. Chapter 5, Send: The Women's Democratic Therapeutic Community in Prison, by Caroline Stewart and Michael Parker, attempts to address the gap in writing about women's experiences of therapy in prison but intentionally excludes detailed reference to clinical work, as the community is still in its formative stages of development, or reference to research for the same reason. The chapter comments on the development of the first women's democratic TC and the difficulties encountered in starting a new community. It describes how the Women's Team in Prison Service Headquarters commissioned research into the needs of women in prison and set about creating a TC to help address them, based on new evidence about women's criminogenic risk factors and needs in prison. All current prison TCs are based in Maxwell Jones' model and in its early days Grendon sent its staff to the Henderson Hospital's annual Group Work Course to train in TC practice. After long experience working with and knowing Maxwell Jones, founder of the Henderson Hospital in the 1950s, Dennie Briggs in Chapter 6, Serendipity or Design? Therapeutic Community History and Maxwell Jones's Theory, attempts to pin down the theory Jones based his work on. He finds that being pinned down, or becoming rigid or fixed was something Maxwell Jones very specifically felt was not helpful to TCs but that they needed to remain capable of change and adaptation over time to circumstances not yet foreseen. Dennie Briggs identifies this capacity to move, adapt, re-think and change to suit new circumstances as the very thing that does characterize Maxwell Jones' method and thought throughout his working life and his theory, clearly a mobile one, is contained within the capacity to change and adapt. Above all, his determination to remain in a questioning and facilitative role so that others can learn, grow and develop must be one of his most important contributions to TC thinking.

Richard Shuker and David Jones in a tightly argued format, Chapter 7, Assessing Risk and Need in a Prison Therapeutic Community: An Integrative Model describe the move from predictive clinical models of assessment to increasingly strict actuarial risk assessment measures and back to more widely based probabilistic forms of clinical risk assessment using a multimodal approach. The authors stress the difficulties but, ultimately, the value of the team approach and the usefulness of combining many different tools in assessment, including assessment of the internal world alongside psychometric tests and the use of the Community and its impressions and viewpoint in forming a view about risk and change in therapy. They propose an integrative model in intervention and assessment using psychological, developmental, offence-related and current behavioural patterns, arguing that these can be explored in relation to each other within the community. Michael Parker in Chapter 8, Supervision of Forensic Group Therapy, attempts to catch the process of identifying patterns of behaviour and focussing the activity of placing observed behaviour into thinking and into patterns that can be named and brought into therapy. Staff's emotional response to the behaviour they are attempting to understand and contain, and its impact on them, is considered and the idea proposed that part of supervisory activity may need to include recovery and recuperation for supervisees from the sometimes destructive or sexually demanding aspects of transference they are subject to. This can easily be lost in the pressure to staff groups in order to keep the Community working. Chapter 9 is entitled, Through-care, After-care: What Happens after Therapy? Past attempts to organize through-care are described here by Alan Miller. The fact that most prisoners return to mainstream prison, 95 per cent at Dovegate, has influenced work at Dovegate and a specific Re-integration programme been devised to help those leaving the TC to cope with life back in mainstream prison. The chapter usefully knits the recent expectation, driven by NOMS, that education forms a core part of sentence planning and TC work is pointed out and the use of peer tutors to help this task is stressed. The chapter describes how to blend OASys, Programmes, TC, and Systemic Family Work together to maximize gains in therapy and adds an interesting perspective on the use of SOTP in Grendon and Dovegate.

The next series of chapters describe the influence of the past in present behaviour and the tendency towards regression in therapy but approaches the question how to harness this to useful effect in therapy? In Chapter 10, 'We used to make a football out of a goat head': Working with Young Offenders in a Prison Therapeutic Community, Teresa Wood outlines the importance of staff modelling socially acceptable behaviour to young offenders and being good enough role models is prioritized. The involvement necessary to do this effectively is underpinned by a need to demonstrate real care and concern about young offenders and their lives. Without these two attributes of good enough modelling and real concern, neither treatment nor containment of young people is likely to be effective. The author highlights young offenders' propensity to act rather than speak their difficulties and points the way to successful treatment as including a multimodal approach using creative arts-based activities as well as engagement in therapy and with the community as a whole. Ronald Doctor in Chapter 11, A Schema for the Transition from Cruel Object to Tender Object Relations Among Drug Users in a Prison Therapeutic Community, proposes the concept of a transference addiction within which can be explored the characteristic splitting and manic-depressive style alternation within the transference between idealization and violent rejection and hatred of the drug, or therapist-as-drug, in transference. It is pointed out that men were required to forgo parole in order to complete sufficient time in therapy in The Max Glatt Unit, Wormwood Scrubs; this is the Unit this chapter is based in and it is sad to note that the Unit was closed in recent years. The typical prison culture of aggression and bravado is described as a problem to contend with but behind which it may be possible to access more real and often vulnerable feeling states that lie behind what may amount to powerful defences of aggression and criminality. In Chapter 12, Internal World, External Reality: From Fantasy to Reality in Violent Offending, Liz McLure illustrates through a vivid clinical example the near re-enactment of Lenny's index offence within the community and therapy group after emotions were stirred up during a Family Day at Grendon. The need for staff and fellow residents to be able to explore difficult fantasies with those in therapy in depth is described. Also explored is the idea that fantasies of grievance, persecution and revenge may have become both ego-syntonic and self-serving but also hold a defensive function that therapy may be able to help modify and change. Work in the Prison Service to help life-sentenced prisoners come to terms with the fact of their sentence while in Stage one, the early part of the life sentence, is described in Chapter 13, Changing a Life Sentence into a Life. Judy Mackenzie points out that the Gartree Thera-peutic Community has a philosophy that includes the possibility of redemp-tion and that the point of such early work in a long sentence is partly to help prisoners adjust to life in prison at a time often characterized by denial and sometimes violent acting out. If therapy is built on the solid ground of trust and a suitable culture and structure, then risk assessment and a more realistic focus on the reality of the offence can be accessed and worked with even earlier in the sentence and arguably progress in later sentence to become more balanced and productive. The repetition compulsion, a very old term coined by Freud is briefly explored by Michael Parker in Chapter 14, Repeating Patterns: Sexual Abuse, Sexualized Internal Working Models and Sexual Offending, in relation to clinical examples of sexual offenders who have been abused and who describe in therapy similarities between their own experience of being abused and the pattern of their behaviour in their index offence. The shock that sexual assault holds for the public may make it difficult to think with interest about the antecedent life history and personal narrative of sexual offenders and why they may commit the crimes they do, and yet this is what must be done to begin to understand why they do what they do. An example is given of offence re-enactment within the transference in the therapy group setting and how difficult it can be to detect such repeti-tions when they are powerful, subtle and strongly defended against. The idea of putting aside time and thought to understand the offender's narrative in his or her own style and meaning is an essential part of any reconstructive therapy and, interestingly, is similar to Shadd Maruna's (2001) recently described ideas of desisters, once repeat offenders, 'making good'. The way in which desisters had been able to build stories about themselves that made sense of their lives to themselves seemed to be essential to the process of their 'making good' and desisting from further offending, as we hope those in therapy will do as they make sense of their lives and regain control, through thinking, in therapy.

In the section on management of the TC, Peter Bennett begins by describing in Chapter 15, Governing Grendon Prison's Therapeutic Communities: The Big Spin, the tension between functions that can materialize and be all too typical of organizational life in the Health and Prison Services. 'The big spin', a prison-wide search for a missing tool early in the life of the new Governor of Grendon, came to symbolize a clash of ideology or power between therapy and security staff responsible for ensuring delivery of the mandatory security rules and regulations in the prison. The argument appeared to be about who gives way to whom and who runs the establishment: which ideology holds pre-eminence? This is an honest and revealing account, seldom seen in the literature but all too often experienced in the workplace and avoided, and it will doubtless provoke controversy but certainly illustrates the very kinds of tensions and disputes that occur in prison TCs and which can affect the overall sense of safety or containment that characterizes the community's working environment. In Chapter 16, Directing Therapy in the Prison Democratic Therapeutic Community, Mark Morris sets out four pillars of therapeutic management for directors of therapy, namely: leadership, ambassadorial, research and gladiatorial roles necessary to keep TCs afloat. Based on experience at Grendon, the author argues in a natural and free-flowing way the importance of these four pillars and of the necessity of creating networks of professional colleagues and of the need to be able to adapt to the inevitable changes created by the external managerial environment. Roland Woodward describes TCs in non-TC environments in Chapter 17, Symbiosis: Therapeutic Communities within Non-therapeutic Community Organizations. This chapter describes the wide and varied role a TC manager has to fulfil and highlights three functions as crucial to this: that of container of anxiety; minder of the unconscious processes driving the organization and lastly, representing the TC language and meaning to the wider organization. The host organization needs to be credited with its valuable contribution where appropriate and worked with closely to avoid the characteristic splits and divisions that can overcome a TC overpreoccupied with its own sense of importance. In Chapter 18, Security and Dynamic Security in a Therapeutic Community Prison, Kevin Leggett and Brian Hirons describe changes in the relationship between the Security department and the therapy teams in one example as moving from conflict to a more collaborative position through the restructuring of senior management team meetings. This is a critical area for the survival of TCs and getting this relationship right for TC managers needs to be placed in their top priority draw. Rather than operate split, the authors point to the need for therapy and security to work collaboratively on matters of safety and threat but still be able to preserve the confidentiality of personal detail. This relationship is illustrated with changes in the use of security information reports.

The next section concerns audit and experience. Experiences from therapy are described in Chapter 19. The four accounts given, which remain anonymous to preserve the confidentiality of offenders and victims, two by men and two by women who have been in therapy for substantial periods of time, say something of the combined thinking and emotional impact that takes place as a result of therapy in prison. Their own words best describe their experiences and they do so with a real conviction about their involvement in what is clearly a difficult but hopefully worthwhile undertaking. It is hoped that they give an idea of the depth and complexity of work in therapy and particularly of the past–present behaviour linkage that is necessary in combined psychotherapeutically and cognitively informed therapy. It may be helpful in future to see more accounts of therapy from the inside of this kind in the TC field. Finally, Danny Clark and Jan Lees in Chapter 20, Auditing of Prison Service Accredited Interventions, describe the shaping of an audit model in which joint work between the Association of Therapeutic Communities and the Prison Service has resulted in a specific audit process for prison TCs. This process joins together the Prison Service's need to address offending behaviour and elicit evidence that offending behaviour work is being done effectively within the Service Standards for TCs. This is a major development and the result of a great deal of work by the Community of Communities, which sets out a demanding self-audit tool for prison TCs, which now have a pass or fail standard to achieve. Perhaps the most difficult component is that of the test of efficacy in tackling offending behaviour and being sure that this is done within the therapy work itself. The chapter outlines the combined approach to auditing this process.

It is hoped this book approaches the clinical inside of therapy a little more closely, as this is where, arguably, change and transformation take place but also where great difficulty, anger and resistance are found. This book also attempts to consider a little more how to deal with such difficulties, think about them without retaliation and cope with them emotionally in the day-to-day business that is work in a democratic TC in prison.

References

Cordess, C. and Cox, M. (2002) *Forensic Psychotherapy: Crime, Psychodynamics and the Offender Patient.* London and Philadelphia: Jessica Kingsley Publishers.

Marshall, W. L., Anderson, D. and Fernandez, Y. (1999) *Cognitive Behavioural Treatment of Sexual Offenders.* Chichester: John Wiley & Sons Ltd.

Maruna, S. (2001) *Making Good: How Ex-Convicts Reform and Rebuild Their Lives,* 3rd edn. Washington DC: American Psychological Association.

McGuire, J. (1995) *What Works: Reducing Re-offending.* Chichester: John Wiley and Sons Ltd.

McGuire, J. (2002) *Offender Rehabilitation and Treatment: Effective Programmes and Policies to Reduce Re-offending.* Chichester: John Wiley & Sons Ltd.

Shine, J. (ed.) (2000) *A Compilation of Grendon Research.* Gloucester: Leyhill Press.

Welldon, E. V. and Van Velsen, C. (1997) *A Practical Guide to Forensic Psychotherapy.* London: Jessica Kingsley Publishers.

Theory: Origins of Criminal Behaviour

Chapter 1

Social Factors and Crime

Joseph Murray, Leonidas Cheliotis and Shadd Maruna

Contemporary therapeutic communities (TCs) aspire to reform offenders by addressing their social, as well as psychological needs. This chapter critically reviews evidence on childhood socialization experiences that predict criminality and later family and employment factors that predict persistence in or desistance from crime. These research findings may be of relevance to TCs seeking to employ an empirically driven approach to offending behaviour work in therapy.

This chapter provides an overview of current evidence and theory regarding social factors and crime. *Social* factors refer to environmental influences that are outside the individual. By this definition, factors such as individual temperament, personality and IQ are excluded from our review. In doing so, we purposefully neglect over 100 years' worth of research on biological and psychological theories of crime. This neglect should not be understood as a rejection of individual-level explanations for criminality on the part of the authors. To the contrary, a comprehensive theory of crime ought to include individual factors, environmental influences, and the interaction between the two. However, over the last 50 years, there has been growing appreciation of the importance of social influences on criminality, and this will be the subject of this chapter.

Social factors have many different levels and types of influence on the individual (Brofenbrenner 1979). Because of limited space, we focus on social factors at the 'micro level'. These are the social interactions that are immediately experienced by individuals and that are most likely to factor into psychotherapeutic or resettlement practice. We will limit our review to three key aspects of social experience: relationships with the family of origin, family relations in later life, and employment[1]. Two social factors that we exclude from this review, but that have received considerable research attention in criminology, are neighbourhood influences and peer factors[2].

We will draw many of our conclusions from evidence collected in 'longitudinal' studies, which follow the same individuals over time, and make it possible to identify social (and individual) factors that predict later criminal behaviour. There are important limitations to these findings. First, prediction of criminal behaviour is not deterministic: social factors are rarely accurate in predicting who will, and who will not, commit crime in the future. Second, even when prediction is relatively good, this does not imply a cause-and-effect relationship. The main problem for identifying a causal relationship is that so many social factors tend to occur together. For example, even though low family income predicts criminality, poverty is associated with many other social factors, making it difficult to disentangle which is the active ingredient in producing crime (Rutter et al. 1998).

There are various methodological approaches to disentangling causes from confounding effects (Shadish et al. 2002). However, one important criterion for suggesting that a predictor causes criminal behaviour is that there is a plausible theoretical link between the two. If there is no credible theory linking the hypothetical cause with its effect, then it is less plausible that the relationship is causal. A number of criminological theories have suggested explanations for the links between social factors and crime. In this review, we focus primarily on criminological theories of strain, social learning, and social bonding/control to explain the empirical findings (Vold et al. 2002). First, we review childhood predictors of crime, including family factors of child rearing, parental conflict and disrupted families, poverty, and family criminality. Second, we review adult family and employment factors related to criminality.

---

1   For a comprehensive, book-length review on antisocial behaviour (including many of the topics covered here) the reader is referred to Rutter et al. (1998).

2   For a review of the literature on neighbourhood effects and criminality, see Bottoms and Wiles (1997); for a discussion of peer effects, see Warr (2002).

Childhood predictors of criminality

The most influential, longitudinal study of offending in the UK is the Cambridge Study in Delinquent Development (hereafter referred to as the Cambridge Study), which has followed the lives and criminal careers of over 400 London boys from age 8–48 (Farrington 2003). The main childhood predictors of crime identified in the Cambridge Study include: poor parental child rearing, parental conflict, broken homes, family poverty, larger-sized families, and criminal parents. These and similar childhood experiences have been identified in many other longitudinal studies (Loeber and Stouthamer-Loeber 1986) and have been found to predict girls' delinquency as well as that of boys (Moffitt et al. 2001).

Child rearing

Lack of parental supervision (monitoring of children's activities) is one of the strongest family predictors of children's later criminal behaviour (Loeber et al. 1986). Harsh or inconsistent discipline of children also predicts later-life criminality. In the Cambridge Study, 27 per cent of boys who had very strict or erratic and inconsistent discipline became delinquent, compared to 16 per cent of boys who experienced other disciplinary methods (West and Farrington 1973). Other longitudinal studies also show that harsh discipline (using physical punishment) predicts children's delinquency (Haapasalo and Pokela 1999). In 1989, Cathy Widom published a seminal paper, 'The Cycle of Violence', which showed that experiencing abuse and neglect as a child increased the risk of juvenile and adult arrests (including, but not exclusively, for violence). However, to date, research has not distinguished the effects of abuse from chronic psychosocial adversities that often accompany abuse, and the causal effects of abuse on offending are unclear. Rutter and his colleagues (1998) conclude that the general climate of the home environment) appears to be more influential than any isolated instances of abuse, suggesting that the 'abusive episode itself probably does not provide the main risk' (p.188).

There are several mechanisms that might link poor child-rearing practices and delinquency. According to Patterson's coercion theory, harsh and inconsistent discipline provokes a cycle of aversive reactions between parents and children: '[Following] parental failure to be contingent ... families produce children who are both socially unskilled and extremely coercive' (Patterson 1995, p.92). During coercive cycles, children learn antisocial behaviour as an effective means to stop aversive experiences and, at the same time, fail to learn prosocial skills and behaviours. Through these processes, children develop an antisocial trait that becomes self-sustaining through events and reinforcements outside the home. Alternatively, social bonding theory (Hirschi 1969) suggests that ineffective child rearing predicts delinquency because children without close attachments to warm and loving parents (and other social 'controls') do not have the same stakes in conformity. That is, they do not perceive the same costs to antisocial behaviour (broken social bonds, social disapproval or shame). Sampson and Laub argue that both the direct effects of child rearing (hypothesized in Patterson's coercion theory) and the indirect controls (hypothesized by social bonding theory) account for the link between poor child rearing and delinquency, because 'direct parental controls are likely to be positively related to relational, indirect controls' (Sampson and Laub 1993, p.67).

Parental conflict and disrupted families

The idea that disrupted families predict delinquency has a long history in criminology (Bowlby 1946). However, different types of family disruption need to be distinguished. For example, homes disrupted by parental death do not predict delinquency as strongly as homes disrupted by parental disharmony (Juby and Farrington 2001). Murray and Farrington (2005) found that separation because of parental imprisonment predicted worse antisocial outcomes for boys than separation for other reasons, even after controlling for parents' criminality. However, most studies of disrupted families have focused on disruption following parental separation or divorce. In general, the risk of delinquency is approximately doubled for children from families where parents have separated compared to children from intact families (Rodgers and Pryor 1998).

Originally, it was believed that traumatic experience of parent–child separation and the disruption of attachment relations caused delinquency after parental separation (Bowlby 1946). However, life-course theories suggest that the effects of parental separation are better explained by stressful events before, during, and after parental separation. For example, McCord (1982) found that, although fatherless families predicted adult offending, there was little difference between boys who grew up in single-parent families with an affectionate mother, and boys in two-parent families with parental conflict. McCord concluded that 'the quality of the boy's home life rather than the number of parents affects crime rates' (McCord 1982, p.124). These and more recent findings (Fergusson et al. 1994; Juby and Farrington 2001), suggest that a life-course perspective best explains the relationship between parental separation and children's delinquency.

Poverty and social disadvantage

Socio-economic disadvantage in childhood is predictive of criminal behaviour in adult life. In the Cambridge Study, family poverty measured at age 8–10 was one of the six most important independent predictors of later offending (Farrington 2003). In a recent meta-analysis (combining results across different studies) family social class was one of the two strongest family predictors of serious and violent delinquency in young adulthood (Lipsey and Derzon 1998).

Different paradigms (for example, strain, socialization and genetic theories of criminality) suggest that the relationship between social disadvantage and crime could be direct, indirect or spurious. *Strain theories*, originally developed by Robert Merton, suggest that coming from a background of poverty, or low social class, directly pressurizes people to engage in crime because crime represents an alternative means to achieve social and economic 'success' (Merton 1995). According to strain theory, offenders experience a disjunction between their aspirations and expectations; crime occurs as a result of desiring conventional goals, but lacking the socially approved means to achieve them. Alternatively, *socialization theories* suggest that the relationship between crime and poverty is indirect, and is explained by the effects of economic strain on family socialization practices. In their study of 585 children from pre-school to grade three, Dodge *et al.* (1994) found that over half of the association between socio-economic status and children's aggressive behaviours was accounted for by socialization factors, including harsh discipline, exposure to aggressive adult models, and lack of maternal warmth towards the child. A third alternative is that crime and family poverty could both be explained by *genetic factors* (Rutter *et al.* 1998, pp.201–202). Some adoption studies suggest that both genetics and the environment account for the association between social class and crime, but further research is needed to examine the relationships more robustly. Therefore, although some prediction of criminal behaviour is possible on the basis of social and economic disadvantage, we cannot draw firm conclusions about the causal processes involved.

Family criminality

Parents with criminal records are more likely to have children with criminal records as well. This has been established in a number of studies: by the Gluecks in 1950, Ferguson in 1952, Wilson in 1987, McCord in 1977, and Robins in 1975 (Farrington *et al.* 1996). Although most studies have only examined the effect of parental criminality on boys' delinquency, Robins found that parental arrests were a strong predictor of girls' delinquency as well (Robins *et al.* 1975).

In the Cambridge Study, parental criminality was one of the most important predictors of later offending among the study's male participants (Farrington 2003). Of those boys whose father had a criminal conviction, 62 per cent were convicted themselves (compared to 30 per cent of boys with an unconvicted father) (Farrington *et al.* 1996). Growing up with a mother who had a criminal conviction also predicted boys' delinquency, as did growing up with convicted siblings. In Pittsburgh, PA (USA), having an arrested father, brother, sister and uncle all predicted boys' arrests, even after controlling for the six other most important predictors in the study (Farrington *et al.* 2001).

Farrington et al (2001) suggested six explanations for the inter-generational transmission of criminality:

1. intergenerational exposure to risk, e.g. parents and children might be trapped in poverty

2. offenders are likely to partner other offenders, and children with two antisocial parents are even more likely to be antisocial

3. imitation and teaching of crime

4. criminal parents tend to live in bad neighbourhoods and use poor child-rearing methods

5. genetic mechanisms

6. official (police and court) bias towards children from criminal families.

Further research is needed to test which of these or other explanations can account for the fact that crime runs in families.

Adult social factors predicting desistance

Criminologists increasingly agree that adult experiences as well as childhood backgrounds can have a significant effect on a person's criminal behaviour. It is now believed that adult experiences can affect the onset, escalation, versatility, persistence in and desistance from offending. Longitudinal and cross-sectional studies (conducted at one point in time) have tried to assess how and to what extent adult experiences such as marriage, parenthood, and employment can account for criminal behaviours. We review this evidence, drawing attention to the difficulties in establishing causal relationships, and specifying the mechanisms by which marriage, parenthood, or employment relate to crime.

Marriage

Many observers believe that criminality partly stems from weakened or broken ties to informal institutions of social control in adulthood as well as childhood. In their re-analyses of the Gluecks' data, Sampson and Laub found that, after controlling for the effects of early childhood experiences, good marital bonds (as indicated by close, warm feelings towards the spouse, and compatibility in a generally constructive relationship) explained significant variations in adult crime, regardless of the spouse's own deviant behaviour. They argued that strong marital bonds reduced criminal behaviour because marriage engenders personal 'systems of obligation and restraint' that impose significant costs for translating criminal propensities into action (Sampson and Laub 1993, p.141). There is an unmistakable note of rational choice theory in these social bonding explanations (Hirschi 1986). Individuals refrain from crime because they fear losing the 'social capital invested in their family lives' (Sampson and Laub 1993, p.141),[3] and 'because a sense of shame is enhanced when the reactions of a significant other person are considered' (Horney et al. 1995, p.70). According to these accounts, what prevents criminality is not the involvement in family per se, but rather the related changes in people's perceptions of consequences of their actions.

Taking Sampson and Laub's analysis one step further, Warr (1998) drew on differential association and social learning theories (Sutherland 1947; Akers 1990) to argue that the positive effects of marriage are due to changes in social networks. The empirical finding that supports this claim is that, following marriage, there is typically a dramatic decline in the time spent with deviant peers. Using data from a longitudinal study of 1725 Americans, Warr (1998, p.211) argued that, as crime is learned and motivated in interaction with others who share deviant norms and attitudes, transition to an intact marriage may discourage offending by 'simultaneously reducing exposure to delinquent associates, whilst increasing stakes in conformity and attachment to conventional others'. Opportunity and routine activity theories provide a similar framework to explain why adult family factors

3   Laub and Sampson borrow the term *social capital* from James Coleman (1988) to describe the investment in social relationships with law-abiding people that help individuals achieve their aims through legitimate means.

may *indirectly* prevent crime: individuals who enjoy a cohesive marriage tend to spend less time 'hanging out' on the streets or in bars, thus being presented with fewer opportunities to engage in criminal behaviour (Felson 1998, pp.25–26; Osgood *et al.* 1996).

In the Cambridge Study, Farrington and West (1995), like Warr, found that an enduring marriage at age 32 predicted lower rates of offending; conversely, separation from a wife predicted later self-reported and official offending. Getting married predicted a decrease in conviction rates relative to remaining single, whilst separation from a wife predicted an increase in conviction rates compared with staying married. Compared to separated men who lived alone, men who were still married to their first wife at age 32 were less likely to self-report offending or have a recent conviction; they were also the most 'conventional' in their self-reported lifestyle, rarely went out at night, and tended not be heavy drinkers or drug users (see also Quinton *et al.* 1993; Rutter *et al.* 1997).

However, the empirical research has not established that marriage *causes* a reduction in criminal behaviour (Maruna 2001). As Farrington and West (1995, p.279) acknowledge, it might be argued that getting or staying married is 'a symptom, a cause, and a consequence of becoming more conventional'. Laub *et al.* (1998) explain in later research that the positive effect of marriage is gradual and cumulative over time, rather than a static condition or event (see also Farrington and West 1995; Horney *et al.* 1995; Laub and Sampson 2003; Wright and Wright 1992). It is therefore imperative that future criminological research explores the strength, quality and interdependence of marital attachments on a longer-term basis. Finally, more research is needed on alternative intimate relationships and cohabitation on patterns of offending, as the institution of marriage has changed dramatically in recent years. Such research may better uncover what it is about marriage that makes it appear to be reformative (Maruna 2001).

Parenthood

The onset of parenthood has also been linked to changes in criminal behaviour. Farrington and West (1995, p.251) argue that 'having a child may have more effect than getting married on social habits associated with offending (e.g. going out drinking with male friends)', and therefore 'it is important to try to disentangle the effects of getting married from the effects of having a child'.[4] However, the evidence on this matter is scarce and inconclusive.

In 1993, Sampson and Laub reported finding no effect of parenthood on offending in the Gluecks' sample. However, their recent analysis of life history narratives suggested that, at least for some offenders, parenthood constituted a significant transition away from crime (Laub and Sampson 2003). The presence of children may increase the perceived costs of offending (e.g. shame for the parent, stigma for children: Gramsick and Bursik 1990). Also, from the perspective of differential association and routine activity theories, the care of young children should reduce individuals' exposure to criminogenic influences or situations (Osgood and Lee 1993). In Warr's study, however, although married men with children had fewer delinquent friends compared to unmarried men without children, married men who had no children also had fewer delinquent friends. Warr (1998, p.206) concluded that 'it is marriage – not the presence of children – that affects relations with friends'. Finally, from the perspective of labelling theory, Matsueda and Heimer (1997) argued that the pro-social label of being a 'good parent' can discourage criminal engagement, a view that receives support from some recent empirical studies (Giordano et al. 2002; Uggen et al. 2004).

Although parenthood is generally thought to discourage offending, it is also possible that having children could increase the likelihood of criminal involvement. This is the line taken by the advocates of strain theory (Agnew 1992), who argue that crime, particularly offences committed for financial gain, may function as a means for already disadvantaged parents to meet financial needs associated with child rearing. Whatever the viewpoint taken, further research is needed to test the overall effect of parenthood on criminality.

Employment

Unemployment has a great deal of common sense appeal as cause of criminal behaviour. In line with strain theory, it is often argued that unemployment causes economic deprivation which, in turn, increases the likelihood of crime. In a review of 63 pertinent studies, Chiricos (1987, p.203) concluded

---

4   A crucial distinction should be drawn here between parenthood within the context of marriage – which is what the vast majority of researchers address – and parenthood outside marriage. In the Cambridge Study, for example, Farrington and West (1995) found that, like separation from a wife, conceiving a child outside marriage predicted later offending independently of all other variables.

that the evidence does suggest that rates of property crime, in particular, are linked to unemployment rates (see also Box 1987; but compare Land *et al.* 1990). An American study of programmes that provide employment benefits to released prisoners in the USA concluded that, 'for ex-offenders at least, unemployment and poverty do cause crime on the microlevel.' (Berk *et al.* 1980, p.784) This link is less clear with young people, but appears particularly strong for persons over 25 years of age (Uggen 2000).

Mechanisms other than economic strain need to be considered in relation to unemployment and crime. From the social bonding perspective, Sampson and Laub (1993) focused on the effects of unemployment and job instability, on how people perceive their bonds to society. They concluded that poor job stability increases the likelihood of criminal activity and deviant behaviour; whereas, social ties embedded in adult transitions, like stable employment, explain variations in crime unaccounted for by childhood propensities' (Sampson and Laub 1993, pp.248–249). Differential association, and routine activity theories may also provide a useful framework for addressing the preventive role of employment, as the time devoted to work-related activities decreases an individual's exposure to delinquent peers or to situations conducive to crime (Horney *et al.* 1995).

In the Cambridge Study, individual crime rates were found to be higher during periods of unemployment, especially for offences involving material gain, yet this effect related only to youths with a prior high risk of delinquency (see also Farrington *et al.* 1986; Farrington 2003 and Caspi and Moffitt 1993). Therefore, as with marriage and parenthood, unemployment does not necessarily cause crime. The crime–unemployment relationship might exist just because pre-existing risk factors (e.g. adverse family background) cause both crime and unemployment, or because antisocial behaviours cause unemployment. As Rutter et al (1998, p.206) put it, 'unemployment does predispose to an increase in criminal activities by individuals already at high risk as a result of their own behaviour, characteristics, and psychosocial background'.

In recent years there has been an impressive revival of interest in the use of programmes reintegrating prisoners into the community through vocational skills training, prison-based work programmes, and, most notably, work-release schemes, in which offenders undertake paid work in free-world settings during the day, whilst spending non-working days and nights in custody. Encouragingly, a recent systematic review of the literature on the effectiveness of work-release programmes showed that such schemes can increase post-release employment rates and decrease the likelihood of re-arrest or re-incarceration, although the underlying mechanisms remain largely elusive (Cheliotis 2006, submitted). Also, research findings from the USA have consistently shown that integrated TC work-release programmes (e.g. the CREST Outreach Center in Wilmington, DE) are more effective than placement in a conventional work-release programme for a number of outcomes, for example re-incarceration, post-release frequency of drug use and post-release frequency of alcohol misuse (Inciardi *et al.* 1997; McCollister *et al.* 2003). It remains to be seen whether these positive findings will generalize to other jurisdictions.

Conclusion

In 1991, the Home Office surveyed nearly 4000 prisoners in England and Wales about their lives inside and outside of prison (Dodd and Hunter 1992). To no one's surprise, the survey revealed that those who are imprisoned disproportionately come from poor and criminal families, have few career opportunities and have a history of being in care and experiencing family problems. Criminology has long identified such social factors as key predictors of crime. Even social factors occurring early in childhood, such as types of parental discipline, or family criminality, can predict future criminal behaviour. We have emphasized caution regarding such predictive statements. Prediction is always imperfect, and it is extremely difficult to establish causality between predictors and crime. Nevertheless, there are plausible theories linking various aspects of family and work life to criminality.

What is striking about the social factors highlighted in this review is the disadvantage they reflect. Crime is a marker of many social ills. From childhood abuse, neglect, harsh physical punishment, parental conflict, parental separation, economic stress, and family criminality, through to failed marriages, stresses of parenthood, and unemployment in adulthood, crime is associated with society's many failures. Of course, many of these social failures may also be the results, not causes, of antisocial behaviour. Evidence also suggests that these social failures have an additive or cumulative effect, making it more likely crime will occur under conditions of multiple disadvantage (Sampson and Laub 1995). To the extent that crime is exacerbated by social factors, TCs might be able to help offenders break out of these coercive cycles and establish new patterns of interaction and relationship. Of course, equal attention needs to be focused on social policies designed to ameliorate family problems and unemployment to prevent criminality before this cycle begins.

References

Agnew, R. (1992) Foundation for a general strain theory of crime and delinquency. *Criminology, 30*, 47–87.

Akers, R.L. (1990) Rational choice, deterrence, and social learning theory in criminology: The path not taken. *Journal of Criminal Law and Criminology, 81*, 653–676.

Berk, R.A., Lenihan, K.J. and Rossi P.H. (1980) Crime and poverty: Some experimental evidence from ex-offenders. *American Sociological Review, 45*, 766–786.

Bottoms, A.E. and Wiles, P. (1997) Environmental criminology. In M. Maguire, R. Morgan and R. Reiner (eds) *The Oxford Handbook of Criminology*, 2nd edn. Oxford: Clarendon Press.

Bowlby, J. (1946) *Forty-Four Juvenile Thieves: Their Characters and Home-Life.* London: Baillière, Tindall & Cox.

Box, S. (1987) *Recession, Crime and Punishment.* London: Macmillan.

Brofenbrenner, U. (1979) *The Ecology of Human Development.* Cambridge, MA: Harvard University Press.

Caspi, A. and Moffitt, T.E. (1993) When do individual differences matter? A paradoxical theory of personality coherence. *Psychological Inquiry, 4*, 247–271.

Cheliotis, L.K. (2006, submitted) *Reconsidering the effectiveness of temporary release: a systematic review of the literature.*

Chiricos, T.G. (1987) Rates of crime and unemployment: an analysis of aggregate research evidence. *Social Problems, 34*, 187–212.

Coleman, J. (1988) Social capital in the creation of human capital. *American Journal of Sociology, 94*, 95–120.

Dodd, T. and Hunter, P. (1992) *The National Prison Survey 1991.* London: HMSO.

Dodge, K.A., Pettit, G.S. and Bates, J.E. (1994) Socialization mediators of the relation between socioeconomic status and child conduct problems. *Child Development, 65*, 649–665.

Farrington, D.P. (2003) Key results from the first forty years of the Cambridge Study in Delinquent Development. In T.P. Thornberry and M.D. Krohn (eds) *Taking Stock of Delinquency: An Overview of Findings from Contemporary Longitudinal Studies.* New York: Kluwer Academic/Plenum.

Farrington, D.P. and West, D.J. (1995) 'The effects of marriage, separation, and children on offending by adult males.' In Z. Smith Blau and J. Hagan (eds) *Current Perspectives on Aging and Life Cycle*, Vol. 4, *Delinquency and Disrepute in the Life Course.* Greenwich: JAI Press.

Farrington, D.P., Barnes, G.C. and Lambert, S. (1996) The concentration of offending in families. *Legal and Criminological Psychology, 1*, 47–63.

Farrington, D.P., Gallagher, B., Morley, L., St. Ledger, R.J. and West, D.J. (1986) Unemployment, school leaving and crime. *British Journal of Criminology, 26*, 335–356.

Farrington, D.P., Jolliffe, D., Loeber, R., Stouthamer-Loeber, M. and Kalb, L.M. (2001) The concentration of offenders in families, and family criminality in the prediction of boys' delinquency. *Journal of Adolescence, 24*, 579–596.

Felson, M. (1998) *Crime & Everyday Life*, 2nd edn. Thousand Oaks: Pine Forge.

Fergusson, T. (1952) *The Young Delinquent in his Social Setting.* London: Oxford University Press.

Fergusson, D.M., Horwood, J. and Lynsky (1994) Parental separation, adolescent psychopathology, and problem behaviours. *Journal of the American Academy of Child and Adolescent Psychiatry, 33*, 8, 1122–1133.

Giordano, P.C., Cernkovich, S.A. and Rudolph, J.L. (2002) Gender, crime and desistance: Toward a theory of cognitive transformation. *American Journal of Sociology, 107*, 990–1064.

Glueck, S. and Glueck, E. (1950) Unravelling Juvenile Delinquency. New York: The Commonwealth Fund.

Gramsick, H.G. and Bursik, R.J. (1990) Conscience, significant others, and rational choice: Extending the deterrence model. Law and Society Review, 24, 837–860.

Haapasalo, J. and Pokela, E. (1999) Child-rearing and child abuse antecedents of criminality: Research design and findings on criminality, violence, and child abuse. Aggression and Violent Behavior, 4, 107–127.

Hirschi, T. (1969) Causes of Delinquency. Berkeley: University of California Press.

Hirschi, T. (1986) On the compatibility of rational choice and social control theories of crime. In D. Cornish and R.V. Clarke (eds) The Reasoning Criminal. New York: Springer-Verlag.

Horney, J., Osgood, D.W. and Marshall, I.H. (1995) Criminal careers in the short-term: Intra-individual variability in crime and its relation to local life circumstances. American Sociological Review, 60, 655–673

Inciardi, J.A., Martin, S.S., Butzin, C.A., Hooper, R.M., Harrison, L.D. (1997) An effective model of prison-based treatment for drug-involved offenders. Journal of Drug Issues, 27, 261–278.

Juby, H. and Farrington, D.P. (2001) Disentangling the link between disrupted families and delinquency. British Journal of Criminology, 41, 22–40.

Land, K.C., McCall P.L. and Cohen, L.E. (1990) Structural covariates of homicide rates: Are there any invariances across time and space? American Journal of Sociology, 95, 922–963.

Laub, J.H. and Sampson, R.J. (2003) Shared beginnings, divergent lives: Delinquent boys to age 70. Cambridge: Harvard University Press.

Laub, J.H., Nagin, D.S. and Sampson, R.J. (1998) Trajectories of change in criminal offending: Good marriages and the desistance process. American Sociological Review, 63, 225–238.

Lipsey, M.W. and Derzon, J.H. (1998) Predictors of violent or serious delinquency in adolescence and early adulthood: A synthesis of longitudinal research. In D.P. Farrington and R. Loeber (eds) Serious and Violent Juvenile Offenders. Thousand Oaks: Sage.

Loeber, R. and Stouthamer-Loeber, M. (1986) Family factors as correlates and predictors of juvenile conduct problems and delinquency. In M. Tonry and N. Morris (eds) Crime and Justice: An Annual Review of Research, Vol. 7. Chicago: University of Chicago Press.

Maruna, S. (2001) Making Good: How Ex-Convicts Reform and Rebuild their Lives. Washington: American Psychological Association.

Matsueda, R. and Heimer, K. (1997) A symbolic interactionist theory of role-transitions, role-commitments, and delinquency. In T.B. Thornberry (ed.) Developmental Theories of Crime and Delinquency. New Brunswick: Transaction Press.

McCollister, K.E., French, M.T., Inciardi, J.A. et al. (2003) Post-release substance abuse treatment for criminal offenders: A cost-effectiveness analysis. Journal of Quantitative Criminology, 19, 389–407.

McCord, J. (1977) A comparative study of two generations of native Americans. In R.F. Meier (ed.), Theory in Criminology. Beverly Hills, CA: Sage.

McCord, J. (1982) A longitudinal view of the relationship between paternal absence and crime. In J. Gunn and D.P. Farrington (eds) Abnormal Offenders, Delinquency, and the Criminal Justice System. Chichester: John Wiley & Sons.

Merton, R.K. (1995) Opportunity structure: The emergence, diffusion, and differentiation as sociological concept, 1930s–1950s. In F. Adler and W. Laufer (eds) Advances in Criminological Theory: The Legacy of Anomie Theory, Vol. 6, New Brunswick, NJ: Transaction Press.

Moffitt, T.E., Caspi, A., Rutter, M. and Silva, P.A. (2001) *Sex Differences in Antisocial Behaviour.* Cambridge: Cambridge University Press.

Murray, J. and Farrington, D.P. (2005) Parental imprisonment: Effects on boys' antisocial behaviour and delinquency through the life course. *Journal of Child Psychology and Psychiatry, 46,* 1269–1278.

Osgood, D.W. and Lee, H. (1993) Leisure activities, age, and adult roles across the lifespan. *Society and Leisure, 16,* 181–208.

Osgood, D.W., Wilson, J.K., O'Malley, P.M., Bachman, J.G. and Johnston L.D. (1996) Routine activities and individual deviant behaviour. *American Sociological Review, 61,* 635–655.

Patterson, G.R. (1995) Coercion as a basis for early age of onset for arrest. In J. McCord (ed.) *Coercion and Punishment in Long-term Perspectives.* Cambridge: Cambridge University Press.

Quinton, D., Pickles, A., Maughan, B. and Rutter, M. (1993) Partners, peers and pathways: Assortative pairing and continuities in conduct disorder. *Development and Psychopathology, 5,* 763–783.

Robins, L.N., West, P.A. and Herjanic, B.L. (1975) Arrests and delinquency in two generations: A study of black urban families and their children. *Journal of Child Psychology and Psychiatry, 16,* 125–140.

Rodgers, B. and Pryor, J. (1998) *Divorce and Separation: The Outcomes for Children.* York: Joseph Rowntree Foundation.

Rutter, M., Giller, H. and Hagell, A. (1998) *Antisocial Behaviour by Young People.* Cambridge: Cambridge University Press.

Rutter, M., Maughan, B., Meyer, J. *et al.* (1997) Heterogeneity of antisocial behaviour: Causes, continuities, and consequences. In R. Dienstbier and D.W. Osgood (eds) *Nebraska Symposium on Motivation,* Vol. 44: *Motivation and Delinquency.* Lincoln: University of Nebraska Press.

Sampson, R. and Laub, J.H. (1993) *Crime in the Making: Pathways and Turning Points Through Life.* Cambridge, MA: Harvard University Press.

Sampson, R.J. and Laub, J. (1995), A life-course theory of cumulative disadvantage and the stability of delinquency. In T.P. Thornberry (ed.) *Developmental Theories of Crime and Delinquency.* New Brunswick, NJ: Transaction Publishers.

Shadish, W.R., Cook, T.D. and Campbell, D.T. (2002) *Experimental and Quasi-Experimental Designs for Generalized Causal Inference.* Boston: Houghton Mifflin Company.

Sutherland, E.H. (1947) *Criminology,* 4th edn. Philadelphia: Lippincott.

Uggen, C. (2000) Work as a turning point in the life course of criminals: A duration model of age, employment, and recidivism. *American Sociological Review, 65,* 4, 529–546.

Vold, G.B., Bernard, T.J. and Snipes, J.B. (2002) *Theoretical Criminology,* 5th edn. New York: Oxford University Press.

Warr, M. (1998) Life-course transitions and desistance from crime. *Criminology, 36,* 183–215.

Warr, M. (2002) *Companions in Crime: The Social Aspects of Criminal Conduct.* New York: Cambridge University Press.

Uggen, C., Manza, J., Behrens, A. (2004). 'Less than the average citizen': stigma, role transition and the civic reintegration of convicted felons. In S. Maruna and R. Immarigeon (eds), *After Crime and Punishment: Ex-Offender Reintegration and Desistance from Crime* (pp. 258–290). Cullompton, Devon: Willan.

West, D.J. and Farrington, D.P. (1973) *Who Becomes Delinquent?* London: Heinemann.

Widom, C.S. (1989) The cycle of violence. *Science, 244,* 160–166.

Wilson, H. (1987) Parental supervision re-examined. *British Journal of Criminology, 27,* 275–301.

Wright, K.N. and Wright, K.E. (1992) Does getting married reduce the likelihood of criminality? A review of the literature. *Federal Probation, 61,* 50–56.

Chapter 2

Psychiatric Factors in Criminality

Jim Ormsby

The links between mental disorder and offending are complex and have been the subject of analysis and debate for many years. On one side of the fence a view that mental disorder implies dangerousness has contrasted with the theory that any associations between psychiatric factors and offending are due to confounding factors such as drug use, social environment or other external factors. Psychiatric factors cover a broad range of characteristics and clinical diagnoses. This chapter will give an overview of the arguments and evidence for links between different mental disorders and offending, and then place this in the context of the current legislative climate, psychiatric service provision and implications for those professionals working within the mental health and criminal justice system.

Evidence from prison populations

The presence of high rates of psychiatric morbidity in prisons has been highlighted in a number of publications since the mid-1990s. A high rate of psychiatric disorder in prisons is not in itself a clear indicator of a role of psychiatric factors in criminality – the relationship is far more complex than that. Risk factors for psychiatric disorder may be shared risk factors for criminality and prisoners may be at increased risk for developing psychiatric illness on imprisonment.

The 1997 Office for National Statistics prison survey (Singleton *et al.* 1998) found high rates of mental disorder in prisoners. This study had the advantage of allowing comparison with general population rates of illness measured using equivalent tools. It is not possible to provide a thorough review here of the study findings, however a brief summary of the data indicates the scale of the problem of mental disorder in prisons. Psychotic disorder had been present (in the year prior to the study) in 7 per cent of male sentenced prisoners and 10 per cent of remanded prisoners. This compared to rates of 0.4 per cent in an equivalent community survey. The data indicated the scale of the problem of mental disorder in prison. Neurotic disorder was present in 59 per cent of remand male prisoners and 76 per cent of female remand prisoners with lower figures for both genders serving sentences. In addition, many other prisoners had neurotic symptoms that may not meet the criteria for mental disorder. The most commonly found symptoms were depression, sleep disturbance, irritability, and worry.

Studies in the USA have drawn similar conclusions recording rates ranging from 10–15 per cent for serious mental illness (Teplin *et al.* 1996; Steadman *et al.* 1987). The Office for National Statistics study also recorded rates of alcohol and drug use in the year prior to imprisonment. There were high rates of both harmful use and dependence on psychoactive substances. Of the male remand prisoners, 58 per cent reported harmful alcohol use in the year prior to imprisonment. Of female remands, 54 per cent fulfilled the criteria for drug dependence with significant rates of prisoners having a history of injecting drug use.

The high rates of substance use and psychosis found in population studies of prisoners may indicate a causal link between the two. Farrell *et al.* (2002) studied 3142 prisoners using structured clinical interviews with 503 prisoners. The study confirmed previous findings of high rates of functional psychosis (10 per cent in preceding year) and high rates of both substance use and dependence. The study showed an association between severe dependence on cannabis or cocaine and psychosis. Interestingly, there was a negative relationship between opioid dependence and psychosis. These findings would be consistent with the theories that amphetamines, cannabis and cocaine can cause an acute psychotic illness and are therefore psychotogenic, a property that does not apply to opioids.

Disorders of adult personality are conditions that compromise ingrained and enduring behaviour patterns that manifest themselves as inflexible responses to a broad range of personal and social situations (World Health Organization 1992). By definition, personality disorders are conditions that are not attributable to mental illness or other mental disorder. They do, however, represent one end of a spectrum of people's characters and behavioural tendencies that may lead to contact with psychiatric services. Prison populations contain high numbers of people with personality disorder. Surveys have consistently reported this finding. The Office of National Statistics survey found 78 per cent of male remand prisoners, 64 per cent of male sentenced prisoners and 50 per cent of female prisoners fulfilled the criteria for personality disorder using standardized diagnostic instruments (Singleton et al. 1998; Coid et al. 2002). These figures compare with much lower rates in the general population with figures varying from 0.6–4 per cent for antisocial personality disorder. The figure of 0.6 per cent comes from a study of individuals living in private households (Singleton et al. 2001) that used similar diagnostic and screening instruments as the prison study described earlier.

Dissocial personality disorder includes characteristic patterns of thought and behaviour that include disregard for social norms, rules and obligations; low threshold for discharge of aggression and violence; and incapacity to profit from guilt. It is, therefore, not surprising that prison populations contain high numbers of individuals with these characteristics. High rates of other personality disorders were also found, particularly paranoid personality disorder and emotionally unstable type (particularly in the female population).

Evidence from community studies

Community studies have focused mainly on the link between mental illness and violence. It is now generally accepted that people with schizophrenia are more likely to be violent than other members of the population. This view is a change from the one held prior to the 1980s and is based on the influence of a number of studies but most importantly the Epidemiologic Catchment Area (ECA) study (Swanson et al. 1990). This study examined 10,059 adults living in the community in the USA. Of those with schizophrenia, 8 per cent were violent. This compared with 2 per cent of those without schizophrenia. The influence of comorbid substance use was striking, increasing the likelihood of violence from 8 per cent to 30 per cent.

Substance use has been cited as a major risk factor for violence in patients who have an underlying mental illness (Soyka 2000). It is not clear, however, whether there are significant confounding factors that influence this relationship. Are those individuals who are more impulsive and reckless (factors that may lead to offending) using more substances as part of risk-taking behaviour? Are those individuals who are associated with a criminal lifestyle and who have antisocial attitudes more likely to offend and take drugs rather than offend because they use drugs? The relationship is likely to be complex and vary from individual to individual.

Estimates of risk of violence in patients with serious mental illness have also been made by looking at inpatient rates of violence or rates in people prior to hospitalization or after discharge. The MacArthur Risk Assessment study (Monahan and Applebaum 2000) recorded violence in the 10 weeks following discharge from hospital. In this time period, 9 per cent of patients with schizophrenia were violent with rates of 19 per cent for patients with depression and 15 per cent for those with bipolar affective disorder. Highest rates were found in those patients with diagnoses of personality disorder or substance misuse.

An Australian study looked specifically at the issue of offending in those patients with schizophrenia (Mullen et al. 2000). The study compared general population controls with two patient groups. The first group had had a first admission in 1975 and the second group in 1985, with one study aim to compare these two groups. The 1975 group were admitted in a time when treatment was focused on inpatient care and the 1985 group in the context of policy focusing on community care. Both of the groups diagnosed with schizophrenia were more likely to have been convicted for all types of offending than the general population (except for sexual offending). Patients who had a comorbid substance misuse were the highest rate offenders. There was an increase in convictions from 1975 and 1985 but this was not specific to those with schizophrenia.

The study provides an interesting breakdown by offence type. Patients with schizophrenia showed a significantly increased risk of property offences (relative risk 3.4 [1.8–6.3] for 1985 cohort lifetime risk), drug-related offences (relative risk 3.5 [1.4–8.9] for 1985 cohort lifetime risk) in addition to violent offences.

Studies following individuals from birth attempt to eliminate bias in selection of groups. A Swedish cohort studied by Hodgins (1992) was followed up for 30 years. Males with mental disorder had a four times increased risk of violent offences compared with those without. The members of the female group with mental disorder were more than 27 times more likely to offend violently. These findings have been supported by other birth cohort studies. Where specific mental disorders have been examined then schizophrenia, alcohol dependence and substance abuse have been associated with an increased prevalence of violence (Arseneault et al. 2000). The Hodgins (1992) study also showed an increase in offending (three times) and specifically violent offending (five times) in men with learning disability. Females with learning disability were 25 times more likely to commit a violent offence.

There is less detailed evidence for links between brain injury and offending. Brennan *et al.* (2000) reported higher rates of offending (particularly violence) in individuals with brain injury. Frontal lobe damage is specifically associated with disinhibited behaviour. Homicide by patients with mental illness attracts strong media interest, often with a criticism of 'community care'. It is now generally recognized that, as with the risk of violence shown above, certain groups of mental disorder are associated with an increased risk of homicide. Taylor and Gunn (1984) found that 11 per cent of those convicted of killing another person had a schizophrenic illness compared with an expected rate of 0.4 per cent. Other studies have shown increased rates of around 8–10 per cent (Wallace *et al.* 1998). Although these rates are high compared to the general population they still equate to an annual risk of 1 in 3000 for males and 1 in 30,000 for females. The rate of homicide by mentally disordered individuals appears to have been relatively stable in England and Wales from 1957 to the present (Taylor and Gunn 1999).

Personality disorder has its origins in childhood disturbance and is by definition a developmental disorder. Therefore, treatment options that address developmental disturbances may be recommended, such as therapeutic communities (TCs), which have been shown to help strengthen personality and behaviour in pro-social, non-criminal ways (Cullen 1994; Marshall 1999; Taylor 2000). Antisocial personality disorder is most clearly associated with criminal behaviour and has a rate of 2–3 per cent in the United Kingdom. It is associated with substance misuse, early school drop out, homelessness and increased mortality in young adulthood (Coid 2003). Developmental research suggests that antisocial personality disorder is influenced by the presence of risk factors including genetic predisposition, perinatal factors and poor family environment. Protective factors may reduce the likelihood of progression from childhood conduct disorder to adolescent delinquency to adult antisocial personality disorder. A subgroup of individuals whose antisocial behaviour persists into adulthood have high rates of offending including violence. Service development in the treatment of personality disorder has recognized that a broad range of interventions across a number of settings is required to address the needs of this group of individuals (NIMHE 2003).

Prison healthcare

The Future Organization of Healthcare published in 1999 (HM Prison Service & NHS Executive 1999) began the process of a move from provision of healthcare by the Prison Service towards responsibility being taken over by primary care trusts in formal partnerships with the prison. This report followed the Chief Inspector of Prisons' recognition of problems in prison healthcare including professional isolation of staff and limited links with the NHS (Her Majesty's Inspectorate of Prisons 1996). This transfer of funding responsibility and commissioning of services has now occurred and has happened alongside an expansion of input from mental health services to the prison population. This is based on an expectation of 'equivalence' of healthcare provision for those in prison to those in the community. Prisoners should in essence be receiving the same level of healthcare as they would were they not incarcerated. Prisons, primary care trusts and mental health providers moved a long way to meeting this need; however, there are areas of ongoing difficulty in the provision of equivalent psychiatric care in prisons. Psychiatric in-reach teams or prison community mental health initiatives have been developed in most prisons and will allow access to secondary care specialist services for assessment and treatment. This means that many of the mental health standards of care set out in the National Service Framework for Mental Health (Department of Health 1999) and in the National Institute for Clinical Excellence guidelines are being met for those prisoners who need the equivalent of community treatment and follow up. There are more difficulties meeting the needs of those inmates who are identified as needing inpatient mental health services. Many of those inmates who have a more serious mental illness will be transferred to a prison healthcare wing. These units are not hospitals and are specifically excluded in legislation (National Health Service Act 1977) meaning that treatment under the Mental Health Act cannot be given there (Wilson 2004). There are delays in transferring prisoners to hospital for inpatient treatment, meaning that often prison healthcare centres are required to manage patients with untreated psychotic illnesses.

Implications for prisons and psychiatric services

In 1939 Penrose proposed a theory that there were a stable number of persons confined in any one industrial society. He found an inverse relationship between prison and mental health populations. If one form of confinement reduces does the other increase? Some would suggest that the reduction in inpatient psychiatric beds has been associated with an increase in the mentally ill population in prison. The studies by Mullen et al (2000) appear to contradict this, suggesting increased offending rates for all members of the population, not just those with mental illness. Those with mental disorder may not be offending more but may still be imprisoned more frequently. This may reflect an increase in imprisonment for minor offences such as public disorder, lack of diversion schemes, or mentally disordered offenders finding difficulty in complying with structured probation orders.

The evidence cited earlier shows links between mental disorder and offending from epidemiological studies. On an individual basis the pathway by which mental disorder leads to offending may be varied and complex. The cases where a patient with a psychotic disorder acts on command hallucinations telling him to harm another person are relatively rare but do occur. More often the links between psychiatric factors and offending will be mediated by factors such as disinhibition, poor impulse control, thought disorder, poor planning and executive function or social isolation. This may mean that a number of patients who were 'revolving-door' patients of the psychiatric institutions become 'revolving-door' patients of the local prisons. Those people who have mental illness complicated by antisocial personality disorder or in the setting of unstable family background, interrupted education, childhood behavioural disturbance and delinquency may find it harder to access those services in the community. They may be non-compliant with medication, may not abstain from substance use and not engage with other social interventions. All of these characteristics are recognizable to those working within the Prison system. This means that the Prison Service has a large population of mentally ill and personality disordered inmates who have high rates of comorbidity and substance use, and who have social and psychological factors that may be associated with a poor prognosis. The Prison Service also has to manage a population who are at high risk of suicide. The number of suicides in prison has increased in recent years (Shaw *et al.* 2004). This issue is not examined in detail here but reflects the complex interaction of psychiatric factors with other risk factors for suicide including substance misuse and withdrawal, and social influences including the prison environment, loss and isolation.

The development of mental health in-reach teams has contributed to an improvement in the provision of equivalence of healthcare to inmates. Services need to continue to be developed inside and outside of prison to address the needs of mentally disordered offenders. These services need to include:

- services to allow diversion of less serious offenders from custody; these should include diversion from police cells, if appropriate, and court liaison schemes
- early intervention for seriously mentally ill patients
- family interventions and social support
- inclusion of mentally disordered offenders in the broad range of disposals available to all other offenders, including bail hostels and probation

- thorough screening processes for receptions to prison

- programmes for monitoring self-harm risk and preventing suicide

- prompt access to admission for patients requiring transfer from prison at all levels of security

- psychological treatment for personality disorder including the use of TCs for those needing a more structured and intensive input or cognitive interventions for those who are more readily able to learn and use thinking skills interventions

- maintenance and improvement of links between the National Health Service and prisons

- the continued development of psychological treatments for offenders.

References

Arseneault, L., Moffitt, T.E., Caspin, A. *et al.* (2000) Mental disorders and violence in a total birth cohort: results from the Dunedin study. *Archives of General Psychiatry, 57,* 979–968.

Brennan, P.A, Mednick, S.A., Hodgins, S. (2000) Major mental disorders and criminal violence in a Danish Birth Cohort. *Archives of General Psychiatry, 57,* 494–500.

Coid, J., Bebbington, P., Jenkins, R. *et al.* (2002) The national survey of psychiatric morbidity among prisoners and the future of prison healthcare. *Medicine Science and Law, 42,* 245–250.

Coid, J. (2003) Epidemiology, public health and the problem of personality disorder. *British Journal of Psychiatry, 182* (suppl.44), s3–s10.

Cullen, E. (1994) Grendon: The therapeutic prison that works. *Therapeutic Communities, 15,* 301–310.

Department of Health (1999) *National Service Framework for Mental Health.* London: Department of Health.

Farrell, M., Boys, A., Bebbington, P. *et al.* (2002) Psychosis and drug dependence: results from national survey of prisoners. *British Journal of Psychiatry, 181,* 393–398.

Her Majesty's Inspectorate of Prisons (1996) *Patient or prisoner? A New Strategy for Health Care in Prisons.* London: Home Office.

HM Prison Service & NHS Executive (1999). *The Future Organization of Prison Healthcare.* Report by the joint prison service and National Health Service Executive Working Group. London: Home Office.

Hodgins, S. (1992) Mental disorder, intellectual deficiency and crime: evidence from a birth cohort. *Archives of General Psychiatry, 49,* 476–483.

Marshall, P. (1997) *A reconviction study of HMP Grendon therapeutic community. Research Findings 53.* London: Home Office Research and Statistics Directorate.

Monahan, J. and Applebaum, P. (2000) Reducing violence risk: diagnostically based clues from the MacArthur Violence Risk Assessment Study. In Hodgins S. (ed.) *Effective Prevention of Crime and Violence among the Mentally Ill.* Netherlands: Kluwer Academic Publishers.

Mullen, P.E., Burgess, P., Wallace, C. *et al.* (2000) Community care and criminal offending in schizophrenia. *Lancet, 355,* 614–617.

National Institute for Mental Health in England (2003) *Personality Disorder: No Longer a Diagnosis of Exclusion.* London: Department of Health.

Penrose, L. (1939) Mental disease and crime: outline of a comparative study of European statistics. *British Journal of Medical Psychology, 18,* 1–15.

Shaw, J., Baker, D., Hunt, I.M., *et al.* (2004) Suicide by prisoners: national clinical survey. *British Journal of Psychiatry, 184,* 263–267.

Singleton, N., Bumpstead, R., O'Brien, M., *et al.* (2001) *Psychiatric Morbidity Among Adults Living in Private Households.* London: Stationary Office.

Singleton, N., Bumpstead, R., O'Brien, M., *et al.* (1998) *Psychiatric Morbidity Among Prisoners in England and Wales.* London: The Stationary Office.

Soyka, M. (2000) Substance misuse, psychiatric disorder and violent and disturbed behaviour. *British Journal of Psychiatry, 176,* 345–350.

Steadman, H., Fabisiak, S., Dvaskin, J., *et al.* (1987) A survey of mental disability among state prison inmates. *Hospital and Community Psychiatry, 38,* 1086–1090.

Swanson, J., Holzer, C.E., III., Ganju, V.K., *et al.* (1990) Violence and psychiatric disorder in the community: evidence from the Epidemiologic Catchment Area surveys. *Hospital and Community Psychiatry, 41,* 761–770.

Taylor, P. and Gunn, J. (1984) Violence and psychosis I. Risk of violence among psychotic men. *British Medical Journal, 288,* 1945–1949.

Taylor, P. and Gunn, J. (1999) Homicides by people with mental illness: myth and reality. *British Journal of Psychiatry, 174,* 9–14.

Taylor, R. (2000) A seven year reconviction study of Grendon therapeutic community. In Shine, J. and Morris, M. (eds) *A Compilation of Grendon Research.* Gloucester: Leyhill Press.

Teplin, L., Abram, K. and McClelland, G. (1996) Prevalence of psychiatric disorders among incarcerated women. *Archives of General Psychiatry, 53,* 505–512.

Wallace, C., Mullen, P., Burgess, P., *et al.* (1998) Serious criminal offending and mental disorder. Case linkage study. *British Journal of Psychiatry, 172,* 477–484.

Wilson, S. (2004) The principle of equivalence and the future of mental health care in prisons. *British Journal of Psychiatry 184,* 5–7.

World Health Organization (1992) *The ICD-10 Classification of Mental and Behavioural Disorders.* Geneva: World Health Organization.

Chapter 3

Psychological Theories of Criminality

Jo Day

Why do people commit crimes? Over the last century this question has been the focus of much theorizing and debate within sociology, biology, psychiatry and psychology, and is one of the reasons for the creation of the discipline of criminology. Within each discipline one aim has been to explore the factors related to why a person commits a crime and enable the development of explanatory theories. A second aim has been to assist in the development of effective interventions that can reduce the likelihood of future offending.

Any theory that attempts to explain offending must take into account that criminality is a multi-faceted and incredibly complex phenomenon. It must therefore not be assumed that crime can be solely explained by theories from a psychological perspective or perhaps any other theory from a sole discipline. A multi-factorial approach to understanding crime is required where the interaction of a variety of biological, social, psychological and environmental factors shown to be associated with offending can assist to explain why any one person chooses to commit crime.

This chapter outlines the contribution that psychological theories have made in understanding why people offend. The main theories outlined include psychobiological, learning, cognitive, control, narrative psychology, and 'what works' in offender rehabilitation. Psychiatric and criminal career approaches to understanding crime are explained in other chapters and will not be attended to here. Throughout the chapter a case study, outlined below, of a fictional male offender – 'Andy' – is used to highlight the application of theory to understanding the reason for someone's offending behaviour.

Andy's offending

Andy is a 39-year-old male convicted of grievous bodily harm, burglary and possession of Class A drugs. He has five previous convictions for violent and theft-related offences. Andy is divorced with three children; he has substance misuse problems and has spent time in care since the age of 10 years. The male members of his family have a long history of involvement in criminal activities. His father had a reputation for serious violence and extortion. Andy has one brother who has no involvement in crime and runs his own business. The last time Andy was released from prison he remained crime-free for a period of 18 months. He was in full-time employment, had moved away from his home area with a new partner and had the support of his non-criminal brother. Prior to the current offences, Andy had returned home after his relationship ended. He resumed illegal drug use and started to associate again with family and peers who were still active in committing crime.

Psychobiological theories

The majority of psychological theories acknowledge the importance of genetic, neurological and other biological factors in human functioning. This is no different when applied to understanding the psychological factors related to criminality. The evidence from research conducted in this area suggests that criminals are born and not made. That is, the role of the environment is considered to have played a minimal part in shaping their behaviour. Seminal work by Cesare Lombroso, a physician and 'criminal anthropologist', proposed that an offender's genetic make up was different from that of non-offenders. He also introduced the concept of 'indirect heredity', where people who spent a lot of time associating with others involved in criminal or antisocial behaviour were also likely to become criminals. In later work he considered other factors such as the environment, but proposed that approximately one-third of offenders were criminal due to a direct genetic link whereas other offenders' behaviour was due to direct heredity or a mix of causes. Later empirical studies focused on families, twin and adoption studies to establish the potential role of genetics in explaining offending behaviour. There is still research to the current day examining the role of genetics in criminality, although there is no longer a search for a specific 'criminal gene'.

For example, Rowe and Osgood (1984) conducted a study to look at the impact of genetic (e.g. whether identical or non-identical twin), environmental (e.g. broken or intact home) and individual factors (e.g. peer group) on self-reported delinquency. They found that the genetic component accounted for over 60 per cent of the interaction between the three factors. Shared environmental factors accounted for 20 per cent and specific environmental factors the remaining 20 per cent. They concluded that offending behaviour has a genetic component but that it is not a straightforward relationship.

Other psychobiological factors that have been considered include chromosomal abnormalities such as XYY syndrome and body build and behaviour, e.g. Sheldon (1942) and Glueck and Glueck (1950).

Psychobiological theories offer an interesting insight into why some people commit crime by indicating a predisposition to offending. Overall, they lack complete explanatory power and further consideration of other psychological, social and environmental factors associated with crime.

Application to Andy's offending

There could be a plausible genetic role in Andy's offending. His family has a history of criminal behaviour. It may be that hormonal and neurological factors play a part, although further information would be needed for this to be clarified. Overall, it could be argued that Andy has a genetic predisposition to commit crime but that other factors need to be taken into account to fully explain his offending behaviour.

Learning theories

The theories included in this section are based on the premise that offending is a learnt behaviour and are differentiated by the processes by which criminal behaviours are proposed to be learnt (Palmer 2003).

Differential association theory and operant learning theory

This approach is based on the work of Sutherland (1947) and built on further by Sutherland and Cressey. The theory describes the necessary social conditions to produce crime but also attempts to explain the processes by which the individual becomes a criminal. It proposes that through contact with other people who hold favourable definitions towards crime that similar definitions are learned. This does not necessarily occur through association with criminals but rather with people who hold definitions favourable to crime; varying definitions can also exist. There are problems in validating this theory such as the difficulty in objectively defining what constitutes criminal and non-criminal definitions and why, given similar conditions, some individuals adopt criminal definitions while others do not (Hollin 1989). Despite these issues, this explanation has provided a foundation for successive theories.

Operant learning theory, as developed by Skinner, proposed that offending behaviour is the result of the environmental consequences for the individual of the 'criminal' behaviour. These consequences can be reinforcing or punishing and lead to a three-term contingency of antecedent conditions for a behaviour that produces consequences. Reinforcement and punishment is said to occur positively and negatively as follows:

- *Positive reinforcement* occurs when performing a behaviour leads to consequences perceived as rewarding

- *Negative reinforcement* occurs when performing a behaviour leads to the avoidance of unwanted consequences

- *Positive punishment* occurs when the consequences of a behaviour are unwanted

- *Negative punishment* occurs when the consequences of a behaviour involve the removal of something desired.

(Palmer 2003, p.15)

Jeffery (1965) integrated operant learning principles into the differential association theory to expand its explanation of crime. Criminal behaviour is argued to be maintained by consequences that are either positively or negatively reinforcing to the individual and include both material and intrinsic consequences. Whether an individual offends or not is a result of their learning history and their experience of the reinforcing and punishing consequences of offending. Palmer (2003) noted a limitation of operant theory is the need for further attention to the internal processes in the learning of criminal behaviour.

Social learning theory

Bandura (1977, 1986) developed a social learning approach to provide further detail on the internal cognitive process and expand on the limitations of operant learning theory. Central to this theory is the proposition that in addition to the experience of the consequences of behaviour, learning can also occur through observing other people perform a specific behaviour. This is known as modelling and two principles of motivation for behaviour are considered to be important:

- *vicarious learning* – observing the positive reinforcing and punishing consequences of behaviours for other people when they behave in a certain way

- *self-reinforcement* – motivations can be determined from inner feelings of self-approval that can lead to a behaviour being repeated.

Social learning theory suggests that through observation, especially if the model is someone regarded as successful or of high status, we learn at a cognitive level how to perform the observed behaviour. Given further opportunities the behaviour may be practised and refined and then reinforced or punished both externally and internally so motivating future behaviour. There are three contexts in which this learning can take place:

1. the family

2. the prevalent subculture in which they live (e.g. friends)

3. the wider culture such as television and books.

However, this theory still cannot explain all instances of offending by all people as it still lacks a full account of the internal cognitive processes involved in criminal behaviour.

Application to Andy's offending

It could be argued that Andy learnt to commit crime through the social contact and observation of criminal activity by his family and peers. From a young age he observed how his father was able to get what he wanted by verbally and physically bullying other people. Positive reinforcers of offending may have been the respect and status he gained in the criminal fraternity. Negative reinforcement may include that he was

> able to get money quickly so did not have to go without illegal drugs. As Andy continued to commit violent crimes, he may have felt a sense of pride in his ability to dominate others, thus reinforcing his use of aggression to ensure that he could get what he wanted.

COGNITIVE THEORIES

The limitations of learning theories in providing detail on the internal cognitive processes in why people commit crimes led to a focus on a cognitive approach to expand the explanation of why some people offend. Ross and Fabiano (1985) made a distinction between two types of cognition:

- *impersonal cognition* – the skills needed to deal with the physical world such as visual perception, memory, intelligence
- *interpersonal cognition* – the ability to understand other people and solve problems in social situations including skills such as perspective taking, means-end thinking, social problem solving.

Yochelson and Samenow (1976) conducted a study that was based on in-depth interviews with a large number of male offenders referred to hospital for assessment of their mental state. They concluded that offenders have a distinct cognitive style referred to as 'criminal thinking patterns', which include lack of empathy, poor decision making, irresponsibility, and a tendency to perceive themselves as victims. There were a number of methodological flaws in their study that has limited the capability to generalize from their work to other offenders. However, this body of work did lead to a growth in empirical studies within psychology to examine the differences in social cognition between offenders and non-offenders that revealed a number of cognitive patterns that appear to characterize offenders. Mixed findings have been reported in various studies that are likely to reflect the fact that offenders are not a homogenous group. The following list can therefore be considered to reflect general 'group patterns' and may not apply to every criminal:

- *poor self-control and impulsivity* – difficulties regulating and managing one's own behaviour and a tendency to act without thinking in a given situation with a reduced ability compared to non-offenders to delay gratification

- *concrete vs. abstract reasoning* – thinking styles are often rigid, action-orientated and concrete in nature and forming abstract concepts may be a problem

- *locus of control* – tendency to attribute behaviour to external forces rather than to own internal control

- *social perspective taking* – lack of ability to see situations from other people's perspectives and perform poorly on measures of social perspective taking

- *social problem solving* – ineffective problem solving skills including difficulties weighing up a situation, generating possible solutions, and considering consequences of different options and planning to reach a desired outcome; it has been suggested that offenders may be able to recognize effective social problem solving strategies but lack the ability to construct these responses themselves.

Recent researchers have attempted to define a more coherent explanation through social information processing models as to how such deficits as described earlier may cause offending. For example, Cornish and Clarke (1986a) developed rational choice cognitive theory. In brief, crime is seen as an opportunity and the offender is considered to be making a rational decision about whether to offend or not, and is therefore considered to be 'a reasoning criminal'. The active weighing up of the costs and benefits of committing an offence takes place and these can differ according to each individual. Their particular poor social cognitive skills may impact on their ability to make an informed decision. Palmer (2003) notes the fact that the decision is made under constraint by social factors (e.g. time) and individual factors mean that in reality the decision is made under 'limited rationality'. Cornish and Clarke distinguish between criminal involvement (the complete process through which an individual becomes involved in offending) and criminal event (the decisions that are made in a specific situation with regard to committing and offence). This theory provides an interactional approach to explain offending and argues that the offender reacts cognitively to the environmental opportunities that occur around them. What is not considered is that some people do not offend even if the opportunity arises, which has led to theories concerned with how people may control themselves so they do not commit crime.

Application to Andy's offending

In addition to the explanation provided by the learning theories, it is likely that further information is required about Andy's internal world and whether there are thinking styles (e.g. he perceives himself as a victim or has a sense of entitlement) and social cognitive deficits, such as poor perspective taking, impulsivity, and lack of long-term goals, which may be present and further assist in explaining his offending.

CONTROL THEORIES

Eysenck's Theory of the Criminal Personality (1964) developed a theory of crime and personality over a number of years. It incorporates biological, social and individual factors proposing that the criminal personality is derived from a stable trait theory of personality. It is based on the premise that through genetic endowment some individuals are born with cortical and autonomic nervous systems that affect their ability to learn from, or more poorly condition to, environmental stimuli. Eysenck proposes three dimensions to the personality: extraversion (E), neuroticism (N) and, psychoticism (P). The latter dimension is thought to describe 'tough mindedness', aggressiveness, and lack of thought for others. The theory predicts poor conditionability for those with high E or N and particularly for those high on both. The principle assumption in explaining crime is that children learn to control antisocial behaviour through the development of a conscience. This conscience is a set of conditioned responses to environmental events associated with the antisocial behaviour. The speed and efficiency of social conditioning will depend on the personality in terms of E, N and P. The prediction would be that high E and N will be over-represented in offender populations and P is argued to be strongly related to offending. However, similar to the finding related to social cognitive deficits, some allowance must be given to the heterogeneity of the offender population.

This theory has generated a great deal of empirical research that has generally found strong support for offenders scoring high on P and N, although had mixed findings for E. It has been suggested that E can be split into sociability and impulsivity and only the latter relates to offending (Palmer 2003). Although there are flaws with the methods used in many of the studies as the majority explored personality traits singly rather than in combination. Overall, there appears to be support for a relationship between personality and crime, although this approach does not explain all crime and is not applicable to all offenders.

Moral development

Palmer (2003) provides a comprehensive overview of Kohlberg's theory of moral development and how it has been used to develop an explanation for why people offend. Kohlberg argues that moral reasoning develops in a sequential manner as a person attains maturity. He described three levels of moral development with two stages in each level (Hollin 1989, p.52).

- *Level one: Pre-morality* – The first stage is punishment and obedience, where moral behaviour involves deference to authority and avoiding punishment. The second stage – hedonism – is indicated by an occupation with own needs regardless of others.

- *Level two: Conventional Conformity* – The interpersonal concordance stage is concerned with conformity and social approval. The second stage is law and order with a commitment to social order for its own sake.

- *Level three: Autonomous Principles* – The social contract stage acknowledges individuals' rights and the democratic process in lawmaking. The second stage is universal ethical principles where moral judgements are determined by concepts such as justice etc. and may override the legal stance.

It is argued that offending is associated with a delay in the development for moral reasoning. Given the opportunity to offend, it is proposed that the individual does not have the internal mechanisms to control and resist the temptation. Empirical studies have tended to explore the moral judgements of offenders and non-offenders. These have provided mixed findings and, despite methodological flaws, there is a lack of evidence of a direct causal link to crime. A criticism of this approach is based on the assumption that there is a relationship between moral reasoning, moral values and actual behaviour. This has been queried on the grounds that several studies have shown that people behave in ways they believe or know to be wrong. Thus it cannot be assumed that moral or social issues are relevant when an offender is deciding to commit a crime. It may be, as suggested by Hollin (1989), that they are more concerned with whether or not they are likely to be successful.

A broader criticism of theories based on personality trait theory is that they are almost inherently static. Longitudinal and ethnographic research on crime over the life course indicates that criminal careers are sporadic, short

---

Application to Andy's offending

To further explain Andy's offending, information would be useful on his current level of moral reasoning and personality traits such as where he lies on dimensions of extraversion, neuroticism and psychoticism. This may provide indications of an inability to resist opportunities to offend.

---

lived and largely shaped by social and developmental contexts. Consequently, a theory of crime needs to rise to the challenge of the need for an explanation of why people commit crime that allows plasticity and change while still acknowledging the role of individual differences in cognition and identity (Maruna 2000). This need to go beyond personality trait theory to understand criminal behaviour has led to two more recent theoretical approaches, namely narrative psychology and the findings of studies based on 'what works' in offender rehabilitation and reintegration.

NARRATIVE PSYCHOLOGY

Shadd Maruna (2000) argues that a true understanding of criminal behaviour can only come through an in-depth analysis of offenders' narratives and connecting them to roles and behaviour. The criminal narratives to which offenders subscribe may lead them to consider their actions as acceptable and not 'criminal'. They may, alternatively, enjoy being part of a group that lives by rules that break conventions. This socio-cultural approach emphasizes how the actions of the criminal are thought to be shaped by his or her social network and also by the way in which the criminal sees his or her world and makes sense of his- or herself. Like all cognition, Maruna argues that criminal cognition is socially situated and the social context of any criminal therefore has a profound relevance for the way in which that criminal's self-identify is determined.

Self-narratives are shaped by experience and then reflected in behaviour. In order to explain why individuals commit crime an analysis is required to understand these internal states. One level is to explore the narrative identity or self concept. It is suggested that traits give only the beginning of the 'whole personality'. To fully understand offending there is a need to move beyond 'stable traits' to explore the 'whole person'. Previous approaches to understanding crime do not take into account understanding of the criminal and this must be supplemented with offenders' perspectives and a review of their unique personal histories to give, as Maruna (2000) describes, a 'full-blooded portrait'.

Narratives of offenders explain their criminal actions in a sequence of events that connect to explanatory goals, motivations and feelings. These then act to shape and guide future criminal behaviour. To date, few empirical studies have addressed the issue of self-narrative identity and desistance from crime and delinquency. Previous studies, however, have found indications that a change in identity and self concept is critical to the process of reform.

In summary, narrative psychology can provide a methodological and theoretical framework for exploring many of the concepts and constructs thought to be related to criminal behaviour. By trying to understand the 'whole person' it is possible to better understand the change and development in criminal behaviour time.

What works in offender rehabilitation

A rehabilitative model is based on targeting risk factors that are associated with offending and addressing those that identify the criminogenic needs of offenders. These are based on meta-analytic studies of 'what works' in rehabilitation approaches that aim to reduce re-offending. A summary by McGuire (2002) of meta-analytic reviews reached the following conclusions.

1. Offenders often have multiple problems and criminogenic needs, and those with many are most likely to re-offend. Interventions that tackle a range of problems will be more effective than those that target a single problem.

2. Offenders may need additional practical support/training in relation to accommodation, education and employment.

The following list describes particular social and psychological 'needs' as being important criminogenic factors found to be empirically related to offending (PSO 4360 Correctional Services Accreditation Panel 2004):

- poor cognitive skills
- antisocial attitudes and feelings, including sexist and racist attitudes
- strong ties to and identification with antisocial/criminal models and impulsive antisocial lifestyle

- weak social ties and identification with pro-social/non-criminal models
- cognitive support for offending: distorted thinking used to justify offending
- deficits in self-management, decision making and problem solving skills
- difficulty in recognizing personally relevant risk factors and in generating or enacting appropriate strategies to cope with them
- poor pro-social interpersonal skills
- dependency on alcohol and drugs
- contingencies favouring criminal over pro-social behaviour
- some adverse social or family circumstances
- weak or fragile commitment to avoiding re-offending.

Application to Andy's offending

First, in addition to the initial understanding of personality traits, the narrative approach would suggest further exploration of the underlying motives, strategies, narrative identity and self-concept held by Andy. This would assist an understanding of why Andy committed his most recent offences. Of particular interest may be the changes in his identity when desisting from crime and how this may have changed as his social and personal context changed in the time preceding the current offences. Second, it may be useful to identify the evidence for and against each of the criminogenic factors in the list given above, specifically whether their presence applies to previous and current offending.

Conclusion

A range of theoretical explanations for criminality derived from a psychological perspective has been presented in this chapter. In attempting to reach a comprehensive understanding of offending behaviour there is a need for a thorough consideration of the interaction of a range and variety of biological, social, psychological and environmental factors demonstrated to be associated with criminality. The empirical evidence suggests that offenders have multiple problems, many of which contribute directly towards their offending and may therefore be termed 'criminogenic'. To understand which are truly related to any one individual who commits crime will require an understanding of that person as a 'whole' including drawing on, but not solely, on theories from a psychological perspective. A therapeutic community (TC) approach provides an environmental setting that can offer an opportunity for an offender to understand the reasons why they committed offences that fits with a multi-factorial perspective. This is due to a similar starting point, which is holistic and based on working with each individual as a 'whole person'.

References

Bandura, A. (1977) *Social Learning Theory*. New York: Prentice-Hall.

Bandura, A. (1986) *Social Foundations of Thought and Action: A Social Cognitive Theory*. Englewood Cliffs, NJ: Prentice-Hall.

Cornish, D.B. and Clarke, R.V.G. (eds) (1986a) *The Reasoning Criminal: Rational Choice Perspectives on Offending*. New York: Springer-Verlag.

Eysenck, H.J. (1964) *Crime and Personality*. London: Routledge and Kegan Paul.

Glueck, S. and Glueck, E. (1950) *Unravelling Juvenile Delinquency*. New York: Harper and Row.

Hollin, C. (1989) *Psychology and Crime: An Introduction to Criminological Psychology*. London and New York: Routledge.

Jeffery, C.R. (1965) Criminal behaviour and learning theory. *Journal of Criminal Law, Criminology, and Police Science, 56*, 294–300.

Maruna, S. (2000) Criminology desistance and the psychology of the stranger. In D. Canter and L. Alison (eds) *The Social Psychology of Crime: Groups, Teams and Networks*. Dartmouth: Ashgate Offender Profiling Series.

McGuire, M. (ed) (2002) *Offender Rehabilitation and Treatment: Effective Programmes and Policies to Reduce Re-Offending*. Chichester: John Wiley & Sons.

Palmer, E. (2003) *Offending Behaviour: Moral Reasoning, Criminal Conduct and the Rehabilitation of Offenders*. Cullompton: Willan Publishing.

Prison Service Order 4360, 25th June 2004, Correctional Services Accreditation Panel.

Ross, R.R. and Fabiano, E.A. (1985) *Time to Think: A Cognitive Model of Delinquency Prevention and Offender Rehabilitation*. Johnson City, Tenn: Institute of Social Sciences and Arts.

Rowe, D.C. and Osgood, D.W. (1984) Heredity and Sociological Theories of Delinquency: A Reconsideration. *American Sociological Review, 49*, 526–540.

Sheldon, W.H. (1942) *The Varieties of Temperament: A Psychology of Constitutional Differences*. New York: Harper and Row.

Sutherland, E.H. (1947) *Principles of Criminology*, 4th edn. Philadelphia, PA: Lippincott.

Yochelson, S. and Samenow, S.E. (1976) *The Criminal Personality, Vol. 1: A Profile for Change*. New York: Jason Aronson.

History of the Therapeutic Community in Prison

Chapter 4

The Historical Development of the UK Democratic Therapeutic Community

Tim Newell and Bob Healey

The mental state of prisoners and the development of treatment options for those presenting particular problems has long been a concern of the Prison Service and its medical officers. As prisons began to be built in the 1840s to contain prisoners over longer periods of time, the regime design of the separate cell and silent system was found to contribute to the deterioration of those so confined and it had to be abandoned. In Victorian times, prisons were built to accommodate and to isolate prisoners who attracted a wide range of labels to describe their condition. Dr Campbell, a prison hulk medical officer in 1850, for example, writes: 'remarks apply with even more force to mental affections which occur among invalid prisoners in every form and degree, from simple weakness of intellect to well-marked lunacy' (Snell 1963, p.176). Dr Campbell later became Governor of Woking Invalid Convict Prison, at the time a radical new establishment, devised for the treatment of invalid prisoners. The prison closed after 26 years and its 'lunatic' wing 2 years later in 1886. In response to the identified need for the containment of the 'criminally insane' Broadmoor was opened in 1863 followed by Parkhurst in 1869.

Parkhurst became a convict prison with separate provision for 'a weak-minded class', which included epileptics, violent men and 'subnormals'. Such men were designated unfit for ordinary penal discipline by reason of some mental defect. Diagnosis and designation into one of these categories was made on the basis of the findings of Sir Herbert Smalley, then Medical Commissioner of Prisons. He presented the problem of mental defectives to the Royal Commission on the care and control of the feeble-minded in 1904. The *Mental Deficiency Act* followed in 1913 (Snell 1963, p.176). In 1932 a report was published by the Departmental Committee on Persistent Offenders, which considered the need for psychiatric treatment of disturbed prisoners in addition to their supervision and appropriate containment. Sir Norwood East was a member of the committee and commented: 'The mental condition of offenders is a matter calling for careful attention. There is reason to believe that certain delinquents may be amenable to psychological treatment' (Snell 1963, p.176). Paragraph 121 of the Report recommended that a medical psychologist should be attached to any penal establishment built to carry out psychological treatments.

The outbreak of World War II temporarily halted progress in the development of the treatment of prisoners. Dr Mackwood joined the staff at Wormwood Scrubs in 1943 as a psychotherapist, which signalled a fresh attempt to treat amenable prisoners. Shortly afterwards therapists were appointed at Holloway, Wakefield and Feltham Borstal. Treatment initiatives developed in many different directions but Dr Mackwood reported back to the Prison Commissioners in 1949 and highlighted some drawbacks of providing treatment in a prison setting. This was a direct reference to the architecture and physical construction of Wormwood Scrubs and Victorian prisons in general. The 'drawbacks' highlighted by Dr Mackwood were rectified and incorporated in the final design and building of Grendon.

The East–Hubert Report of 1939 (East and de Hubert 1939) suggested that a special institution should be built to serve four main functions:

1. To be a clinic and hospital where cases could be investigated and if necessary, treated by psychotherapy and other means as well as a centre for criminological research

2. To be an institution in which selected cases could live under special conditions of training and treatment to achieve alterations to their behaviour

3. To provide a colony for the offender who proved quite unable to adapt himself to ordinary social conditions but for whom reformative measures, however specialized, seemed useless

4.   To be a unit for Borstal inmates who because of mental abnormality appeared unsuitable for or had failed to respond to ordinary Borstal training.

Snell added to the four functions that the standard and accepted methods of training and discipline inherent in mainstream prisons 'will be included among those adopted at Grendon' (Snell 1963).

Early development of Grendon

The concept of a prison that would house offenders deemed to be in need of some form of psycho-therapeutic intervention was born out of an investigation conducted at Wormwood Scrubs in 1939. Sir Norwood East, Director of Prison Medical Services and Lecturer in Forensic Psychiatry at the Maudsley Hospital Medical School, in his presidential address delivered on 12 October 1943 to the Psychiatric Section of the Royal Society of Medicine, said in their report, *The Psychological Treatment of Crime*, that:

> As a result of investigation ... Hubert and I recommended the establishment of a special institution under the administration of the Prison Commissioners for the abnormal and unusual types of convicted offenders ... The institution would serve as a clinic or hospital where convicted prisoners could be investigated and treated by psychotherapy and other means, and as a centre for criminological research.'

> (The Grendon Courier 1963, p.14).

Sir Norwood East was assisted in his research by Dr W.H. de B. Hubert, Visiting Consultant from St Thomas's Hospital, and the eventual report took 4 years to complete. The embryonic institution was initially called 'The East–Hubert Institution' before being referred to as Grendon Psychiatric Prison or occasionally HM Regional Training Prison. Sir Norwood added, 'Here offenders who suffer from abnormal mental conditions, but are not certifiable...and those for whom an ordinary prison is inappropriate would receive the individual attention they require.' Sir Norwood as a former Commissioner of Prisons, who also had a psychiatric background, lent great credibility to the notion of a 'special establishment' and, after 17 years of planning, East's and de B Hubert's dream was realized in 1962 with the laying of Grendon's foundation stone by R.A Butler.

This new and innovative thinking on psychotherapeutic intervention was not confined to East and de B Hubert nor to prisons. The drafting in of British psychiatrists and psychoanalysts to the military at the end of World

War II to preside over residential treatment units for returning POWs, seems to have been the spark that triggered the idea of the therapeutic community (TC). The recommendations and plans for the treatment of 'mental disorder' in offenders and the development of a special institution to accommodate this group was interrupted by the outbreak of World War II. During the 1940s, Dr Maxwell Jones at Mill Hill, then Belmont Social Rehabilitation Unit in South London and Dr Tom Main, together with John Rickman, S H Foulkes and Harold Bridger at Northfield Military Hospital, Birmingham, developed the concept of the TC. Wilfrid Bion wrote of the first attempt at a TC in *Experiences on Groups* (1961) but was 'retired' some 6 weeks after being given charge of the first Northfield Experiment because the Unit was thought too anarchic for a military hospital by his commanding officers. Despite this, the seeds of psychoanalytically based socio-therapeutic treatment seemed to have been sown at both Northfield and Belmont Hospitals. On the other hand, some might argue that the origins of the TC could be traced back even further to 1911. At the turn of the twentieth century Alfred Adler broke with classical Freudian psychoanalysis and attached greater significance to the social context of human behaviour. The development of group psychology, it might be reasonable to assume, is perhaps attributable to the theoretical work of Adler.

Even earlier developments towards the social and communal aspects of the TC in Britain can be found in the remarkable developments in mental healthcare brought about through The Retreat in York in the 1790s, when the first communal approach to the care of mentally disturbed people under Quaker inspiration began. This work reflected the value-based approach to the treatment of individuals that runs through therapeutic community experience. The importance of the person and their capacity to bring about their own healing in relationship with others are key themes that persist from The Retreat into today's institutions.

Captain Alexander Maconochie R.N. and the Transformation of Norfolk Island

A Scotsman, born in 1787, Maconochie ran away to sea and fought in the Napoleonic Wars, during which he was captured and imprisoned for 3 years, perhaps a seminal experience. After the war, and his release, he tried his hand at farming before moving to London, where he became Professor of Geography at London University. He was subsequently appointed private secretary to Sir John Franklin, Governor of Van Dieman's land (now Tasmania).

In Tasmania he accepted an invitation, made by the Society for the Improvement of Prison Discipline, to investigate the state of the convict prison system. His report was so critical and his recommendations for reform so radical at the time that his position as Franklin's secretary became untenable. Franklin was on the point of sending him back to England when instead he sent Maconochie to be Superintendent of the Norfolk Island Penal Colony – situated on a small (6 square miles) Pacific island 1500 miles from Australia.

In March 1840 Maconochie arrived on Norfolk Island with his wife and six children. In only 4 years Maconochie turned brutalizing and degrading conditions into an enlightened and liberal regime, which he called the 'Mark System'. The central principle of Maconochie's system was that each prisoner took responsibility for his crime and for his role as a member of the group with whom he lived. He abolished floggings and tried to give prisoners the opportunity to take responsibility of a sort which the previous repressive regime prevented. For example, to celebrate Queen Victoria's birthday, he opened the gates of the prison and allowed the prisoners to wander at will and to toast the Queen with diluted rum. However, the constraints placed upon Maconochie proved insuperable and, tired of receiving his prolix memoranda for change, the Governor of New South Wales sacked him.

A portrait of Maconochie hangs in the Governor's office at Grendon as a reminder to continue the tradition of challenge and reform for which Maconochie stood.

However, it was Tom Main who first coined the phrase 'therapeutic community' in 1946 as a result of his experiences at Northfield Military Hospital, Birmingham. At the same time in Mill Hill and later Belmont, Surrey, Maxwell Jones envisaged a range of treatment approaches in hospitals as well as prisons (Cullen *et al.* 1997, p.50). The legacy of Jones and Main can be seen in the NHS today at the Henderson and Cassel Hospitals, both of which operate as TCs. The Henderson offers an entirely group-based therapy regime and provides the model on which the regime of Grendon is based. The Cassel Hospital on the other hand has used other forms of therapy, particularly individual analysis. Michael Selby, former Governor of Grendon, wrote an obituary for Maxwell Jones in *The Independent.*

HM Prison Grendon opens

Despite the fact that Sir Norwood East referred to his 'special establishment' many times to the Commissioners, it is not clear what his thoughts or strategies were about how it should be staffed or run. Plans for the prison had been drawn up by 1956 and construction began on 20 acres of a 132-acre site already occupied by an existing open prison, Springhill (a prison with its own history), in 1959.

The Rt Hon R.A. Butler, once described as the best prime minister we never had, Conservative MP for Saffron Walden from 1929–1965, was sympathetic to the idea of de B Hubert and East's 'special institution'. R.A. Butler was in the Treasury as Chancellor of the Exchequer at the time Grendon was planned but left to take up the position of Home Secretary. Butler was a very senior man in the Government; it has also been said that he was 'positive and wanted to make it' as Home Secretary. Michael Selby describes this time in history as a 'positive situation, when everything seemed possible. ... There was group counselling going on all over the place' (Snell, p.179). Butler sought funding from the Treasury and finally laid the commemorative stone in Grendon's 'centre' on 1 July 1960. R.A. Butler said at the time 'The regime must be flexible with the accent on treatment; and success will depend above all on an enlightened staff–inmate relationship, together with close cooperation at all levels between the different members of the staff' (Snell 1963, p.179).

Grendon was built by Turriff Construction Corporation, including around 30 subcontractors, and took 3 years to complete. Its reputed cost was £1.25 million. Once the contractors moved out the clearing up began. This muddy work was undertaken by working parties of up to 60 prisoners from Wormwood Scrubs. They were accommodated on B wing and were subject to a more traditional prison regime and discipline as they were not 'patients'! The planning and building of Grendon attracted quite strong local opposition and petitions were raised. One candidate at the local elections remarked that if he was elected he would insist that a siren should be installed on the prison roof to be sounded if a prisoner escaped. Grendon, when it opened, took a placatory step and threw open its gates to the general public. On one day alone 250 people were said to have visited the prison to see for themselves what lay behind the alleged mysterious perimeter wall!

Dr Bill Gray was appointed as the first Medical Superintendent and Governor. Bill Gray, a man of considerable authority and with an international reputation, worked at Grendon for 14 years and was awarded the *Companion of Bath* for his services there. He was the only prison governor to receive the award. Adrian Arnold came as an administrator and was, as a prison governor, Dr Gray's deputy. However, as it turned out, Adrian Arnold became more interested in therapy and Bill Gray found himself in the position of having to do more administration than he would have liked to have done! This set a precedent for following deputy governors, all of whom were being inspired by therapy. John McArthy, later Governor of Wormwood Scrubs, and Wilf Booth are two notable names amongst a long list of Grendon's deputy governors. Dr Gray was quoted in *The Observer* (16 Sept. 1962) as:

[He] and his staff avoided formulating a treatment policy at this early stage. This was all to the good, for too much of prison life was handicapped by bureaucratic rigidity, and at Grendon there are signs that genuine scientific experiment will be the order of the day.

Grendon eventually opened its gates and accepted its first six 'patients', who were already undergoing group therapy at Wormwood Scrubs, on 13 September, 1962. The policy was to build up slowly and by May 1963 the number of patients had reached just over 100. It was originally designed to provide accommodation for 250 men, 50 boys and 25 women. Grendon opened as an experimental (a label lost only in recent years) psychiatric prison in accordance with Section 72 of the Mental Health Act 1959 and under the direction of a medical superintendent.

The concept of a therapeutic regime within a prison setting spread to a number of other countries. The Max Glatt Centre (The Annexe) at Wormwood Scrubs and the special unit at Barlinnie prison in Scotland were set up post Grendon, both now sadly closed. The former concentrated on psychotherapy, individual counselling and life and social skills training. The latter catered for the needs of a smaller, more disruptive group of men, seeking to help them through to their release from prison. Further afield Denmark built Herstedvester, a special institution that provides psychiatric therapy for 131 prisoners. The treatment includes the use of psychotropic medication and, in contrast to Grendon, this may be administered on an involuntary basis. The La Paquerette Centre in Champ–Dollon prison in Geneva was modelled specifically upon Grendon, though it only accommodates 12 prisoners. In the USA, the Clinton Diagnostic and Treatment Center, which opened in 1966, houses 100 inmates. The treatment programme at Clinton is specifically geared towards the re-education and re-socialization of persistent offenders (Genders and Player 1995, pp.10–11).

In England, the growth of democratic TC places in prisons is increasing with the opening of a large set of five communities of 40 men in Dovegate Prison in 2001 in a private prison environment. The success story behind this new venture will be worth another book in the course of time. The development of a TC in a Cat C (lower security) prison at Blundeston for 40 men has also been a considerable achievement. The Gartree Therapeutic Community has been operating in a top-security setting for lifers for the past 10 years and has an excellent regime within a positive environment. Aylesbury Young Offenders Institution houses a therapeutic community in the Chilterns Unit, a small TC for young men, established soon after Grendon temporarily closed for re-wiring in 1990. In April 2003, in a continuation of the UK prison service's determination to provide therapeutic community facilities for those who need a more intensive regime intervention, HMP West Hill appointed the first staff and began what HMP Send now continues: the first women's Democratic Therapeutic Community. The community at Send has now been in operation since March 2004, has a full staff team and is building its numbers up to 40 women.

The survival of the therapeutic community prison within an increasingly managerialist prison service with the erosion of public service ideals and the growth of reliance on evidence-based practice for legitimacy was achieved by the incorporation of the prison within the larger prison services systems. The leadership of medical officers in the first 20 years of Grendon's life gave way to the appointment of a generalist governor with accountability through the line as other governors. This could have been very threatening to the medical ideal of the regime, but through a typically English system of checks and balances a committee to hold the ideal of therapy was established under the chairmanship of the Director of Prison Medical Services and helped the governor keep to the therapeutic straight and narrow. The future of the prison was more secure as there was now a clear strategy for therapeutic development and a focus on the need for research into effectiveness. Themes for this strategy involved:

- the treatment of 'sociopaths', currently possibly referred to as those with dangerous and severe personality disorders

- the treatment of sex offenders and their incorporation within the regime alongside other prisoners

- managing the long-term population, and in particular life-sentenced prisoners

- preparing possible release plans for difficult prisoners.

The prison continues to work with these strategies within a context of evidence-based practice, sound research and a dependence on basic therapeutic community principles.

References

Cullen, E., Jones L. and Woodward R. (eds) (1997) *Therapeutic Communities for Offenders.* Chichester: John Wiley & Sons.

East, W., N. and de Hubert, W.H. (1939) *The Psychological Treatment of Crime.* London: HMSO.

Genders, E. and Player, E. (1995) *Grendon: A Study of a Therapeutic Prison.* Oxford: Clarendon Press.

Marshall, P. (1997) *A Reconviction Study of HMP Grendon Therapeutic Community, Research Findings No 53.* London: Home Office Research and Statistics Directorate.

Snell, H.K. (1963), The New Prison At Grendon Underwood. *Medico-Legal Journal, 31,* 175–18.

Chapter 5

Send: The Women's Democratic Therapeutic Community in Prison

Caroline Stewart and Michael Parker

The idea of a women's therapeutic community in prison is not new. In 1963 Dr Snell outlined the plans for a new experimental prison: 'Grendon Prison is an integral part of the prison service and has been designed to accommodate between 325 and 350 men, women and young offenders' (Snell 1963, p.178). This chapter describes the development from plans to actuality of the first women's democratic therapeutic community, first in HMP West Hill, later in HMP Send.

Origins in the Women's team

The recent origins of the women's democratic therapeutic community (TC) go back 10 years to the mid-1990s. In 1994 a task force looked at TCs in prisons and recommended their expansion. Some time after that, the then Women's Policy Group, now Women's Team, and the then Prison Health Policy Unit set up a small working group to look at the feasibility of a women's TC in prison. They commissioned research into the numbers of women who might benefit from a TC regime. The resulting research found that at that time, when the women's population was around 2000, there were between 120–150 (6–7.5 per cent) women suitable for and who could usefully benefit from treatment in a TC (Kennedy 1998, unpublished report to the Women's Policy Group). These conclusions were in line with Maden *et al.*'s findings that 5 per cent of men and 8 per cent of women prisoners met diagnostic criteria for personality disorder or substance abuse, making them suitable for TC treatment (Maden *et al.* 1994, p.234) An earlier study in 1991 had found that 65.6 per cent of sentenced women prisoners attracted a psychiatric diagnosis regardless of whether they received treatment or not (Gunn 2000, p.333). It seemed clear that there was a considerable potential need for treatment of varying kinds, but including TC treatment, for a greater number of sentenced and remanded women than were receiving it.

The working group, which included members of staff from the prison establishment that was to house the community, went on a number of familiarization visits to other communities and residential units in prisons and hospitals to find out more about how TCs worked in secure settings and what the treatment needs of women in particular might be. Contact was also made with professionals in the Association of Therapeutic Communities, and advice sought from those with experience of prison TCs.

The policy environment of the last 10 years has supported the development of the women's TC and evidence from research into women's needs has lent support to the idea that there is a need for a more rounded and holistic treatment type that will enable emotional and psychological factors to be given time and attention in treatment. Growing numbers of women receiving prison sentences during the 1990s led to a renewed interest in the needs of women in prison, and a commitment by the Prison Service has been made to ensure that policies and practice reflect the needs identified. The Women's Team in the Prison Service was set up to take the lead in this work.

This period also coincided with the setting of Prison Service targets for the reduction of risk of re-offending: the What Works agenda, and the emphasis given to developing offending behaviour programmes, drug interventions and resettlement strategies. The Correctional Services Accreditation Panel (CSAP) was set up to oversee the accreditation of such programmes. TCs have been fully integrated into this agenda. A model for the accreditation of therapeutic communities by the Correctional Services Accreditation Panel has been developed, and the Send Therapeutic Community participates in this accreditation process by annual audit, having been accredited in March 2004 together with the male TCs in the prison estate. Funding under the Spending Review in 2000 and 2003 was used to support these priorities and a business case submitted for the development of a women's TC was successful. Full running costs were made available from 2003.

The Women's Team took the lead in co-ordinating the development of the women's TC during the early stages. A Steering Group, whose members included the Head of the Women's Team, the Area Manager and the Therapeutic Community Policy Manager, was drawn together to provide a top level strategic overview of the work. A Project Management Group was set up and chaired by the Governor of the HMP West Hill to begin with and members included staff at that establishment and others with specialist knowledge of TCs. It was responsible for the details of the planning, selection and recruitment of staff and the day-to-day development of the community at West Hill, later Send. Now that it is up and running, the Therapeutic Community Steering Group maintains oversight of the continuing development of the Community, offering advice and support as needed.

From evidence to policy

The high level of emotional and psychological needs of women in prison has been well documented (HMCIP 1999; Singleton *et al.* 1998; Prison Reform Trust 2003; Howden-Windell and Clark 1999; Clark and Howden-Windell 2000). The picture emerging in the 1990s when this early work was being done has been confirmed by a more recent study (Hollin and Palmer 2005). While sharing many of the same criminogenic needs and risk factors as their male counterparts, women's needs differ in significant ways. Women show higher needs in relation to: financial matters; family and marital relationships; accommodation; companions; alcohol and drugs, and emotional and personal factors (Hollin and Palmer 2005).

Additionally, women in prison show high levels of imported vulnerability. Studies of women in prison have reported that:

- many are mothers and primary carers: 55 per cent have children under 16, and 33 per cent a child under 5; 20 per cent are lone parents, and 80 per cent lose partner support while in prison

- many have experienced housing difficulties and inadequate housing. Many have had chaotic housing histories, for example, abandoned tenancies and rent arrears; 30 per cent lose their homes while in prison

- substance misuse is a major issue: 50 per cent report being drug dependent in the previous year; 43 per cent of remands and 23 per cent of sentenced women report heroin dependency; many are poly-drug users (6–9 substances) and 40 per cent report excessive alcohol use

- mental health problems also characterize women in prison: 80 per cent have diagnosable mental health problems; 66 per cent report symptoms of neurotic disorder; 50 per cent display features of personality disorder; 40 per cent of women report having had treatment for mental health problems prior to imprisonment and 15 per cent of sentenced women have been admitted to a psychiatric hospital prior to sentence

- many women in prison report experience of abuse: 50 per cent report domestic violence and 30 per cent sexual abuse

- 10 per cent of the sample of women engaged in deliberate self-harm.

(Singleton *et al.* 1998)

In their recent study of criminogenic risk factors and pathways into offending among women offenders, Hollin and Palmer (2005) address the issue of how such adverse life events impact on the development of criminogenic need. They report that women with higher levels of involvement in crime were more likely to have been exposed to violence as a child; experienced sexual abuse; had a violent partner; experienced extreme problems in caring for their children; had an alcohol or a drug problem, and standing out particularly as a risk factor was having been referred to a psychologist or psychiatrist. They conclude that 'there is growing evidence for a link between adverse life events and the development of criminogenic needs' and that 'we need to understand more about the relationships between factors such as abuse, self-harm, parenting, mental health, and their links with criminogenic needs and offending' (Hollin and Palmer 2005). What emerges from these studies seems to be a need in the treatment of women to attend to the whole person in relation to the range of risk factors evident.

Starting the Therapeutic Community at West Hill: Hope and idealization

In April 2003, the TC was started at West Hill, a small prison on the side of HMP Winchester, a local male prison, which had a bed capacity for 80 women. A part-time director and senior psychologist were appointed and began work developing marketing literature to send to other women's prisons and to use within West Hill and to generate an understanding of this new venture. Women expressing an interest in joining the Community were offered interviews and information, and a holding group was started in August and September 2003 – the beginnings of the Community meeting, for those expressing a continuing interest in joining the TC. Nearly all women's prisons were visited, literature distributed and talks given to staff about who the Community was for and how it worked. Interest was mixed as the Community was not yet up and running and many wanted to know whether it would succeed. External referrals from other establishments tended to be of women who seemed to be stuck where they were and for whom progress and onward movement in sentence seemed a problem.

By August and with the arrival of the full-time Director of Therapy (DOT), thoughts turned to how to expand the community and when to start the therapy groups in which to focus therapy targets. It was agreed to begin the first therapy group in September with four women. The Psychologist and the DOT jointly facilitated the group to help it become established. Community meetings had begun a little before and were characterized by high levels of anxiety about what was going to happen, what we would do in the Community, and featured many complaints about the facilities at West Hill but everyone turned up for these meetings and participation was lively.

TC staff met together with the non-TC staff team at West Hill at 08.00 as part of the development of the TC. Both Governors attended these meetings, which took on a valuable role as forums in which daily issues, both TC and non-TC, could be discussed before the day began. This morning meeting has continued after the TC left for HMP Send as part of the daily routine at West Hill. Additionally and to help develop the culture, a staff–residents consultation meeting was started, in which everyday complaints and concerns of a more practical kind in the Wings could be aired. These were stormy at first then became established and well used. The Governor attended these meetings and this clearly made the women feel they were being taken seriously as individuals in the establishment and that the TC was also being taken seriously as a new venture within it. Later, after the recruitment of the Probation Officer, a second group was started in January 2004 with three women and, again, the DOT joined the group, on invitation, for 2 months to help establish this group.

Both new groups were stormy early on. The idea of working on personally identified issues – current behaviour as it was on the wings; offending and offending behaviour as set out in the Core Programme Model – was not what some wanted from a TC and was angrily resisted by some very vocal women to begin with.

The idea of clear targets in therapy and of offence-focussed work was a shock and it was disturbing to some, who left after finding, for one woman that exploring offending behaviour resonated with prior sexual abuse and she did not want this. Others did want this and, though they found it difficult they stayed and worked with issues of abuse. In another case, work in therapy was not possible as active involvement in the commission of her offence was denied once in therapy; she gave as her reason for joining the Community that she wanted 'to help others'. Both women had read and agreed the community's rules and compact (see pages 1–4) both had agreed initially to the idea of exploration of their offending behaviour. What began to emerge in the clinical material was a great difficulty in managing hostility or anger to self or others within groups or community and a strong trend towards placing this into the staff members' remit to 'do something with'.

Another major initial difficulty emerged from a tendency to attribute to the Community all that each woman wanted it to be: a place of rest, a hideaway – 'a beautiful island' – and this re-arranging of aims included attempts to distort the normal prison rules: 'we are in the TC and we do it different here'. While true in one sense, this was used as a means to try to bypass prison rules, which had to be thoughtfully resisted by the staff team and resulted in more disappointment and conflict. Work in the Community was fraught and rather chaotic to begin with as the difference between wish, hope and offending behaviour-based reality became clearer.

The useful aspects of hope and longing for difference and change provide the spur to joining such ventures as TCs in the first place and to match this, staff needed to be able to convey an idea of hope to those joining the Community. 'The instillation and maintenance of hope is crucial in any psychotherapy. Not only is hope required to keep the patient in therapy so that other therapeutic factors may take effect, but faith in a treatment mode can in itself be therapeutically effective.' (Yalom 1995, p.4) Idealization led to disappointment and the feeling, often expressed by the women, that the staff had let them down, disappointed them and not measured up to the ideals: we never could. However, as a team we tried to hold on to the sense of hope and wish to develop a Community that could deal with some of the important issues women choosing to come to the community demonstrated and we were careful to hold and contain their ideals despite their almost daily change of shape. More practically, an art group was set up for women in the Community together with a cookery group and educational aims drawn into the therapy targets to be considered as part of the total treatment aims. At West Hill, women were able to support each other naturally by being locked up behind their Wings rather than in their cells and a natural support system developed among the women in the Community, which they found invaluable.

Literature was produced and re-written several times to advertise the TC. Roadshows were organized to other women's prisons between April and December 2003 to describe and explain who the Community was for and how it worked, and HMP Durham was visited in the New Year. Roadshows were delivered to a mixed and sometimes sceptical audience. The one difficulty standing out in recruitment work was the cautious response received from several establishments. In one instance we were told: 'we have several women we would like to refer but we want to see how it develops first.' Awkward as it is to recruit on that basis, nevertheless, referrals did begin to be made and eight women from West Hill who saw what was being attempted applied to join early on in Autumn 2003.

As the non-unified staff members' efforts gathered momentum unified staff became interested and two men and three women staff members put themselves forward to join the TC, making a colossal difference. Over 2 months in New Year 2004, the support network spread from daytime to more or less 24 hours a day with their help on night and weekend duties. This had a very positive and settling effect on the Community and so there was real sadness and anger that the women who had joined the Community would lose these staff members who had been there with them in times of difficulty and anxiety, when the move to Send was announced in March 2004.

The move from West Hill to Send

In the wake of population pressures in the prison estate and a sharp unanticipated rise in the numbers of men coming into prison, HMP West Hill, the new women's TC, was re-rolled as a prison from female to male in March 2004 and the TC was obliged to move to HMP Send. After consultation between the Governor of Send, Head of the Women's Team and Director of Operations in the Prison Service, it was agreed that Send was the most suitable site for the women's TC in the long term and anxieties that had generated into real difficulty about the possibility of a further move were put to rest by the Director of Operations that the Community was to have its home in Send.

The move took place within two weeks during late March 2004. Strategic thinking at operational level was that a long drawn-out move might make matters worse and so the staff and prisoner group were obliged to move as quickly as possible. There was a meeting at West Hill with Governors, staff members and prisoners from West Hill and Send to field questions about what Send was like and to go over details of the physical move itself. Prisoners were to be moved as close together in time as possible so that there would be as few separations of women from each other as could be managed. A-wing was allocated as the TC wing at Send.

The move produced a strong reaction among the women, who felt they had lost their safe base: the Community as they knew it together with the unified TC staff team at West Hill, who had become familiar to them and their work in therapy. The TC unified staff team there had been present intermittently in groups during the week but most importantly had been with them during evenings and weekends, when support was often needed. Their contribution was invaluable and they had, as a team, begun to function in a way that combined good sense discipline with a caring and supportive approach, which enabled the first women in the Community to feel supported and to a considerable degree understood. Only the DOT, Senior Psychologist and Probation Officer moved to Send with the women in the Community. All the unified staff members without exception were unable to move with the Community and there was a complete loss of the evening and weekend staff base that had become so important to the women prisoners and to their sense of safety. Some of these prisoners were very angry indeed, blaming staff members. They felt there was nowhere else to locate these feelings, articulating specifically that they felt unsafe with staff at Send, who did not know how a TC worked. Send, initially, was a new environment, unfamiliar with the way a typical TC operated. This was coupled with a certain amount of obvious misgivings and uncertainty by staff members at Send about having a therapeutic community thrust on them. The shock was too much for some women community members who left the community.

Four women prisoners left the community in angry protest after a May Bank Holiday, 2 months after the move to Send. They felt the gap in time between meeting with TC staff on weekdays and the absence over the weekend, when there were no TC staff on duty, was too great for them to cope with (there were no unified TC staff yet appointed to the Community in Send). Another woman, feeling the same lack of support from Community-familiar staff, also withdrew shortly afterwards. The Community had halved in numbers and this produced further anxiety and fear that the whole venture would collapse.

Work in the therapy groups came to a halt while these worries were addressed issue by issue and we entered a crisis of confidence in which all thinking was focussed on whether the TC would continue or not and both therapy groups were joined together for a time while anxiety was at its highest. A sense of crisis continued until more women were accepted into the Community and it became clear that there was an intention to make the Community work. These anxieties also affected the staff team, who were unsure for a time whether their work had a future or not and we discussed among ourselves how to manage our own anxieties and worries in order to try not to place too much undigested worry of our own onto Community members, who were clearly very concerned and looking to us to see them through this uncertain transition.

The majority of the difficulty expressed in the Community lay in the gap between daytime, when non-unified staff members were running the Community, and night and weekend times, when there was felt to be an absence of understanding of the emotional responses often generated in therapy. The four women who stayed had decided that, come what may, they were going to remain and continue what they had started in therapy. The staff and external support team – the women's team and the management team at Send – worked to think how to resolve these difficulties and planned a hard-hitting advertising campaign locally in Surrey to recruit unified TC staff to work in the Community to bridge this clear and important gap in continuity of care, as few staff from Send expressed an interest in applying to join the TC, at least initially.

Early life at Send

Hope and idealization of the untested idea of 'what the TC would do for me' came into conflict, this time with the rules and security baseline of the prison and a sense that 'they think they are special', from existing staff; this became a minor theme reverberating in the staff group in the wider prison for a period in early 2005, once the Community had moved to HMP Send. Difficulties arose with the main prison hosting the TC in such matters as being in cell on time at roll check, wishes to decorate cells with pictures beyond the limits laid out, or anxiety about the misuse or overuse of the newly created Buddy system, in which women could buddy up with each other after lock up time if in real crisis, instead of using the Listeners' scheme. TCs expect to observe the ordinary rules of prison but there was great pressure not to do this from women in the TC in the early days of the Community's life and to create instead an entirely different, idealistic environment with a different rule base than was wise or possible.

The Community had to adapt to its new host environment. At West Hill women Community members were free after lock-up to come and go within the Wing and into and out of each others' cells as they wished. With this freedom a natural support system could be and was developed, though not without some unwanted pressure at times. It remains a hope to resume this free movement after lock-up behind the Wing gates as a particular feature of the women's TC into the future once it reaches its intended population of 40 women. In the meantime, the Community was operating without unified staff and this presented a major problem.

Completing the staff team: the advert

A proposal was made in the Women's Team to advertise for staff to work for the Community after a successful campaign had been run to find staff for a Young Offenders' prison. An advertising company, Barkers, was contacted and they quickly met staff from Send and from the TC, asking questions to establish the nature and purpose of the TC. They produced a highly effective campaign, accurately capturing the purpose and spirit of TC work in two meetings and advertised in local papers and on a bicycle outside the local train station in Woking. This worked very well and a group of potential staff contacted the prison, were interviewed and the majority offered posts in Send TC.

Some staff already at Send wanted to work in the community, though this did take longer to emerge. All were obliged under the What Works in Prisons Accredited Therapeutic Community Manual guidelines to be interviewed for suitability for TC work specifically, and all existing staff expressing an interest were offered interviews. By early summer 2005, the TC had achieved a full staff complement and unified staff members were able to join the therapy groups once more. The next task remains to complete induction and training for the whole staff team. Individual and group supervision has been in place for those involved in therapy group work since 2003 but those not in groups will not have a natural means of taking part in group supervision.

Disturbances in the Community and changes in population

It has not been the intention to describe the clinical work at Send in detail here nor research: this will be undertaken when the Community is further established and when research recently started can complement descriptive clinical narrative. However, some particularly strong themes have emerged in the life of the Community that seem worth comment as they generated both conflict and disruption in the Community and need to be understood. These themes emerged as argument and angry responses in the life of the Unit and caused some women to leave the Community prematurely. This is not entirely unusual and Penelope Campling, after Rapoport (1960), writes of 'the repeated cycle of oscillations: times of healthy functioning, when residents were well able to manage responsibility and a level of therapeutic permissiveness; other times when high levels of disturbed behaviour meant that staff had to take a more active role.' (Campling 2001, p.397) More healthy, stable functioning alternating with mood changes in the Community and periods of anger or hopelessness are predictable features of TC life and can be perplexing to staff new to TC functioning. Such oscillations have been evident in the short life of the Send Therapeutic Community but seem linked to identifiable actions or difficulties in a way that is less random than is sometimes described. In two of the examples cited below (2 and 3), the move to Send and discussions about the involvement of probation work seemed to be involved at the start of the difficulty. The other example (1) appears due more to a process of Community members projecting wished-for fantasies onto the idea of the TC and, while anger was directed at staff members, appeared to originate more in their own wishes and needs than anything the staff had or had not done.

A very simple bar chart below shows numbers of women resident in the Community plotted against major disturbing themes evidenced in Community meeting records, therapy group records and the wing chair's log. The chart could appear to show that periods when women chose to leave prematurely may be linked to the themes idenftified in Figure 5.1.

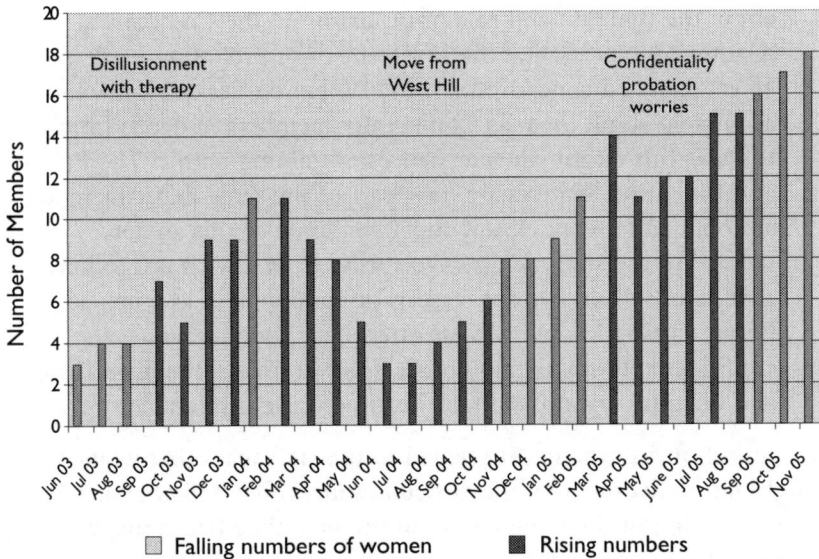

Figure 5.1 TC membership.

The three main themes emerging in Community discussion were as follows.

1. *Disillusionment with therapy:* Two women left because it was not the nurturing, all-embracing Community they imagined it to be. There was disillusionment on discovering that the Community was not a sanctuary, a place where women would be looked after.

Anger was focussed on the notion that there might be work to complete in understanding offending and offending behaviour coupled with refusal to do this.

2.   *The move from West Hill*: Five women left angrily after the move to Send in March 2004, when the entire unified staff team who had supported them during evenings and weekends was lost. They felt the gulf between meeting non-unified staff in the weekdays with no TC unified staff members to help tide them over evenings and weekends was too great. They also felt that it was too difficult for them to tolerate the variation in styles of care and support between unified and non-unified staff members that became evident in interactions on the Wings outside weekday times.

3.   *Probation and confidentiality worries*: Two women left the Community in the wake of angry and unresolved discussions about the function and role of probation in the Community. Alarm was expressed at the involvement of probation work and an exaggerated concern that if the Probation Service knew more accurately about them as Community members in depth from therapy, this might worsen chances of gaining parole. The Prison and Probation Services are now part of the same department and are obliged to work closely together. Some of this anxiety seemed to the staff members to spring from a wish not to have aspects of self known for reasons of concealment as much as because being known was a matter that should remain confidential to the therapy process; nevertheless, the disturbance and hostility towards staff at this time was considerable.

In each period of disturbance, it seemed to the staff team that women left who might not have done so if the difficulties identified had not taken hold in the dynamic life of the Community in the way they had done, but it is impossible to be certain about this.

The themes in numbers 1 and 3 above are also suggestive of difficulty looking at the details of personal involvement and motivation in offending. The four women leaving did so at points at which they had begun to be asked to look more closely at the nature and pattern of their offending behaviour and the extent of it, and all four were finding it very difficult to do so. In each of the four cases in numbers 1 and 3, issues involving anger and rage were present in the clinical material and appeared particularly difficult to work with, as anger was directed towards staff. It seemed safer to enact the difficulty and attack the staff and Community, and split off the difficult thinking that work in therapy presented. This may be in keeping with the findings of Zamble and Quinsey (1997) that the emotional state of the offender at the time of the offence was an important factor in understanding the dynamics of offending and this was the area the therapy team were trying to approach. Leaving could be understood as a defence and resistance to attempts to engage with such understandably difficult recall and its consequent dynamics in current feeling states.

Hollin and Palmer point out in their research on women that: 'It is the Emotional and Personal subscales of the LSI-R that is predictive of reconviction.' (Hollin and Palmer 2005, p.54). This set of factors needs to be addressed in order to improve the likelihood of reducing reconviction in women but it also seems to be the case that such a return to thinking about the offence may resurrect difficult, traumatic or otherwise carefully defended thoughts and feelings. Within this cognitive series of connections in offence thinking may lie painful, aggressive or otherwise destructive aspects of self and sense of being re-traumatized by re-entering the thinking associated with the offence. Clinically, this area of work needs to be treated with the greatest respect and understanding due to the inevitable regression and increased vulnerability brought about by the process of re-visiting old behaviour patterns and what they mean, and what they have meant in the past. For those periods when staff might appear to be involved in the origin of difficulties, such dynamics are taken into the staff supervision process normally or into the staff consultation group for understanding and where needed, changed as well as can be done, though it is clearly difficult to avert every and any situation that might present difficulty.

Two accounts from women who have taken part in the TC at Send so far are included in Chapter 19 and give a clear indication of what might be done in therapy and what time in a TC might be like from the direct perspective of women in therapy.

Acknowledgement

Jane Roberts, Psychological Assistant at HMP Send, kindly produced the chart indicating the numbers of women in the community plotted against dominant disturbing themes in the community records at the time.

References

Campling, P. (2001) Therapeutic communities. *Advances in Psychiatric Treatment, 7*, 365–372.
Clark, D. and Howden-Windell, J. (2000) *A Retrospective Study of Criminogenic Factors in the Female Prison Population*. London: Home Office.

Howden-Windell, J. and Clark, D. (1999) *Criminogenic Needs of Female Offenders: A Literature Review.* London: HM Prison Service.

HMCIP (1999) *Thematic Review: Women in Prison. Her Majesty's Chief Inspector of Prisons.* London: HMSO.

Gunn, J. (2000) Future directions for treatment in forensic psychiatry. *British Journal of Psychiatry, 176,* 332–338.

Hollin, C. and Palmer, E. (2005) *Criminogenic factors among women offenders. Research Study for the Women's Team, HM Prison Service.* London: Crown Copyright.

Kennedy, H. (1998) (unpublished study). *Women's Therapeutic Community Feasibility Study.* London: Prison Service Women's Policy Group.

Maden, T., Swinton, M. and Gunn, J. (1994) Therapeutic Community Treatment: a Survey of Unmet Need Among Sentenced Prisoners. *Therapeutic Communities. 15,* 229–236.

O'Brien, M., Mortimer, L., Singleton, N., *et al.* (1997) *Psychiatric Morbidity among Women Prisoners in England and Wales.* London: Office for National Statistics.

Prison Reform Trust (2003) *Report of Wedderburn Committee.* London: Prison Reform Trust.

Rapoport, R. (1960) *Community as Doctor: A New Perspective on a Therapeutic Community.* London: Tavistock Publications.

Singleton, N., Meltzer, H. and Gatward, R. (1998) *Psychiatric Morbidity among Prisoners in England and Wales.* London: Office for National Statistics.

Snell, H. K. (1963) The New Prison at Grendon Underwood. *Medico-Legal Journal, 31,* 175.

Yalom, I. (1995) *The Theory and Practice of Group Psychotherapy.* New York: Basic Books.

Zamble, E. and Quinsey, V.L. (1997) *The Criminal Recidivism Process.* Cambridge: Cambridge University Press.

Chapter 6

Serendipity or Design? Therapeutic Community History and Maxwell Jones's Theory

Dennie Briggs

Our last conversation on 8 August 1989 began by Maxwell Jones suggesting I ask him what scientific 'proof' he had as to the effectiveness of his work. I thought it a leading question as we had often discussed the difficulties of evaluation. But he immediately took the question as a touchstone to reflect on his work, which he now saw as having moved toward a paradigm: '…the accumulation of knowledge which can be added to, or subtracted from, in light of further information.'[1] He continued:

> Those of us who are working in the field like yourself, are comfortable with the idea of a paradigm because it's no longer seen as irrational, or lacking in proof. It's knowing when to get away from objective reality which is so stultifying and so characteristic of our industrial age. More and more people in the pure sciences, too, are moving into paradigms.

1   This, and the following quotes, are excerpts from our conversation which was recorded on videotape and will be available in the Maxwell Jones's Archive at the Planned Environment Therapy Trust and Study Centre (PETT).

I pointed out that he had previously used the term 'evolutionary' which was unsettling to a lot of people as being too vague, and that paradigm connoted something more definitive, yet remained fluid.

> Right, but the paradigm that we've gone by in open system work has its own dangers. Because a paradigm tends to reinforce its own beliefs, you get the danger of a fixation which really blinds you to other possibilities that you're missing by focusing on the central theme. So, everything fits into your preconceptions. I've had that criticism all my life: people have said, "It's your manipulating the system." And I've never liked that. I think that it's overlooking the essence of the open system in that leadership is increasingly shared, emerging from the bottom, which means that there are checks and balances. If I say that we really ought to have an extra meeting for research every week, I'll be opposed by some people while others will express their support; we are now in a position to learn.
>
> Now, some people point out that we're paying too much attention to reality in the objective sense, and we're going to reinforce the rational approach, the very thing we want to get away from, to be able to think freely, beyond the limitations of the five senses, time and space.

Max later gave the example of meditation as an attempt to listen to something other than the outside world, 'to my true self.'

Open systems and the process of change

Then Max began to sketch some specifics of an 'open system', commenting that he believed that social organization (as differing from social structure) implies constant flux, leaving reality and rationality if it is to grow. That, he said, was the most important or primary aspect for change. A key to achieving that kind of organization was Max's unbending insistence on multiple leadership. His view of this included everyone in the community: leadership was fluctuating and leaders arose to the occasion. He had relied heavily on James Tyhurst's studies of disaster situations where the most unexpected source could come through, to which Max added that everyone has such 'latent possibilities'. I reminded him of the many people who had credited him as being a charismatic leader. From that unexamined insinuation we looked at the influence of the Eastern guru, and mythologically at the function of the 'awakener', one who inspires, either by example or in teachings. What the critics stamp as 'charisma' seems to overlook its context in an open system, where there are constant checks and balances to prevent cultism, which many religious and pseudo-religious organizations lack. Max stressed the need for a facilitator in bringing about change to an open system; he often described this role as a 'neutral outsider,' and suggested that:

...Everyone is a facilitator at some time and, finally, the idea of a process review, you're really getting a structure which is forever changing....The essence of change in the social learning context is that each of us listens to everyone who communicates in the group setting and...you then incorporate the idea which becomes a part of you. You may or may not even be conscious of this process.

To me, the *process* becomes more important than the goal: treating patients or helping prisoners, or whatever. *Process* means that you're not taking a straight line to develop a more articulate group of prisoners. What you're doing is allowing the paradigm to grow, in light of your information and your own interaction. As it grows, everyone is changing in harmony. It's a very subtle thing. A truly open system is a most sensitive body and everyday it changes. But, that doesn't mean that it's unstable; it really means that it's flexible.

We then spoke of how programmes can lose their vitality in an effort to preserve their structure, which Max referred to as 'addiction to a system', or 'paradigm fixation' when we 'get lulled into complacency by our own brilliance....The dynamic of a therapeutic community (TC) is that it's constantly changing, even from minute to minute.' He commented that in his work he came to the point where he almost welcomed a crisis, '...Because then one saw how people had to operate without time to consider or censor their thoughts.' 'Crisis', Max continued, 'means that the social organization is challenged and that it responds with heightened morale and togetherness. It tests the depths of the integrity of the group as a whole.'

Max focused on the quality of communication and that as it becomes more open and trusting, the level of consciousness changes: 'You become less tied to the objective. You begin to allow for some latitude in entering the world of fantasy or dreams and the abstract; even the spiritual begins to creep in.'

Adaptability in prison work

Maxwell Jones's last direct contact with prisons, I believe, took place after he retired to Nova Scotia. He had been contracted to do a written evaluation of Canada's Therapeutic Community Programme at Springfield Medium Security Federal Institution. At the time of this consultation (June, 1983) the programme for 100 prisoners had been in existence for 14 years, started by a psychiatrist, who still came by every two weeks, and several correctional officers, some of whom who had been there since its beginning. He was impressed with the programme and the possibilities that it could be spread to the other 300 prisoners, making it a total therapeutic institution.

Prior to moving to Nova Scotia, Maxwell Jones had been involved in a therapeutic community project in the Maracopa County Jail in Phoenix, Arizona, beginning in 1978, with Chief Psychiatrist Leonardo Garcia-Buñuel. His participation lasted until 1982, when he arrived in Canada. The project began with a trial run to determine the feasibility of this approach in the jail, both in terms of acceptance by the administration and the diverse population they wanted to engage (prisoners with schizophrenia and character disorders). From this experience, they modified their modus operandi and began a longer term programme that lasted over the following decade.

The pilot phase lasted 18 months and consisted of 16 prisoners who volunteered and were selected by the psychiatrist, one-quarter being diagnosed as schizophrenic. Not only was the project able to blend the two diverse populations, but, as Max had foreseen, it 'tapped the creative potentials', especially of the 'clients' manifesting personality disorders. Looking back, Dr Buñuel recalled:

> It was very moving to see how some of our recalcitrant social offenders were able to respond to many of these 'crazy' patients and how they even helped them with elementary personal hygiene needs. It was an unforgettable lesson for all of us, including Max, that scoundrels and madmen could work together and even offer and receive help to and from one another. (Garcia-Buñuel 1991, p.131–137)

The group aspects of the programme consisted of a 15-minute staff meeting that included four inmates elected monthly by the Community, a 50-minute Community meeting followed by a process review of equal time, again with the elected representatives participating. The Community meeting aimed at sharing information, interaction, listening and problem solving. He saw the staff members as examples for the members to learn the fundamentals of group dynamics, problem solving and decision making by consensus.

Developing a therapeutic culture

Max listed a number of stages, processes, or principles in developing 'a therapeutic culture in a therapeutic community as an example of a system for change within a fairly typical jail.' He emphasized the importance of administrative considerations, drawing on his knowledge of organizational development (Jones 1980).

The overall goal of the project was to develop a therapeutic culture: a system of attitudes, values and beliefs, aimed to tap the latent and manifest creative potential of both clients and staff. Now the question could be posed: would this different social environment modify clients' asocial values, attitudes and beliefs? As a treatment mode, Max reiterated his stance that it was not primarily concerned with intrapsychic conflicts, but rather focused on environmental influences, social relationships and change as a result of social learning. The concept of 'treatment', he maintained, was an existential one in which the individual and the group seek a feeling of purpose in relation to society. A key element, especially in the pilot phase, was exploring 'mechanisms' in conflict resolution that were developed and employed in the jail programme. Maxwell Jones delineated:

1. *confrontation*: a different kind from the Synanon type, where, after a period of several months, conflicts between clients and staff played themselves out slowly as clients tested the staff on the safety of confrontation

2. *compromise*: for example, application of institutional rules enforced by custodial staff; here the social work staff facilitated compromise, while for the most part upholding the spirit of the rule

3. *integrating opposing ideas and practices toward new solutions*: a third and most important mechanism. In the day-to-day operations of the unit in the jail, conflicts arose between behaviour that could jeopardize the programme and enforcement of the rules. Cohesiveness resulted in creative solutions being generated between the community, clinical and custodial staff that protected all parties.

There were many ups and downs as the programme proceeded; there were setbacks, many due to changing the higher level administration, which had conflicting ideas about the programme. At one point, Max withdrew completely, but returned under a new administrative structure. The programme, nevertheless, continued. Much of what Max taught us (Garcia-Buñuel 1991) survived for over 10 years, which in a jail setting is little short of miraculous. A therapeutic community operating within a jail system may not reach more than a negligible percentage of the inmates but if it succeeds at changing the social structure of the organization within which it operates, modifying the power structure and the exercise of autocratic, even if benevolent, paternalism, then the effort has been worth its while many times over (Garcia-Buñuel 1991, p.134).

Professor Hans Toch of the State University of New York arranged a two-day seminar on 'Therapeutic Communities in Corrections' at the Institute of Man and Sciences at Rensselaeville, New York, in December 1978. Max and Fritz Redl were the featured seminal thinkers joined by others who had experience in applying the concept to correctional settings (Toch 1980).

Max listed 21 'desirable features' for such a project beginning with modifications in the organization and functioning of the correctional institution if it was to be conducted within its confines. Identified changes included modifying rules and regulations to accommodate an 'atypical social system', to confidentiality, to a definitive chain of command. The point of departure for the project itself had been largely those social learning principles he had already illuminated from his work at Henderson, revised by his experiences in mental hospitals.

Flexibility in leadership style

Then Max concentrated and enlarged on the role of the staff: 'Growth in the direction of social maturity is an immediate goal for the staff and ultimately for the clients too'. 'Treatment and training', he continued, 'overlap, so that one can talk of treating staff and training clients as well as vice versa.' A precept that became apparent to him back in his days at Henderson when he wrote to the effect that meetings for the patients and staff were probably best kept separate until the patients could be told the full truth. At the seminar he also mentioned that the staff had to 'be prepared to recycle basic principles as required'. That adaptability will be evident as the 'oscillatory process has peaks when clients assume considerable responsibility and the staff becomes largely supervisory, and times when this process is reversed.' (Jones 1980, pp.34–35)

As for the clients, they 'should have as much responsibility and authority as they are competent to manage.' He suggested action-oriented roles, for example they should nominate their own leaders as representative 'culture carriers' for new clients (e.g. a committee, as he'd experienced at Durango Jail). He went on to say that, in time, discipline and decisions could be delegated to that committee, a procedure he'd learned from his experiences with former prisoners-of-war (POWs): at the start, they'd demanded order and control from authorities.

In the area of leadership, Max reiterated his views that

a well-balanced social structure assumes that everyone has his area of competence, and recognizes it. In Chino Prison, for example, leadership emerged from the most unlikely places, and was changing hands daily. There was no assumed authority structure. (Jones 1980, pp.106–107)

In the fourth Isaac Ray Lecture to the American Psychiatric Association in 1960 Max focused on 'Social Psychiatry in Prisons'. He said, 'We seem to be dealing with a population which cannot easily be fitted into any psychiatric classification although many would belong under the general heading of Personality Disorders. They cannot be isolated as clearly defined medical or social categories' (Jones 1968, p.78).

He cited the California Department of Corrections' classification system, which took into account legal, social and psychological factors in determining the type of confinement and rehabilitation measures to be undertaken. Max singled out the experimental use of a prediction device in which certain factors, available at the time the inmate entered the correctional system, could forecast the chances for recidivism among various groups. In addition to its probability function, he called attention to the 'base expectancy' device as being useful in planning programmes for offenders making maximum use of prison facilities (space, education, 'treatment', parole supervision and so on). Maxwell Jones devoted considerable room in his lecture to describe the use of a different method of evaluating personality:

> ...An attempt is being made to assess personality integration. This is an interesting attempt to introduce a classification system which promises to be more appropriate for a prison population than any psychiatric classification yet devised. ...This theory describes seven maturity or integration levels (I-levels) which represent successive stages of growth in the capacity to perceive self and the environment without distortion. This implies an increasing capacity to form social relationships and to integrate more realistically and effectively with one's environment. (Jones 1968, p.81)

With this knowledge of a different means of personality assessment in which a rather specific goal of treatment would be to raise the social maturity level, Max went on to describe further experiments in a US Naval prison. There inmates, grouped by I-levels, were assigned to 'living groups' of 20 under the guidance of three Marine non-commissioned officers and a psychologist. The groups consisted of high and low I-levels, and some were mixed. The other interesting facet of the experiment was that the Marine supervisors were also rated by the same method (that is to say, groups of high, low and mixed I-levels of prisoners were matched by staff of the same or varied levels). The studies represented a first attempt to study the effectiveness of:

1. kinds of treatment for kinds of offenders

2. the outcome of interaction of staff and inmates.

One of the findings of the Naval prison research was that treatment goals could be enhanced by matching I-levels of confinees and staff while the reverse was found by mismatching them.

Here, Max detailed his prototype for a therapeutic community in prison, drawing on his experiences beginning with the former POWs and from Henderson, and incorporating his knowledge of social maturity and living groups. To begin, he advised that youthful first offenders with higher social maturity levels and better chances of success be chosen among volunteers.

The model followed his practice of 80–100 in size, composed of volunteers, with daily community and small groups, a common work project, and so on. From the obstructions and difficulties of operating his community at Henderson within the confines of Belmont Hospital, he recommended the first study be carried out in one of the forestry camps, which were relatively autonomous from the parent prison. This project was followed by a comparable one within a minimum-security prison. Max and his long-time colleague, Joy Tuxford, a psychiatric social worker, assisted in orienting the prison staff about the therapeutic community and training the project staff. With modifications, his scheme was implemented for older recidivists with lower social maturity levels, first in two experimental projects and then extended to ten more in a total programme that was in lieu of building a prison for 1200 inmates. A further similar project was developed for narcotics addicts and extended to a new total institution for 2200 addicts under civil rather than criminal commitment (Briggs 2000).

Maxwell Jones's treatment rationale, for want of a better term, can be traced back to his initial exposure to psychiatry during 5 years with David Henderson at Edinburgh University. Max became his senior assistant and in 1935, a lecturer in psychiatry. He found Professor Henderson's psycho-biological orientation to psychiatry was not what he was looking for:

> Anyone with an inquiring mind was driven to seek an orientation which seemed to offer promise for the future and some sort of satisfaction to the patient. Psychoanalytic training offered one such choice, but this was frowned on by the Professor, and out of necessity I was driven to explore the biochemical and endrocrinological fields in relation to psychiatry. I had the opportunity to work with Professor Aubrey Lewis....I became interested in physical methods of treatment, in particular insulin coma, only to be again disappointed in this approach. The war years were my salvation. (Jones 1953, pp.15–16)

It was here that serendipity set in. Beginning with physiological studies of soldiers with neurocirculatory asthenia, alongside a known cardiologist, after a year and a half, the two physicians concluded that the symptoms were largely psychological rather than physical. 'Treatment' then assumed an educational turn and in order to teach the patients to understand and cope with their condition, he undertook classes for the 100 soldiers which soon became a 'community.' Now roles and relationships became the grist for the treatment workshop. He began to talk about re-socialization rather than treatment, a term which he carried over into his next project, that of working with former POWs.

> This presented an ideal opportunity for us to extend our interests from a predominantly psychosomatic field to a predominantly social one. We developed a 'transitional community', which helped to rehabilitate men who had been shut away from ordinary society for up to 5 years and who had to try to adapt to a world which had largely forgotten them. (Jones 1968, p.1)

Max cited Adam Curle from his work with ex-civilian resettlement personnel, to begin to formulate the process of internalization which later, during his psychoanalysis with Melanie Klein, would become refined in her theory of object relationships:

> Curle believes that it is the internal assimilation and integration of culture that is primarily disturbed in the process of desocialization in the ex-POW personnel. This would appear to be largely true in the case of our chronic unemployed population. It would also be true to say that we have made great efforts to develop a suitable hospital culture in an attempt to resocialize the patients. (Jones 1968, p.17)

At Henderson in 1947 Max took on still a new challenge: the rehabilitation of chronically unemployed, socially nonconformist individuals. By now, he had a method that had worked well in two very different treatment situations and he had trained a core staff who were committed to the venture. In addition to enhancing opportunities for relationships between patients and with staff, he was aware of needing to know more about the culture of the community and its effects on change. This was when he enlisted the aid of seven behavioural scientists, who, over a period of 3 years, intensively studied the workings of the programme. What happened there over the next 12 years, while he refined and modified his basic plan, is history. Going back to his original intentions, he summarized his work:

> You see, it all boils down to what we did originally which was merely to take a proactive stance and try to promote change in the established hierarchies of the various helping professions – to make better use of the environment....In my own work I saw the humanizing of hospitals and the professions as the major contribution. Our goal was to recognize the patient or client as a person and demonstrate the power of his peers to change things.

The ultimate goal was for each person to achieve fulfilment. (Briggs 2003, p.320)

Maxwell Jones's principles of social learning

This discussion returns us to his use of paradigm to encapsulate what he also spoke of as an open system. In his later years, Maxwell Jones, referring to himself as a social ecologist, abandoned the term *treatment*, replacing it with *social learning*. He enumerated five general conditions for social learning to occur:

1. people who are motivated to change or grow

2. the presence of a facilitator with skilled neutral leadership

3. the creation of a group setting or milieu where those people can communicate openly and freely together leading to an appropriate level of feeling with one another (a 'challenging uncomfortableness' in contrast to 'rigidifying panic')

4. face-to-face confrontation, occurring around an individual or more general problem area

5. timing of interventions.

(Briggs 2005)

Schematically, his prototype includes these five essentials and their bearing on one another, to which can be built in more enhanced procedures such as systematic observation or research, action, and changing consciousness. These three elements have been demonstrated in projects with prisoners and youth studying their community, becoming change agents, and altering their perceptions of reality (Briggs 2004).

Wrapping up, Maxwell Jones developed a system for change whereby individuals could achieve social maturity, personality integration, and fulfilment, be they children or youth, practitioners, or victims of psychological trauma. He focused on a basic social organization that was flexible, adaptable and able to 'recycle' its basic principles, not dominated by the limitations of 'objective reality'. His tactic was one of being proactive, using appropriate measures to break through the 'trances of ordinary life' when, in an unsettled state, new learning could occur. He termed it *social learning*. Unafraid of leaving outmoded reductive viewpoints, he was able to embrace consciousness changes, including the effects of spiritual elements, enhancing his understanding and practice into a holistic one. Did he come about his philosophy by chance or was it a product of intent and *design*? I hope to have conveyed the notion of consistency in Maxwell Jones's work, not as a static, but as an active process that took into account those undetermined elements that are displayed in situations and relationships. I also used the word *serendipity* – as the variable – with the definition of 'making useful discoveries by chance'. This changing, fluctuating element we can see in all his undertakings. In conclusion, it might be closer to the truth to say the question is not *or* but rather *and*, for it is clear he used both elements. The unification of the two was part of his ingenuity.

References

Briggs, D. (2000) In Prison. Online Occasional Papers 1–3. *Planned Environment Therapy Trust and Study Centre.* www.pettarchiv.org. uk/publications.htm.

Briggs, D. (2003). Summing up: A day with Maxwell Jones. *Therapeutic Communities, 24*, 301–325.

Briggs, D. (2004). *In School 4: Youth Action Team.* www.pettarchiv.org.uk/publications.htm.

Briggs, D. (2005). Learning to Live: Social Learning in Practice. *Occasional Paper, 11, PETT Archive.*

Garcia-Buñuel, L. (1991). Penal developments in Arizona. *International Journal of Therapeutic Communities, 12*, 131–137.

Jones, M. (1953). *The Therapeutic Community: A New Treatment Method in Psychiatry.* New York: Basic Books.

Jones, M. (1968) *Social Psychiatry in Practice: The Idea of a Therapeutic Community.* Harmondsworth, Middlesex, England: Penguin.

Jones, M. (1980) Desirable features of a therapeutic community in a prison. In H. Toch (ed.) (1980) *Therapeutic Communities in Corrections.* New York: Praeger.

Toch, H. (ed.) (1980) *Therapeutic Communities in Corrections.* New York: Praeger. (Proceedings of the Rensselaerville seminar.)

Further reading

Briggs, D. (2002) *A Life Well-Lived: Maxwell Jones – A Memoir.* London: Jessica Kinglsey Publishers.

Briggs, D. (1972) A transitional therapeutic community in a prison. In S. Whiteley, D. Briggs, and M. Turner. *Dealing With Deviants.* London: Hogarth Press.

Jones, M., Briggs, D and Tuxford, J. (1964) What has psychiatry to learn from penology? *British Journal of Criminology, 4*, 227–238.

Jones, M. (1962) Society and the sociopath. *American Journal of Psychiatry, 119*, 410–414.

Jones, M. (1957) The treatment of personality disorders in a therapeutic community. *Psychiatry, 20*, 211–220.

Jones, M. (1956) The concept of a therapeutic community. *American Journal of Psychiatry, 112*, 647–650.

Method and Practice

Chapter 7

Assessing Risk and Need in a Prison Therapeutic Community: An Integrative Model

Richard Shuker and David Jones

Work in a therapeutic community (TC) requires constant attention to the different skills and experience contained in a team of multiprofessional and resident (or attendee) members. While such work can produce great power and energy, a team can be prone to schism and disintegration if individual or professional needs and strengths are not felt to be afforded sufficient value. This is particularly evident in the area of assessment, where actuarial methods of assessment have competed with clinical judgement. This chapter describes ways in which a range of assessment models can be brought together to provide a picture that is both informative and retains potential for surprising change and growth. The difficulty with actuarial methods has been that although they may provide a comforting feeling of certainty for some, they offer little hope for the client or help for clinicians. The overall model also has to encompass the notions of 'criminogenic need' coming from the field of forensic psychology and the 'internal world' coming from the field of psychoanalysis. The former claims to itemize specific issues or attitudes that contribute to criminal behaviours and to intervene directly. The latter is concerned with the modification of internal, often perverse, relationships: a concept that is much more slippery and difficult to demonstrate or test.

A further element, which is in urgent need of research and discussion, is the contribution that can be made by other residents. The prevailing view is that in a prison setting men are open to bullying or other forms of compromise, so it is unrealistic to expect them to make a decisive contribution to the assessment process. The role of the prisoner in contributing to the assessment process is discussed.

This chapter is a good example of the kind of teamwork described earlier. The product in a working TC is more akin to an emulsion, where contributing elements separate out if left alone but can combine effectively when carefully tended, than a solution where the integrity of the substance is retained. In this fashion, the first part of the chapter is written by Richard Shuker, a forensic psychologist, who thus appears as first author, and the second part is written by David Jones, a psychoanalytic psychotherapist.

Development of a model of structured clinical assessment

Models for clinical assessment with forensic populations have evolved significantly since risk assessment models first developed in the 1980s. Purely predictive models of offender risk assessment lost their status as having an overarching and unchallenged legitimacy and a new generation of assessment models emerged, providing a fresh impetus and direction to forensic risk assessment. A redefinition and renewed conceptualization of 'clinical' assessment supported by encouraging levels of predictive validity allowed non-actuarial or 'probabilistic' approaches to reclaim some authority. Furthermore, the emerging evidence base for multimodal interventions in the treatment of personality disordered populations called for an increasingly diverse range of assessment methods drawing from different theoretical perspectives. Meta-analytic studies within forensic research pointed to the need for clinical focus on criminogenic factors when targeting recidivism and assessment methods that were capable of responding to relevant attitudinal, affective, and interpersonal factors became increasingly called for. Responding to this need approaches emerged that were able to identify a diverse range of treatment needs and provide a means to define and measure offence-related risk.

TCs offer unique and potent opportunities for assessment in forensic populations. Perhaps their most defining feature is the conscious and explicit use of the wider institutional structures to provide opportunities for learning and change. The overt use of the internal institutional mechanisms as central components of intervention ensures a diverse and multimodal treatment structure. This simultaneously provides a rich and diverse range of information on which to measure therapeutic change and, in forensic settings, forms the basis for the assessment of offence-related risk. This chapter will advocate a model for clinical assessment that can incorporate structured approaches to the assessment of treatment need, risk reduction and therapeutic progress by integrating a range of assessment methods from psychodynamic, cognitive and social learning perspectives. In doing so, a broader range of clinical knowledge can be incorporated to enhance clinical case conceptualization, comprehensively define individual treatment need, and establish individually relevant treatment plans.

Research in the field of risk assessment was approached with renewed vigour since the 'nothing works' consensus in the field of offender rehabilitation was challenged in the 1980s (McGuire and Priestley 1985; Losel 1995; Lipsey 1995). Monahan (1981) concluded that the poor prediction made by psychologists and psychiatrists of future violent behaviour was due to the inadequate, arbitrary and idiosyncratic use of relevant predictor variables and the lack of clarity to the measurement and definition of violence. Large-scale studies such as the MacArthur Violence Risk Assessment Study (Steadman *et al.* 1998) have helped contribute to evidence-based risk assessment approaches and a development in clinical practice that has seen an integration of actuarial with clinical approaches in the assessment of risk of violence (Webster *et al.* 1997). As a reaction to the strongly subjective nature of risk assessment methods where the charismatic authority of the assessor could dictate what and what was not construed as relevant to risk of violent recidivism a series of what were coined a 'second generation' of risk assessment methods were generated (Menzies and Webster 1989; Monahan 1984) namely 'actuarial' approaches to assessment. Actuarial risk assessment procedures involve employing mathematical formulae to quantify levels of risk to make risk *predictions* and provide probabilistic estimates that a specific behaviour may occur within a given time frame (Hanson 1997; Hanson and Thornton 2000). The aim of actuarial assessment is to provide an estimate or probability of reconviction. In the field of violent reconviction the Violence Risk Appraisal Guide (Quinsey *et al.* 1998) is the most widely used measure of actuarial risk. It consists of 12 weighted mainly 'static' risk predictors and provides a probability of violent reconviction over a seven- and ten-year follow-up period.

Recent shifts towards integrating actuarial with clinical approaches to risk assessment have been referred to as the third generation of risk assessment methods (Grann and Pallvik 2002). The structured clinical approach provides a focus or guidelines to clinical assessment by 'anchoring' the clinician's judgement around the relative value of historical and static factors. The

Historical, Clinical and Risk Management 20 (HCR-20; Webster *et al.* 1997) is the best known instrument combining relevant historical factors with specified clinical and risk management items to make decisions about risk of violence. This method involves an empirically guided approach to clinical judgement by providing a structure to decision making. In doing so, the parameters for risk assessment are defined by those clinical variables considered to be of relevance to violence. This approach can be conceptualized as an *aide-memoire* that attends the clinician's attention to important information that otherwise may be overlooked by drawing on findings in the risk assessment literature (Blackburn 2000).

Difficulties in measuring clinical change with forensic populations

Finding appropriate criteria with which to evaluate treatment efficacy presents challenges. Reconviction provides an unsatisfactory means with which to measure treatment outcome as crime surveys suggest that the vast majority of offending behaviour goes undetected (Myhill and Allen 2002; Harris and Grace 1999). For example, Lloyd *et al.* (1994) estimate that only 3 per cent of all offences result in a criminal conviction. Psychometric evidence is another method routinely used as a measure of treatment efficacy. Whilst psychometric measures are able to consistently demonstrate at least short-term change in key treatment domains such as behaviours, cognitions and attitudes across different forensic populations (Blud 2003; Wilson *et al.* 2003), the evidence supporting their ability to predict long-term behavioural change and future offending has not been demonstrated with any level of certainty. Raynor (1996) argues that only limited evidence supports a relationship between treatment change assessed through psychometric measures and reconviction. Furthermore clinically significant change has mainly been used to evaluate the *short-term* impact of treatment (Beech *et al.* 2002). In addition, Shuker and Newton (2004) found that improvements in EPQ-R Psychoticism (Eysenck and Eysenck 1991) were negatively correlated with reconviction.

Traditional approaches to assessment of offenders in forensic settings use a model that attempts to establish 'risk factors' from file reviews and predict their manifestation within the custodial setting (McDougall and Clark 1991). For example, instrumental aggression during a robbery committed to fund a drug habit may demonstrate itself in the form of bullying other prisoners for drugs or currency with which to obtain drugs. This method has been criticized for its lack of predictive validity as there is no evidence that this technique is likely to identify risk factors actually associated with offending (Towl and Crighton 1995).

Therapeutic communities as an assessment model

Assessment methods in TCs have drawn from different assessment methodologies. The approach perhaps most representative of wider TC practice and values has been to allow clinical/professional judgement to form the basis of an inclusive approach in which all members of the community (both staff and residents) are jointly involved. Whilst standardized psychometric measures have been incorporated into assessment practice, the approach has traditionally been 'client centred', allowing the clients' needs to emerge as an intrinsic consequence of the nature of the therapeutic relationships within the TC setting. The use of diagnostic clinical and empirical assessments has not featured as a central part of conceptualizing the clients' needs.

This assessment model has shifted significantly in recent years, particularly within prison-based democratic TCs. The assessment and conceptualization of individual needs centres around a multimodal approach incorporating clinical information from diverse sources (Democratic Therapeutic Communities Theory Manual 2004). TCs that target offending behaviour as a specified outcome measure rely as much on historical and collateral information including detailing offence histories, custodial behaviours, previously defined 'risk factors', and psychosocial assessments as they do on clinical information obtained from the treatment setting. Into this is incorporated evidence drawn from psychometric, behavioural, psychosocial and structured empirical or diagnostic assessments to establish treatment targets that reflect and identify criminogenic, social functioning, emotional and motivational needs.

The clinical basis for TC intervention is drawn from the focus on behaviours displayed in the treatment setting to which the therapeutic process can then respond. As a core principle, therapeutic communities rely on a therapeutic structure that enables these pathological patterns of behaviour to emerge and be used as a basis for intervention. Treatment is underpinned by practices and structures that allow clinically relevant behaviours to be observed, registered and monitored. This provides a basis for an explicit assessment methodology.

Therapeutic community structures and offence-paralleling behaviour

Jones (2004) critiques the McDougall and Clark (1991) risk assessment model by arguing that offending behaviour and its parallels within custodial settings is not a static process or single event but rather a sequence of behaviours in the form of a chain of events. Consequently, he argues that offence-paralleling behaviours may have representations in terms of cognitive, affective and behavioural indices that may not have immediately obvious similarities to the offence. The patterns of thoughts, behaviours, emotions and fantasies experienced in the treatment setting may not always have clear and obvious parallels with the offence itself but may nevertheless form reliable predictors of relapse. Whilst it may be mistaken to assume that an individual will exhibit the same behavioural patterns in similar settings an individual's unique construal of the situation will lead certain cross-situational parallels in behavioural response. Shoda (1999) argues that although people can be inconsistent across different settings, characteristic behaviour can emerge through an interaction of situational and individual factors. This has implications and opportunities for clinical assessment within the context of forensic settings.

Jones (1997) describes offence-paralleling behaviour as establishing links between relapsing behaviour within the treatment setting and offending patterns. This extends the McDougall and Clark (1991) risk assessment strategies incorporating the theoretical perspective that behaviour is a sequential process and parallels or approximations to offending behaviour can be drawn at cognitive, attitudinal and affective levels. As suggested by Jones (2004) within the treatment environment of a TC this allows an exploration of which *behaviours*, displayed in which *situations*, encountered in which particular *emotional states* are of relevance to offending.

TC practice rests on a set of guiding principles that define a distinctive treatment ethos and culture (Genders and Player 1995; Haigh 1999). The potency of this model is derived from a set of structures and activities that both establish and maintain this culture. Specifically, practices that promote therapeutic exploration, debate, enquiry, participation and empowerment are central components of an intervention where different arenas of experience can be used for therapeutic value and where distinctive opportunities for risk assessment and treatment emerge.

In a model developed by Shine and Morris (2000) the forensic TC model extends this practice so that, and this is of considerable value in intervention *and* assessment, psychological or developmental, offence related and current behavioural patterns can be explored in relation to each other (Figure 7.1).

For example, take Clive and the domains of offence-paralleling behaviour demonstrated in Figure 7.1.

- In the developmental domain, the assessment indicated borderline, avoidant and antisocial features. He has a pervasive lack of trust, is exceptionally self-critical and believes himself to be worthless and unlovable

- His offence was committed upon consumption of alcohol and involved attempting to set fire to his flat after the termination of a 'relationship'.

- Recent Wing behaviour involved isolating himself during the Wing sports day following a dispute with another member of the Community and 'barricading' himself in his cell.

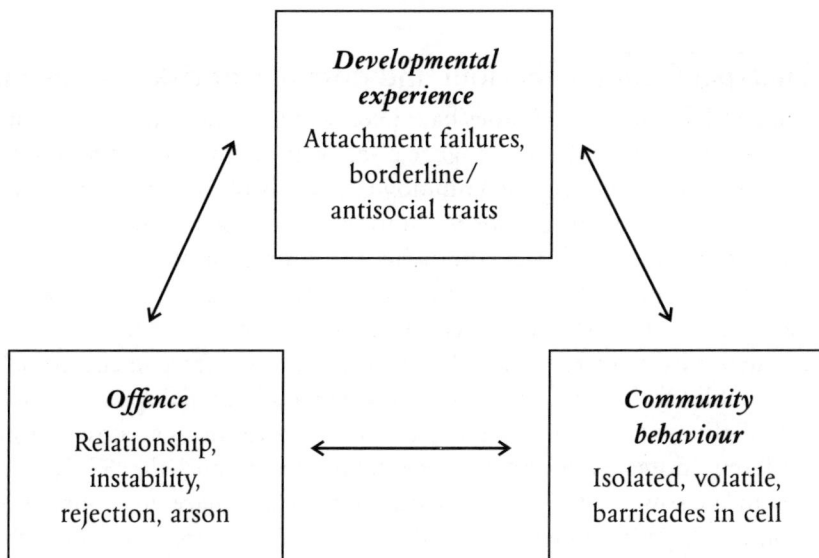

Figure 7.1 *Three domains of offence paralleling (adapted from Shine and Morris 2000).*

The therapeutic group is able to focus on the patterns of interpersonal difficulties, social isolation, and impulsive behaviour that became established during his early development. Likewise therapeutic attention is equally given to the behavioural sequences observed on the Wing and links made with the behavioural chain associated with his offending.

Of particular importance in the analysis of the factors contributing to offence-paralleling behaviour is a treatment setting that is able to adequately contain and manage behaviour. Cullen (1997) emphasizes the need for the custodial setting to allow the individual to behave in ways that 'mirror' the behaviour whilst at liberty. Institutional procedures that inhibit, suppress, or do not contain the opportunities for patterns of offending behaviour to emerge will lead to a sterile environment where it is unlikely that offence-paralleling behaviours will routinely feature in prisoner's behaviour. The custodial environment needs to reflect diversity in the form of relevant social, interpersonal and situational factors of relevance to offending behaviour. Crucially, it is important that the custodial setting has procedures that encourage and emphasize the value of all components of the prison regime: work, education, leisure, and domestic responsibilities, as an integral part of the treatment structure and that facilitates the 'feeding back' of prisoner behaviour within the settings into the core therapeutic process.

Offence-paralleling behaviour and domains of risk assessment

Unstructured treatment modalities have been widely criticized as those with which offenders are unlikely to engage effectively and are considered to be of little value in addressing the criminogenic needs of offenders (Andrews 1995). Clearly treatment groups without either defined structure or prescribed content may well lack the focus to be of clinical relevance with offending populations if they were not rigorously anchored in the therapeutic principles and practices described earlier. Where they are structured they offer a method that offers a clear focus on cognitive, affective and behavioural variables from within the different therapeutic domains.

The earlier example of Clive can be extended to illustrate how within the different domains of offence-paralleling behaviour, the TC model enables an assessment of the individual's needs to take place on a number of different levels (Shine and Morris 2000). Figure 7.2 demonstrates how the incident highlighted is routinely fed back by gym staff and other Community members into the TC and so begins the exploration of the cognitions, affect, fantasies and behaviour that underpinned it. Clive is supported in identifying the parallels between the three domains. His behavioural responses typify indirectly channelled aggression. This takes the form of arson, in the case of the offence; barricading his cell, in the Wing-based behaviour and 'nuisance' letters during the developmental domain. A sequential pattern can also be traced in the parallels between fantasies experienced (patterns relating to revenge, power and idealized intimacy) in each of the domains. Patterns in affect can also be identified across the domains (themes of depression, despair and isolation) and in cognition (perceptions of worthlessness, social undesirability). The multi-faceted nature of the therapeutic regime allows these behavioural patterns to emerge and be identified in different settings that enable a clear focus for the assessment of clinical need, offence-related risk and an exploration of any relationship between the two.

Developmental domain

Cognitive: I'm inferior, powerless and unlovable
Affective: Depression, isolation, anger
Fantasy: Idealized representation of intimate relationships
Behaviour: 'Harassment' of women in unwanted attention, letters etc.

Offence domian

Cognitive: I'm worthless, rejected and made to look a fool
Affective: Depression, anger, humiliation
Fantasy: Being important, respected, powerful
Behaviour: Sets fire to flat

Current behaviour

Cognitive: I'm not valued, repected or important
Affective: Anger, depression, hopelessness
Fantasy: Revenge, control, being 'noticed'
Behaviour: Barricades cell, threatens self-harm

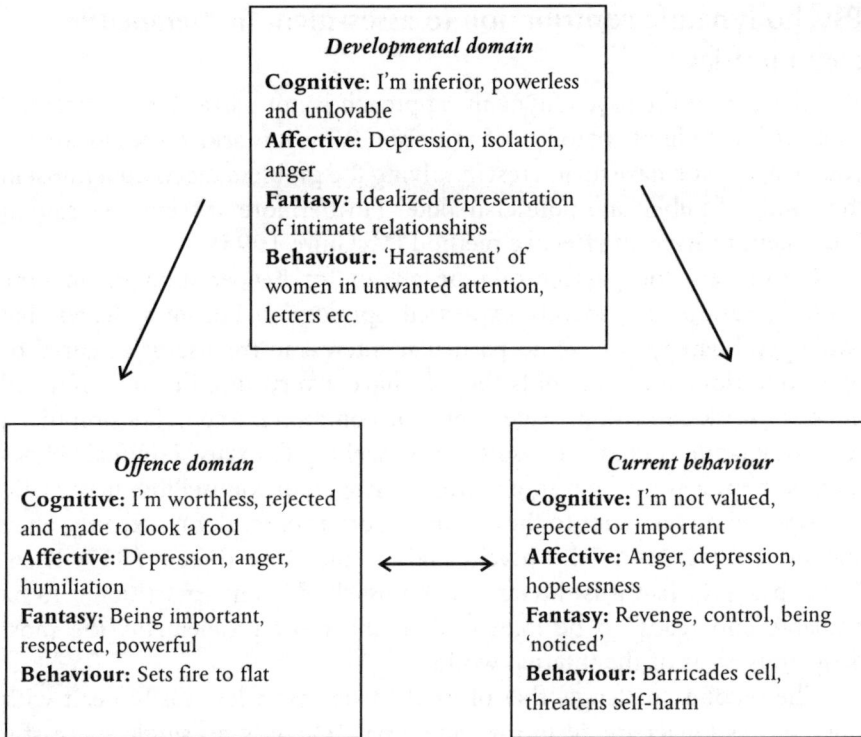

Figure 7.2 Levels of offence-paralleling behaviour in TC assessment (adapted from Shine and Morris 2000).

Extending this idea to a risk management strategy, Jones (2004) points out that developing models of offence-paralleling behaviour can inform effective risk management strategies. The technique enables those involved in clinical case management, in both lower security custodial and community settings, to develop an understanding of the patterns of behaviour associated with relapse, allowing supervisors to have a more informed knowledge of which potential behaviours may be indicative of increased risk. For example, boundary violations and causing splits or divisions amongst the various case workers may be indicative of offence-paralleling behaviours that are associated with increased risk.

Psychodynamic contribution to assessment in therapeutic communities

To suggest that the psychodynamic approach is not particularly concerned about risk is to invite parody and criticism. Why, it is asked, should we pay you a wage if you have no interest in solving the problem that is uppermost in the minds of public and politician alike? Furthermore, it seems, we cannot even claim to have an effective method (McGuire 1995).

Fortunately the passage of time allows for deeper thought and the gradual erosion of stridently expressed opinions. It becomes clearer that while psychoanalysts have no particular interest in the use of actuarial or other questionnaire-type tools they do have a very specific and continual interest in risk and risk management. The common misapprehension that a psychodynamic approach is a soft option seeking to excuse criminal behaviour, perhaps arising from some forms of Rogerian counselling, may easily be dispelled by reference to the extensive corpus of work on sexuality, envy and destructiveness in the psychoanalytic literature (Freud 1917; Klein 1952, p.63). In fact it is the task of the psychodynamic practitioner to be available and ready to be immersed in the most problematic, the most dangerous areas of the internal world.

The second challenge, that of ineffectiveness, is less easily dealt with since professionals are all in the same boat. There is no single successful approach to the problem of criminality and dangerousness but there are at least indications that personality disorder and psychopathy can respond to psychoanalytic psychotherapy, which is a major element of the TC approach (Bateman and Tyrer 2004; Salekin 2002; Adshead 2001). It is the application of a range of different modalities within the TC framework that holds out greatest promise but it is the psychoanalytic model that is the founding discipline and the bedrock of TC practice (Hinshelwood 1999).

The purpose of assessment

There is real meaning behind the question: what is the purpose of assessment? Generally speaking TCs in prisons are working with a therapeutically unusual client group. The clients are often from a highly disadvantaged background, perhaps with a history of physical and sexual abuse. Their educational level may be rather low and their motivation may be questionable. Given that psychotherapies are sometimes criticized for preferring to work with the 'Young, Attractive, Verbal, Intelligent and Successful' (YAVIS) together with the industrial nature of prison therapy, which combines high numbers of prisoners working with low staffing levels of largely untrained staff, the likely outcome would seem to be somewhat unpromising.

This underestimates the real nature of psychotherapeutic work. When psychotherapy begins to challenge rigid and dysfunctional internal structures, whoever the patient is, resistance is always encountered and this has to be recognized and disarmed before progress can be made. Although the YAVIS patient may appear to be perfect for private practice the reality of cutting-edge psychotherapy is always with more problematic patients in less than ideal settings. The skill lies in finding a way to engage the client in developing an interest about themselves so that at least a part of them is working on your side.

Assessment is seldom a static procedure. It is dependent upon the strength and resilience of the treatment agent whether this is an individual practitioner or a Community. Much of the difficulty that we encounter in TC work occurs because of the fragility of the treatment culture. This varies from hour to hour and day by day according to a number of factors:

- the quality and experience of the membership of the TC
- the experience of the staff
- the capacity of the TC to understand and contain powerful transference relationships
- the underlying strength of the culture
- the ability of the TC to withstand external pressures. This is particularly important in an institutional setting such as a prison service, when the operation framework may have limited understanding of the process and be made anxious by a degree of disruptive behaviour
- morale.

The implication of this is that the TC will be able to work effectively with more disturbed, more difficult members the stronger it is and the better it is running according to the criteria set out elsewhere in this book. In addition, this means that one needs to be continually assessing and reassessing at both the group and the individual level.

None if this is meant to imply that assessment is unimportant – only that it is more difficult than one might think. The individual who seems most unlikely in one situation one day may be quite suitable in a different situation at a different time. His capacity to engage and work effectively may be influenced by a chance encounter with a staff member who is felt to understand and sympathize with him and champion him (Wilson and McCabe 2002) There are, however, important considerations to be borne in mind, particularly the need to avoid harm to the prisoner and to your colleagues. For example, Rapoport's finding that some men with a fragile ego structure may be damaged in a TC remains valid today (Rapoport 1960). Staff members who are vulnerable may be similarly affected, particularly if they have limited training and support. Not only will their individual mental health be affected but also, if the psychodynamic symptom goes unnoticed, there is a chance that it will 'snag' upon the psychopathology of a prisoner, provoking an unacceptable acting out in either or both of them (McLure 2006).

Where in the internal world?

When somebody new comes to a TC they bring something with them. They bring a part of their external reality but they also contribute something of their internal world. This idea of the internal world is crucial to an understanding of the potential for violence and risk generally since, if we insist on hearing and giving credence only to the surface meaning of the words that are spoken, we run the risk of missing the most unstable and dangerous part of the prisoner's psychopathology. Of course in prisons there is often an assumption that the prisoner is dangerous; it can be taken as read but if it is simply assumed rather than 'heard' then the subject may feel misunderstood and be further alienated.

The internal world can be understood as that mental space where our mind lives. At the deepest levels it is always chaotic and unpredictable while at the level of conscious awareness it will be more stable. It is characterized by a complex and rich set of internal relationships that constantly shift in direction and in intensity. These interactions will tend to coalesce into certain formations, for example akin to a nurturing mother or a critical father. Although some of these internal relationships and the way they are represented may predominate, they are by no means unchanging. It is the conception of the dynamic nature of these internal relationships and the way in which they can colour the experience of the external world, transference, that differs from the more static, schema-based model (Young 2003).

The configuration of these internal relationships and their qualities will determine the nature of the experience of other, external relationships and the degree of satisfaction with life. By gaining an understanding of this inner life it is possible to make a formulation and to test it out. The psychodynamic formulation takes into account three areas of object relations (Hinshelwood 1991): current relationship life – the external world and infantile object-relations – and fantasy life: the internal world. The third component of this model would usually be the relationship with the assessor, which is understood as representing the transference relationship. In the TC it is possible to utilize not just the relationship with the assessor but with a number of other actors as the relationship with the members of the TC evolves.

Current life

When new in a TC prisoners often begin by talking about current life events, the things that are bothering them. These early descriptions that prisoners give of their life situation often differ markedly from material as presented in their own written applications or in other reports. Often these early presentations, their insistence on current life events or seemingly petty demands and needs, can be irritating to staff who may see them as irrelevant. For example, very soon after he arrived in the TC Graham started complaining that outside he had a baby daughter who was being withheld from him. This was new information and threatened to put his place at risk so agitated and distracted did he seem. We wondered whether he had the mental space and strength to do any psychological work on himself. He would become very angry about the situation and swore revenge on the child's mother, whom he experienced as being spiteful and vindictive. He would tell his story in such a way that he easily gathered support from other prisoners, despite the fact that he had physically abused the mother and he had no record of offering consistent care to the child. His story was easy for other prisoners to identify with because of their own experiences of neglect and ill treatment.

There was a strong element of self-justification in his account and behaviour, which caused the team to worry about his commitment and ability to empathize with others, in this case the mother of his child. However, it can be seen also as a snapshot from his internal world and one could hazard a guess that there had been some experience of cruelty and deprivation in his own life. His anger and resentment was in part about the way in which his childhood, his internal baby, had been stolen from him.

The internal world

There is already a clue to at least one aspect of his internal world in the previous piece of information. Further description of his early life and memories told of a father who was often absent and whose return was feared because of his drunkenness and the beatings he gave to Graham. His mother was a prostitute, who also beat him and his brother, the only other child. Both parents abused him physically and sexually and he had to learn to look out for himself from a relatively young age. As a result, he had developed an extremely tough and seemingly impenetrable carapace. He had little love for his parents, both of whom were dead. It was as if the repetitive model in his mind was of having gone to them and they had let him down and disappointed him. His own relationships with women had all ended when violence towards his partners developed and he began to believe that they too were letting him down and going with other men. His internal world was dominated by harsh parental figures who ignored and betrayed him and it was the interplay between his internal world and the life that he lived with the people around him that was so crucial to the catastrophic course that his life took. In his relationship with the TC he became a leader of sorts, a leader of siblings like Jack in Lord of the Flies, 'See? See? That's what you'll get! I meant that!' (Golding 1959, p.181). This message was largely unspoken but conveyed through his presence and appearance.

The transference relationship

He related in different ways to me and to his Community. To me he was like a little boy. He tried hard and wanted to succeed. I became the father that he wanted to look up to, who he came to for help. My internal feeling was that it was too much. I could not meet his need and I was tempted to push him away thinking that there must be someone else better fitted to look after him. In real life he had actively sought help from various mental health services over a 10-year period. This was rather unusual for a man in his situation but he had felt disappointed and let down by each of these encounters and one can imagine how helpless each therapist or counsellor felt. The TC was more hopeful, however. They were less overcome by his neediness and more able to see the part of him that was seeking to make a change to himself and his life. In fact his relationship with the Community was more paternal and he quickly became Wing Chair.

The central situation

The theme that ran through each of these areas, the current life, the internal world and the transference relationship was to do with neglectful and cruel parents, betrayal and the more hopeful determination to remedy the course that his life was taking. His rage at his former partner and wish to gain some control over his child seemed like a re-enactment of his own childhood, an identification with the child and a wish to make something good. His attention was directed towards staff suggesting that initially at least; sibling rivalry was not a pressing issue. The difficulty for Graham would be the inevitable disappointment that he would experience in his treatment. Of course he would have to experience this disappointment in order to make progress and the therapeutic agent, the TC would need to be strong enough and benign enough to contain the rage of his disappointment without falling into the trap of repetitive punishment. The amelioration of this harsh internal world is the work of therapy and the judgement that has to be made during assessment is whether the ego structure is open enough to allow for the possibility of change but not too exposed and vulnerable that it will fragment under pressure.

The risk

If we return to the idea of risk we can see that the degree of risk will depend upon the nature of relationships in the internal world and the integrity of the ego structure that contains this. It is common for all of us to experience violent, even rapacious, fantasies but it is at the point when the fantasy of the internal world becomes a reality projected onto some external subject that the danger increases.

For some men the line between fantasy and reality is easily crossed; they are an obvious risk. Other men are more problematic. They may seem well balanced and socially minded but as therapy proceeds further difficulties emerge and their institutional risk level may even increase. Some men remain so highly defended that they remain problematic in terms of potential behaviour and hard to engage emotionally. They may even appear to be engaged and working well while in the background their thoughts follow quite different lines related to a set of needs and interests that are quite different to those presented to staff or even other inmates. This 'psychopathic' defence is challenging to work with and can be disabling for a Community, which may be duped by such a presentation or intimidated by the individual concerned. Despite this caution the TC with its wide range of social interactions provides the ideal setting for the close examination of behaviours, linking them with the psychopathology of the individual.

Conclusion

This chapter argues that the forensic risk assessment paradigm is greatly enhanced through incorporating a psychodynamic formulation into risk assessment activities. Exploring internal relationships and transference reactions enhances understanding of a resident's emotional, cognitive and interpersonal world. Structured empirical formulations of risk are improved through using the therapeutic relationship (with staff and the community) to provide a crucial source of information about the residents' needs. Strong emotional reactions, the re-enactment of repetitive self-defeating behaviours, and resistance or ambivalence about treatment engagement can be better understood with an integration of psychodynamic concepts. Attempts to operationalize psychodynamic assessment have recently been made (OPD Task Force 2001) demonstrating that structured frameworks can be used to complement and augment psychodynamic approaches to assessment.

The TC model provides a well-crafted clinical process where the internal world of the resident, the complex interpersonal relationships that emerge, and opportunities for behavioural observation present significant sources of information for risk assessment that can be more effectively captured through the integration of divergent risk assessment modalities.

References

Adshead, G. (2001) Murmurs of discontent: treatment and treatability of personality disorder. Advances in Psychiatric Treatment. *British Journal of Psychiatry, 7*, 407–416.

Andrews, D. (1995) Clinical conduct and effective treatment. In J. McGuire (ed.) *What Works: Reducing Reoffending*. Chichester: John Wiley & Sons.

Bateman, A. and Tyrer, P. (2004) Psychological treatment for personality disorder. *Advances in Psychological Disorder, 10*, 378–388.

Beech, A., Friendship, C., Erikson, M. *et al.* (2002). The relationship between static and dynamic risk factors and reconviction in a sample of UK child abusers. *Sexual Abuse: A Journal of Research and Treatment, 14*, 155–167.

Blackburn, R. (2000) Risk assessment and prediction. In J. McGuire, *et al.* (eds) *Behaviour, Crime and Legal Processes: A Practical Guide for Forensic Practitioners*. Chichester: John Wiley & Sons.

Blud, L., Travers, R., Nugent, F. *et al.* (2003) Accrediting offending behaviour programmes in HM Prison Service: 'What Works in Practice'. *Legal and Criminological Psychology, 8*, 69–81.

Cullen, E. (1997) Can a prison be therapeutic? The Grendon template. In E. Cullen, L. Jones and R. Woodward (eds) *Therapeutic Communities for Offenders*. London: John Wiley & Sons.

Eysenck, H.J. and Eysenck, S.B.G. (1991) *Eysenck Personality Scales (EPS Adult)*. London: Hodder and Stoughton.

Freud, S. (1917) *The Sexual Life of Human Beings. In Introductory Lectures on Psychoanalysis*, Vol. 1, Pelican Freud Library. London: Pelican Books.

Genders, E. and Player, E. (1995) *Grendon: A Study of a Therapeutic Prison*. Oxford: Clarendon Press.

Golding, W. (1959) *Lord of the Flies*. Berkley Publishing Group.

Grann, M. and Pallvik, A. (2002) An empirical investigation of written risk communication in forensic psychiatric evaluations. *Psychology, Crime, and Law, 8*, 113–130.

Haigh, R. (1999) The quintessence of a therapeutic environment: five universal qualities. In P. Campling and R. Haigh, (eds) *In Therapeutic Communities: Past, Present and Future*. London: Jessica Kingsley Publishers.

Hanson, R.K. (1997) *The Development of a Brief Actuarial Risk Scale for Sexual Offence Recidivism* (User Report No 1997 – 04). Ottawa: Department of the Solicitor General of Canada.

Hanson, R.K. and Thornton, D. (2000) Improving risk assessment of sex offenders: A comparison of three actuarial scales. *Law and Human Behaviour, 24*, 119–136.

Harris, J. and Grace, C. (1999) *A Question of Evidence? Investigating and Prosecuting Rape in the 1990s.* Home Office Research Study No. 196. London: Home Office.

Hinshelwood, R.D. (1999) Psychoanalytic origins and today's work, The Cassel heritage. In P. Campling and R. Haigh (eds) *Therapeutic Communities; Past Present and Future.* London: Jessica Kingsley.

HM Prison Service (2004) *Democratic Therapeutic Communities Model. Theory Manual.* Submission to Correctional Services Accreditation Panel.

Hinshelwood, R.D. (1991) Psychodynamic Formulation in Assessment for Psychotherapy. *British Journal of Psychotherapy, 8,* 166–174.

Jones, L. (1997) Developing models for managing treatment integrity and efficacy in a prison-based TC: the Max Glatt Centre. In E. Cullen, L. Jones and R. Woodward. (eds) *Therapeutic Communities for Offenders.* London: Wiley.

Jones, L. F. (2004) Offence paralleling behaviour. In A. Towl and G. Towl (eds) *Needs: Applying Psychology to Forensic Practice.* BPS, Oxford: Blackwell.

Klein, M. (1952) The emotional life of the infant. In *Envy and Gratitude (1975),* London: Hogarth Press, p.63.

Lipsey, M. (1995) What do we learn from 400 Research Studies on the effectiveness of treatment of juvenile delinquents? In J. McGuire. (ed.) *What Works: Reducing Offending,* Chichester: Wiley.

Lloyd, C., Mair, G. and Hough, J.M. (1994) *Explaining Reconviction Rates: A Critical Analysis.* Home Office Research Study No. 36, London: HMSO.

Losel, F. (1995) The efficacy of correctional treatment: A review and synthesis of meta evaluations. In J. McGuire (ed.) *What Works: Reducing Offending.* Chichester: Wiley.

McLure, L. (2006) Support and supervison for staff in a therapeutic community. In D. Jones (ed.) *Humane Prisons and How to Run Them.* Abingdon: Radcliffe Press.

McDougall, C. and Clark, D. (1991) A risk assessment model. In S. Boddis (ed.) *Proceedings of the Prison Psychology Conference.* London: HMSO.

McGuire, J. (1995) *What Works: Reducing Offending.* Chichester: John Wiley & Sons.

McGuire, J. and Priestley, P. (1985) *Offending Behaviour: Skills and Strategies for Going Straight.* London: Batsford.

Menzies, R.J. and Webster, C.D. (1989) Mental disorder and violent crime. In N. Weiner and M. Wolfgang (eds) *Pathways to Criminal Violence.* California: Newbury Park, Sage.

Monahan, J. (1981) *Predicting Violence: An Assessment of Clinical Techniques.* Beverly Hills, California: Sage.

Monahan, J. (1984) The prediction of violent behaviour: Towards a second generation of theory and policy. *American Journal of Psychiatry, 141,* 10–15.

Myhill, A. and Allen, J. (2002) *Rape and Sexual Assault of Women: The Extent and Nature of the Problem.* Home Office Research Study 237. London: HMSO.

OPD Task Force (2001) *Operationalized Psychodynamic Diagnostics.* Göttingen: Hogrefe and Huber.

Quinsey, V., Harris, G., Rice, T. and Cormier, M. (1998). *Violent Offenders: Appraising and Managing Risk.* Washington DC: American Psychological Association.

Rapoport, R. and Rosou, I. (1960) *The Community as Doctor: A New Perspective on a Therapeutic Community.* London: Tavistock Publications.

Raynor, P. and Vanstone, M. (1996) Reasoning and Rehabilitation in Britain: The results of the straight thinking on probation (STOP) programme. *International Journal of Offender Therapy and Comparative Criminology, 40,* 272–284.

Salekin, R. (2002) Psychopathy and therapeutic pessimism: Clinical lore or clinical reality? *Clinical Psychology Review, 22,* 79–112.

Shine, J. and Morris, M. (2000) Addressing criminogenic needs in a prison therapeutic community. *Therapeutic Communities, 21*, 197–219.

Shoda, Y. (1999) Behavioural expressions of a personality system: generation and perception of behavioural signatures. In D. Cervone and Y. Shoda (eds) *The Coherence of Personality: Social – Cognitive Bases of Consistency, Variability, and Organisation.* New York: Guildford Press.

Shuker, R. and Newton, M. (2004) Do psychological test score changes predict risk of reconviction. Paper presented at Division of Forensic Psychology conference, Leicester.

Steadman, H.J., Mulrey, E.P., Monahan, J. *et al.* (1998) Violence by people discharged from acute psychiatric inpatient facilities and by others in the same neighbourhood. *Archives of General Psychiatry, 55,* 393–401.

Towl, G.J. and Crighton, D.A. (1995) Risk assessment in prisons: a psychological critique. *Forensic Update, 40,* 6–14.

Webster, C., Douglas, K., Eaves, D. *et al.* (1997). *HCR-20. Assessing Risk of Violence.* Version 2. Vancouver: Mental Health, Law and Policy Institute.

Wilson, D. and McCabe, S. (2002) How HMP Grendon 'works' in the words of those undergoing therapy. *The Howard Journal of Criminal Justice, 41,* 279–291.

Wilson, S., Attrill, G. and Nugent, F. (2003) Effective interventions for acquisitive offenders: An investigation of cognitive skills programmes. *Legal and Criminological Psychology, 8,* 83–101.

Young, J.E., Klosko, J. and Weishaar, M. (2003) *Schema Therapy.* New York: Guildford Press.

Chapter 8

Supervision of Forensic Group Therapy

Michael Parker

Forensic work with prisoners in psychotherapy, cognitive therapy or in therapeutic communities (TCs) involves attempts to form working professional relationships with men or women who have committed criminal offences and who tend at times to reproduce their offending behaviour styles in the prison setting. This has been called offence re-enactment (Lewis 1997), the tendency to repeat patterns of offending behaviour at differing levels of seriousness but which mirror the sequence of events in the index offence. Staff and Community members may become subject to such re-enactment as one aspect of communal life in a typical forensic TC. This happens in a more concentrated way in the therapy groups but can take shape in all aspects of Community life. Re-enactments of this nature may present significant difficulties to both staff and Community members when prisoners are '...relating to the rest of society through unwelcome deeds, rather than through words.' (Gunn in Cox and Cordess 2002, p.xii).

This chapter points to some basic requirements of the structure and task of supervision and tries to offer guidelines on what staff responses to such behavioural enactments might be, focussing on three key areas in forensic therapy supervision:

1. the *framework and structure* necessary to contain supervisory thinking

2.   the *clinical task and teaching function* that provides learning for therapists in the supervisory process

3.   *recuperative space* for supervisee wellbeing. This third element is offered to ensure staff in forensic settings are neither overwhelmed nor overloaded by the nature of the task they undertake.

Figure 8.1 highlights these three areas.

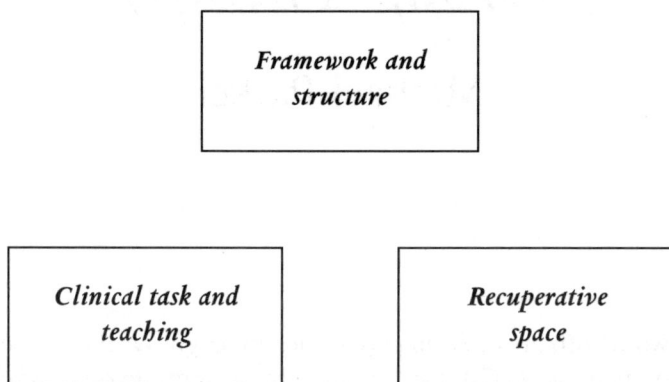

Figure 8.1 The key areas in forensic therapy supervision.

This chapter is written for staff in prison democratic TCs for whom there is a specific task, to address or challenge offending behaviour and to help make meaning of such behaviour: to 'think under fire' (Downie 2004) and be able to hold in mind or 'mentalize' (Fonagy and Bateman 2004) the work in therapy to avoid the natural defensive tendency to act to shun behaviour that may at first seem provocative, unfamiliar or unwelcome.

Framework and structure in the supervisory process

The managerial task

Line management accountability to the organization, the Prison Service and its core purpose, dictates some of the work to be done in therapy and so forms part of the structure of the supervision process. This managerial element (Hawkins and Shohet 1989, p.44) may be more marked in prison work as those in prison are liable to engage more often in offence re-enactment (Lewis 1997) or offence-paralleling behaviour (Jones in Cullen *et al.* 1997) while in prison. It is now a requirement that such behaviour is commented on in the risk assessment process and is tracked in the annual audit cycle so that it can be seen that offending behaviour is tackled and hopefully changed. Those in therapy subject to Multi Agency Protection Panel (MAPPA) procedures are required to be risk assessed and therapy work includes the obligation to offer written evidence on any progress made or not made in therapy and in the Community. Therefore, there is an obligation on the therapy teams to join clinical with managerial accountability in the area of risk assessment. The inclination to split the two functions may be understood differently as part of the cut and thrust of TC life (Morris 2004) or as a problematic and defensive splitting process likely to be associated with the pathology of the offender driving the split. Such splits can lead the team off-task and into regime drift. Such splitting activity should ideally be drawn into supervision for discussion by contrasting areas of therapy work that have become known with areas that remain left aside or hidden, and what difficulties these hidden areas might represent both for the offender and for therapy staff.

Case example

Pressure to stretch time boundaries may be made when angry demands are made for groups to run over time or to re-meet almost as soon as they have ended. On one occasion this happened in a very direct manner after groups had just ended and one resident came to the staff office at 10.35am to announce the immediate need for another meeting. When asked what the trouble was she replied, 'What's the problem, you don't really care if you can't spare half an hour do you?' We asked for time to think about what was making it so urgent. Normally all staff attend emergency meetings. As supervisor, I looked around the team and simply asked: 'Do we need to go at all or do we all need to go?' My own view was that we did not but should communicate this clearly and say why. The decision remained with the supervision group, who then discussed this and decided that one resident's particular upset, following very painful and upsetting discussion of issues concerning maternal separation, was obviously being felt hard to contain by her but also by other Community residents, who were not felt to be good enough at this particular time. It did not seem necessary for us all to attend and we reasoned that there was a replay of not being able to be separate or be separated taking place in her case that probably we ought not to re-enact in our own actions as a staff team by going along with her request immediately. One of the team relayed to the Wing Chair and to the woman requesting the immediate meeting that two of the staff team would be happy to meet with the community at 11.45am, but not before. We hoped this would be a gentle indication of the possibility of being separate and of separation not necessarily being disastrous through this non-immediate but thought-through response. This was accepted and allowed the staff to review the morning's groups and attend to the needs of the staff team to de-brief. The decision enabled staff to think about the urgency of the request rather than act on it immediately. The Community did seem up to the limit of their tolerance with this particular member's anxieties and needs at this time, and were less able or willing to help, therefore, it did seem helpful that we agreed to meet, but later in the morning.

The time frame

Group supervision takes place with the staff group of that morning directly after the client group session; this lasts for 1 hour and is led by the wing therapy manager. Individual supervision with a designated clinical supervisor from within the team takes place in addition to group supervision to enable more time to be devoted to each team member's own professional development. The times, days and room in which group supervision takes place remain the same. It is the supervisor's role to maintain time boundaries, if these become shaky, and to ensure that these are adhered to, not obsessively or rigidly, but so that the supervisory frame remains safe, consistent and predictable: a time and place in which supervisees know when this activity will happen and how long it lasts.

If, however, a Community member has self-harmed or there is a violent incident in the Community, this will need to be attended to straightaway to contain anxieties and take appropriate medical or other appropriate action.

Privacy and consistency of the setting

There needs to be privacy, no interruptions to the process and the supervisory group need to have no other commitments that would intrude into the supervision time, unless these are operational emergencies. Supervision needs to remain time to think about the clinical material emerging from the previous sessions and more broadly over time as the group evolves. Attending supervision is mandatory for those working in democratic TCs and a commitment honoured by the whole organization, not just the Community itself.

Case example

An example of difficulty in staying in the supervision session occurred one day when one member of a therapy group team began to find reasons to do urgent work on the Wing in supervision time and appeared to find it difficult to stay in the group for the hour. His therapy group was one in which a combination of aggressive and very challenging behaviour towards staff was combined with accounts of sexual offending and it was clear that staff in this group were on the receiving end of some very personally focused and angry interactions, fuelled with hatred and rage. With a little encouragement from both the supervisor and members of the supervision group, the member of staff was able to see that rather than think about the material in the group, he was acting to keep away both from the discomfort of the clinical material if recounted, but also from some of his own angry and poten-tially aggressive reactions to one member of the group in particular, propelled by a need to get up and get on with something to distract from the emotional demands placed on him. Bringing this way of responding to attention as something that may have a wider meaning (than just needing to go and fill in the detail) seemed to make it easier for him to stay in the group and think about his responses in relation to this group member's behaviour.

Treatment integrity

The theoretical framework for prison TCs is outlined in the prison service's *Theory, Assessment and Programme Manuals* (HM Prison Service 2004). These describe clinical aspects of work that need to be undertaken in forensic therapy, focusing on past and current offending behaviour patterns and changing these. In the psychodynamic frame real outside life events and rela-tionships – past and present, as well as current behaviour within the Com-munity – emotional reactions or psychological behaviour patterns emerging in the Community will be included to give therapy a realistic balance. Criminogenic risk factors to be addressed include aspects of family life and pro-social support systems, work and education outside prison, emotional responses, work skills, education, drug and alcohol difficulties, identified offending behaviour targets in the initial assessments and participation in Community life. These factors correspond with the LSI-R identified criminogenic risk factors now forming part of the OASys Two assessment system into which TC therapy targets are assimilated; they should cover the same ground. All will be important and appropriate subject matter for the group to discuss and develop. It is for the group and staff together with the supervisor to judge what is relevant at what time and in which order of priority, without swerving from the agreed set of targets, but with sensitivity to each group member's different responsivity (Andrews and Bonta 1998) and ability to accommodate.

It may not be possible, however, for a man to feel victim empathy for a woman he has sexually assaulted if the therapy process results in a strong resonance in him 'according to his own individual disposition on the specific level of regression, fixation or developmental arrest on which his main disturbances and conflicts operate' (Foulkes 1990, p.298) and acts to trigger reaction to his own experience of abuse. Quite often men seem unable to understand, let alone feel victim empathy at first, if personal experience and re-enactment appear inextricably tangled up. Men may find it difficult to contemplate the idea of victim empathy at all if empathy has rarely been shown to them and they have little experience of having received it personally in their own lives. It may be that some experience or demonstration of real empathy and understanding shown to them has to take place in the life of the Community before they are in any real position to begin to comprehend the business required in therapy of victim empathy. For some this can be a difficult issue better understood as a part of the wider context of therapy rather than made a target in its own right.

Fonagy (2001) and Fonagy and Bateman (2004) stress the activity of 'mentalization' as essential to the process of therapy to enable stuck, complex, disturbing mental states to be translated into words and, therefore, be able to be thought about, 'mentalized', rather than simply repeated or reacted to in the circular process outlined in the 'cycle of violence' (non-thinking) Cathy Widom describes (Widom 1989). We might think of treatment integrity including the ability of the therapists, via training and supervision, to achieve the capacity to 'mentalize' the experiences of those in therapy themselves and frame the difficult behaviour they are hearing into understandable structures and, therefore, being able to reflect back and attempt to make the behaviour understandable in its origins and in its impact on others combined.

Attempts to 'mentalize' denied or frozen-in-time abusive experience, or to engage with what is mirrored in fellow group members will often vividly rekindle previous emotional and mental states that can be ferociously defended against and launched at staff as attacks, particularly, as authority figures, in a verbally or physically violent or sexualized, literal way. At times we may wonder whether engagement and the attempt to give feedback is a useful thing to do but residents of TCs have said often enough, 'I know I need to work through this' after exploding into rage that it does seem necessary, but perhaps not with the most strongly defended psychopathic individuals for whom seeing the self can be both hateful and seem an attack in itself. It is important not to become too lost in the intricacies of therapeutic detail that the overall objective of ensuring the targets identified in therapy are met and the responsivity principle is addressed, within which the right kind of intervention style is used that meets the offender's ability to understand and respond (Andrews and Bonta 1998).

Case example: Omnipotent control of the content of therapy, the therapist and the community

In one interchange I gave what the supervision group and wider team thought was a necessary piece of feedback to a frighteningly aggressive man, Jeremy, that his behaviour was 'frightening to others' in as matter-of-fact and undramatic way as I could when it was evident one day in a Community meeting. This was thought necessary by the team, including me at that time, as part of the reality confrontation that was designed to help develop understanding of how others saw you and so, begin to be able to think about this, reflect and be able to change. This was intolerable or indigestible to him, and I think I was carefully placed in the front line to do this by the team and Community as it was so clearly difficult to actually say the words, while almost everyone on the Wing thought them and felt hopelessly stuck and afraid of him but could not quite say anything about it. In retrospect I think this interaction was probably pointless and it might have been better to try to contain the staff need to give this feedback and think why such defensive aggression had become so necessary a part of his defensive life. After a period of days of extraordinary rage in response to this it was said to a colleague in a very concrete way, pupils dilated: 'he's going to be my next victim', referring to me. The next day, when confronted furiously by him in the staff office, I noticed a quietly gathering group of unified staff collecting behind him as he vented his rage at me. We were both standing up in the staff office, him facing inwards, staff gathering outside and behind him. I realized I was in a very real situation of danger. His frightening behaviour could not be spoken about, it seemed, at any cost: he had to be in control of what was and was not spoken about. In our team discussions we wondered whether this particular man's fragility was still so great that any slight or challenge, however well intended, could not be understood as anything other than attack. From what little we were ever allowed to know about him, which was almost nothing, we conjectured he had been subject to some form of abusive or neglectful attachment style for a long time, and was unable at this time to do anything other than act to defend himself against me when feeling under attack. Attempts at understanding have no necessary bearing on risk and in this case the team jointly felt this man remained at high risk of future violent offending under sufficiently provoking circumstances. Such a demonstration of aggression may fall into the category of 'predatory violence' (Meloy 1992, pp.236–241), a course of action thought out and serving a strong ego-syntonic, unbending purpose and it may have been that without the enormously strong deterrent of a life sentence, violence could have taken place in this case. This is a good example of supervisory acting out: I should not have taken on such a role and might have been better remaining in the role of trying to help the team think about what his behaviour meant and what to do, or not to do about it, rather than sail into action with such team-propelled certainty.

The difficult role in prison therapy work lies in the area of when and how to try to raise issues with men, women or young offenders about their behaviour and its effect on others: to challenge or not to challenge. It does seem important to aim to be able to offer well-constructed challenges that are thoughtful and aimed to help the process of self-understanding. It rarely seems possible to do this with a likelihood of success until a good enough relationship with the Community member in question, the team and the Community has been established, and perhaps this is the first supervisory rule of any confrontation: no confrontation unless within the context of a well-formed enough therapeutic relationship.

Verbal reconstruction of the therapy session as a supervisee task

Reconstruction of the therapy session by supervisees of their group in chronological sequence from memory, not from notes, is advised as good practice to ensure a consistent way for the supervisee to present his session. This practice enables variations from such a chronological presentation to be evident and, therefore, to be available for group and supervisory comment and search for meaning if obviously avoided or found difficult (Langs in Martindale et al 1997).

Practice in this activity of recounting the material of the group in more or less chronological order and in detail will help the supervisee to learn to think about the group he conducts and help him to hold varying and, at times, conflicting ideas concerning group members in mind at any one time. Recalling the detail of the group also helps the supervisee remain with the activity of thinking rather than being emotionally propelled away onto other topics by the difficulty of facing, for example, an aggressive transference response or a consistent attempt to undermine what he has been trying to say or draw attention to in the session. Notes could be used but can be used defensively and can be read and worked with to ensure they are accurate in individual sessions and for audit checking. Ultimately, it will become important for the developing group facilitator to be able to keep the group in mind, however complex it is, without recourse to defensive activity and remain able to continue thinking about what is being said, what has been said before in the group's history, what is being omitted from discussion in the group now, and to be able to select what may be a useful intervention now, on this day in this group and why.

The supervisor, then, needs to help encourage the supervisee in the direction of being able to think at the same time as feel and respond to the emotional dynamics emerging in the group. Resistance of any kind, however, will usually be unconscious, and in order to become increasingly able to bear and contain these dynamics in mind, very clear avoidances of important dynamics in the group by the supervisee will need to be enquired into and drawn attention to in an encouraging but clear way. Strong emotional reactions in the forensic setting with prisoners in therapy can be tumultuous, aggressive, murderous or sexually evocative at times, and may occur in many combinations at once in the same group and be distressing and frightening. There needs to be time set aside in supervision to focus on fear generated in the therapist or on being emotionally overwhelmed if this dominates in any session and it is clearly not possible to focus on the chronological presentation in the usual way. Group and supervisor will have to decide when attention to the therapist needs to be prioritized over presenting the material of the session.

Professional distance

Sufficient professional distance between supervisor and supervisee is advised to enable the supervisor to use her or his authority when this is needed in either a directive or advisory way (Driver in Driver and Martin 2002). To veer away from the frame and become too friendly may indicate attempts to placate an aggressive or demanding supervisee or represent embarrassment and attempts at compensating for feelings of not under-standing or being good enough at the task of supervision. Such behaviour is liable to obscure any difficulties emerging in the supervisee's presentation, as the supervisor's emotional focus becomes occupied in essentially defensive activity, rather than in remaining hawk-like to the task at hand: the clinical material of the current session and the supervisee's thinking and emotional response to it.

Clinical and offence-focussed work combined: the supervisory task

The team as therapist

In forensic therapy work of whichever discipline 'Forensic psychotherapy always involves a tripartite relationship…the therapist, the patient and soci-ety's criminal justice system. The setting is of utmost importance for both therapist and patients whose problems involve acts against society' (Welldon and Wilson 2005, p.355). The Institutions of the criminal justice services play an essential role as container of the difficult behaviour that is worked with in therapy. It is likely to actually be dangerous to conduct therapy without the safety of institutional containment because '[t]he forensic patient is unable to think before the action occurs' (Welldon and Wilson 2005, p.355). The supervisory frame must, therefore, include society, client and therapist in therapeutic work and be a team effort to contain the inevita-ble splits and probable aggressive and sadistic attacks that are generated in complex forensic transference patterns. It is an additional factor without which therapy would be impossible. Society has to be represented in the therapeutic contract as it has been offended against in a very concrete way. Figure 8.2 illustrates these components.

The emerging therapeutic relationship

Bottoms (2004), in researching alternatives to prison has commented on the re-emergence, in probation work, of the importance of the nature and quality of the client–professional relationship after a period of political unpopularity. This is timely, as programmes and TC work require careful attention to the nature of the staff–prisoner relationship. Continual attention needs to be paid by the supervisor to the development or absence of devel-opment of a therapeutic relationship between supervisees and those in his group. Indications of difficulty in engaging with one or some in the group will become areas for the supervisor to enquire about to try to find ways to make engagement more possible. The supervisee needs to remain in the

```
┌─────────────────────────┐
│                         │
│        Prisoner         │
│                         │
└─────────────────────────┘

┌─────────────────────┐           ┌───────────────────────┐
│                     │           │    Criminal justice   │
│  Clinical supervisor│           │       services        │
│                     │           │                       │
└─────────────────────┘           └───────────────────────┘

          ┌───────────────────────┐
          │                       │
          │   Therapist as team   │
          │                       │
          └───────────────────────┘
```

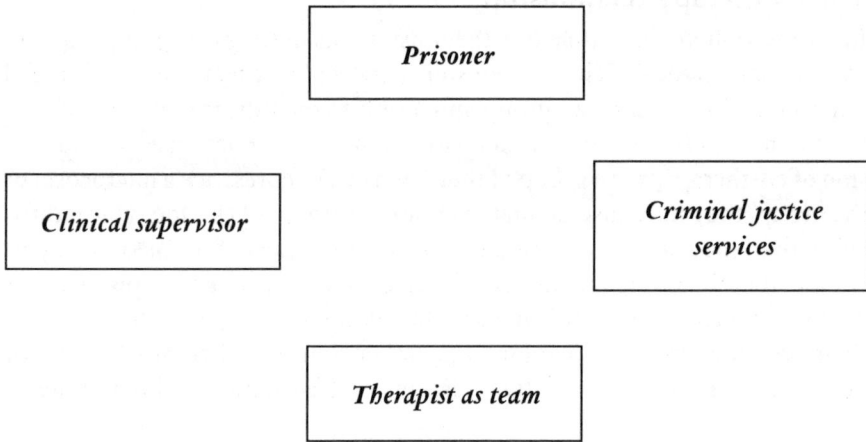

Figure 8.2 *Components of the supervisory frame.*

'learning position' and so open to thinking and emotional development of his own (Del Pozo in Martindale 1997). The learning position is more likely to be a useful position for both supervisor and supervisee to engage with throughout the course of both their professional lifetimes.

Interaction between supervisor and supervisee: Transference and countertransference

Interaction between supervisor and supervisee is an important area of thinking and emotional activity for the supervisor (Searles 1986). Her emotional reaction to the supervisee is likely to provide a clue to the transference that may develop between them, wanted or not, and may also take on aspects of (unintended) parallel process, mirroring in supervision what is taking place between therapist and prisoner in therapy. The supervisor is well advised to have his or her own supervision to ensure he or she remains on-task and to ensure that any strong feeling, stuckness or dislike of the supervisee is able to be discussed in a safe place and difficult aspects resolved, if possible, externally to the supervisory frame after which any issues causing difficulty can be returned in a more processed and thought-through way to the supervision session.

The co-therapy relationship

In settings where more than one therapist works in the same group, Yalom's view is unequivocal: 'The relationship between co-therapists is of crucial importance for the therapy group and, not infrequently, the supervisor may be maximally effective by focusing attention on this relationship.' Supervision of co-therapists in a group of their own often represents 'a microcosm of the group' they have just facilitated (Yalom 1995, p.521). One typical difficulty that may arise is competitiveness and rivalry for making expert comment in the group and thereby being a good, effective therapist. Groups pick this up and can be affronted at the taking away of what they view as their potential space for exploration, rather than the therapists' space for demonstrating expertise. Co-therapists may differ in their ability to tolerate

---

Case example

On one occasion the preoccupation of the therapist, who had worked on her own in the group for a long period, was centred on the personal nature of the anger shown towards her in a therapy group where all the women in the group had complicated experiences with mothers, outlined in the initial therapy assessment. The anger was intense, the therapist was useless, the group said, and the criticisms appeared designed to hit the mark and hurt or make the point that the therapist was failing. Preoccupation remained with thoughts about how to respond to this, what to say and what to avoid. Comment was made in the supervision group that there were many similarities between the women in this group and the main one was that they were all dissatisfied with their mother and angry at some level with her. They could not in reality be angry with mother as this was plainly said to risk completely wrecking what was already a fragile relationship. One of the team said, you are catching all the mother transference at once and with this the group's therapist just said, 'Yes', hugely relieved, as though not having thought about this before and the group were able to continue to talk about how important this anger and discontent seemed to be in reality and how it was impossible to express it to the real mothers in real life outside prison. This seemed to help the therapist make sense of the powerful confluence of anger resonating in the group all of a sudden and all aimed at her at once. Accurate interpretation such as this may help unlock therapists from difficult, seemingly embattled scenarios that may feel very personalized.

accounts of abuse or trauma in personal life or violent or sexually harrowing offence accounts. Co-therapists' ability to take a cue from a colleague and run with it, rather than compete against it, is a mark of some degree of maturity in working together. What may be most important is that the relationship remains open for exploration and is able to be examined in supervision either for dynamic parallel process repetitions from the group or for signs of difficulty in co-operating with each other.

It is critically unhelpful for a team in a forensic setting to find themselves engaged in the battle of therapeutic modalities, though not unusual, one struggling with the other for voice, pre-eminence or power. This engagement takes the emotional energy of the staff so pre-occupied into an off-task activity and it may be helpful to name this kind of defense, if present, as this can free the group up to on-task activity once the difficulty is identified. If matters are more problematic than can be resolved, it may fall to the supervisor to decide at what point a co-therapy relationship might need to be ended or changed.

In forensic settings it is always advisable to work as co-therapists, not singly. It may be better to reduce the frequency of the sessions in the week that struggle on trying to cover what might be a more or less impossible task with the staff group available. Not only is there safety in numbers when the dynamics are difficult but co-therapy offers the chance for co-therapists to share observations about what went on in the group with each other together with the supervisor.

Supervisory teaching and the educative role of supervision

Any supervisory teaching given needs to be predictive and consistent with the guidelines indicated in the DTC Training Manuals to avoid regime slippage. Wider trainings such as individual, group analytic training or cognitive therapy training also need to fit with the Training, Assessment and Programme Manuals Manual (HM Prison Service 2004). Collectively the forensic team uses a continual examination and search for meaning in the current thinking and behaviour of the Community members or in clearly important current or outside relationship life. Typical material for supervision will include whether supervisees are able to notice and make reference to any destructive or self-destructive behaviour that may be unfolding in the prisoner's pattern of behaviour on the Wing. If other Community members in the group are able to confront problematic, offence-paralleling behaviour when this arises, this is a valuable part of the group process and just as valuable as reference to it by staff. There needs to be a clear consciousness on the part of supervisees of whether each member of the group is developing and has begun to tackle the wide-ranging therapy targets outlined in the initial assessment in therapy, which must include offending behaviour as well as other relationship, substance abuse, education, work skills, emotional, family relationship and post-discharge supportive contacts and Wing-based targets in therapy. The supervisor's comment, instruction or feedback, therefore, should remain focused on these issues and targets on this day's therapy group and of the clinical content that has emerged in the group context over time.

Engaging with resistance and avoidance of the task

There may be strong attempts by prisoners to focus away from their behavioural problems, such as verbally threatening and abusive behaviour, especially if the behaviour is ego-syntonic and self-sustaining. This can be difficult for staff to hold in mind and contain emotionally within themselves, particularly so when actively resisted by verbal threats to leave the identified behaviour alone. Deviations too far from the clinical material to be presented may represent difficulties with the material of the session and what has happened in it. In each case it is the supervisor's task to try to elicit where the difficulty lies and help resolve it, if the group does not.

The supervisor needs to remain alert to whether or not this may need to be drawn into the session for exploration and attempt to understand what the difficulty might relate to in the supervisee's own experience. This is not something for the supervisor to say out loud but would need to remain an area of active thinking engaged with in the way that Patrick Casement describes the analyst developing her own 'internal supervisor': a running commentary self to self about what is taking place overtly and unconsciously with the supervisee in relation to the unfolding clinical material in the session and thinking about what might be a way to approach the difficulty without personalizing it onto the supervisee.

Repetition and re-enactment: The re-enactment of offending behaviour

Attention to the development of any re-enactment or parallel process in the therapy and in the supervision group is an important supervisory area of attention. When a similar dynamic begins to develop in the supervision session between supervisor and supervisee(s) to that evident in the therapy group between Community members and therapists, a parallel process may be taking place (Doehrman 1976). This represents a form of enactment on the part of the supervisee taking place without this necessarily being conscious or intended; it simply begins to form itself in the behaviour and relationship life between supervisor and supervisee: the same dynamic simply taking place in both settings.

Case example

In one example, a therapy group as a whole found difficulty in being straightforward about saying what offences they had committed and seemed to become a quasi-nurturing group with exclusive talk of support, but one in which areas of conflict, dangerousness and aggression were avoided: this in a group in which the main offences were violence, sexual violence and armed robbery. The therapist in supervision became more and more reluctant to say what was happening in his group and it very much began to feel like his personal group run according to his personal set of rules. Eventually, when asked one day, he would not say what was happening at all and failed to be able give an account of the clinical material and transactions in the group. A hidden issue emerging later on involved well-constructed, seductive invitations by a sex offender to meet the therapist outside work on discharge from prison and this, when it came to light, was viewed as potentially dangerous to the therapist, especially if remaining outside the supervisory process for discussion. This man's offence had involved abduction, tying up and sexual attack. A form of parallel process developed in this scenario where an enactment was taking place in the group: slow careful cultivation of the therapist to not notice major problem behaviour: seduction. The Supervisor pointed out this developing omission and possible seduction to the therapist and, while difficult, the interaction seemed to begin to allow the dynamic to be named and discussed within the group.

A repetition of this then took place in the supervision group in which the therapist behaved with the supervision group in such a way that the material of the group was not available for discussion and the group's issues were left vague. A pattern developed in which the supervision group was inveigled into not noticing major problem behaviour he had become entangled in. The supervisor and supervision group did draw this to attention and gradually the group's business was able to become known but not without a struggle.

In another scenario, the therapist may be mirroring the prisoner's emotional difficulties and responses and instead of being able to process them and think them through as issues to be worked with, becomes engaged in absorbing, re-enacting and repeating them. This may be in identification with the process or as a means of coping with it or avoiding something difficult, or through resentment at having to bring difficult material not well understood to the supervision session at all and feeling ashamed at not knowing.

A focus on being combative with the supervision group and the supervisor may, initially, be easier to talk about than a powerful eroticized transference or potent sense of threat and fear of a member of the therapy group the supervisee is finding shameful, provocative or intolerable to deal with.

Personal resonance: Supervisee with prisoner

Resonance on the part of the therapist to the prisoner's clinical situation in which there are difficult similarities in the emotional or relationship life of both may occur. This can be a very powerful and disturbing experience to therapists taken unawares. The supervisor should refrain from pointing this out too directly, unless wanted by the supervisee, as this kind of difficulty normally belongs in the supervisee's personal therapy; the possibility of a link of this kind could be pointed to tactfully in individual supervision time and aspects of any similarities that create defensive and rejecting responses from the supervisee worked with to help move beyond the defence to a re-engagement with the material to be worked through in therapy.

The supervisor should avoid responses that propel the supervisee into transference reactions, and hence any tendency to regression, as supervision and therapy should not be confused but kept as separate areas of activity (Grinberg in Martindale 1997). The supervisor may notice the dynamic in the supervision group and be able to act on the information evident in the supervision session without making direct transference-style interpretations. Instead he or she can use the information to guide thinking about the clinical material that seems troubling and consider responses that help work them through. This might address both supervisee and prisoner's dilemmas but supervisory work remains the task of helping the supervisee work effectively with the prisoner's therapy.

Splitting of supervisor from supervisee experience

A particular area of defensive activity in supervisors has been pointed out by Graham Fuller. The supervisor may fail to acknowledge to himself or herself memories of his or her own learning experience as a supervisee, particularly the difficult or emotionally painful experiences that may have taken place. He or she may convey a sense of freedom from difficulty that can foster a form of splitting characterized by valvular, one-way communication, focusing exclusively on the supervisee's difficulties (Fuller in Sharpe 1995). A clear danger here is that unconscious projection from supervisor to supervisee is made easier the stronger the tendency for valvular communication becomes. This is likely to stop the process of dialogue in supervision, often a sign of defensive or projective activity in itself, adding to a sense of distance, unhelpful hierarchy and an absence of thinking within the supervisory setting. It highlights the importance of thinking being a two-way process and of supervision being a shared activity with a sense of reciprocity between supervisor and supervisee.

Functional balance and location of managerial, teaching and recuperative roles

The clinical material emerging in the Community as a whole and in therapy, the emotional and mental health issues and their place within the cognitive structure of Community members are the main task of supervision. However, other matters stray into the frame that might not be so usefully included, such as poor performance of the core task or problematic behaviour when a member of the team demonstrates they cannot respond to invitations to explore and alter aspects of their work in the normal way. Such issues as aggressive, abusive, or bullying by staff towards colleagues or clients, when unable to be commented on readily in supervision, are more effectively and appropriately dealt with by the line management and disciplinary function within the Unit. It may be that the supervisor needs to make such a change of function from supervision to line management clear to the supervisee if it is necessary to discharge both functions. It can cause confusion to try to include such disciplinary or line management responsibilities within what amounts to the wrong framework and seriously inappropriate behaviour is better dealt with outside the supervisory setting.

An inability to operate appropriately within different frameworks at the right time: clinical, supervisory or managerial, may include a tendency to deal with problem issues by 'taking it to the group'. This may happen when an issue is found to be particularly difficult and while 'taking it to the group' is normally useful, automatic, unthinking practice of it can be used to divert the problem elsewhere and so become an avoidant or defensive response. It may function to hide a difficult issue in the group process and it remains a function of the managerial and supervisory leadership of any TC to be responsible for distinguishing between what is a matter for the team as a whole and what must be dealt with by them, as clinical supervisor, in role, or in more problematic cases, what may need to be taken into the line management function for further action. An ability to be clear about the location of such different tasks helps to relieve the team of unnecessary burdens of responsibility.

Recuperative space and supervisee wellbeing

It is useful to think of a balance between several areas of activity that contribute to the overall wellbeing of supervisees and a simple diagram (Figure 8.3) shows three areas: training and learning; countertransference from the supervisor and the preservation of supervisees' own personal space in the supervision process.

No therapist can work well unless clear enough about the task they are responsible for and unless they are well trained enough to do it. Easily overlooked, attention to the level of emotional stress and total workload faced by supervisees needs to be regularly thought about and reviewed by the supervisor with their supervisees. This attention needs to include whether training appropriate to the task has been organized and undertaken. This is a priority in Prison Service TCs and induction within the first month and completion of the 3-day Training Module One within the first year is an audit requirement in recognition of the importance of training for TC work.

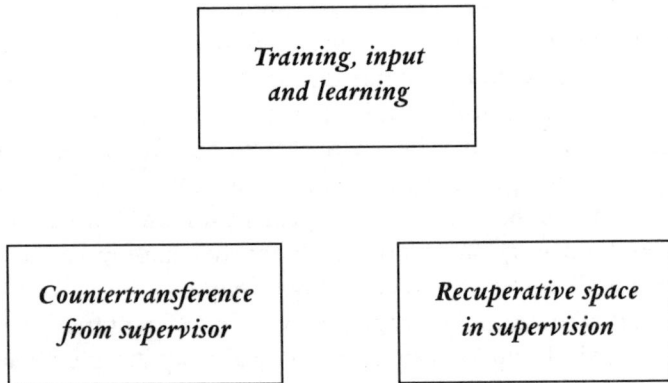

Training, input and learning

Countertransference from supervisor	*Recuperative space in supervision*

Figure 8.3 *Essentials of supervisee wellbeing.*

Supervisor countertransference

At times unhelpful dynamics may take shape between therapist and supervisor. It is difficult to acknowledge this at times in the open setting of the supervisory group. A most likely blind spot of a well-defended or rather narcissistic supervisor will be confusion between the supervisor's personal reaction of dislike or disapproval of a supervisee's course of action and a sense that the supervisee is genuinely making a mistake or missing the point. One of the most difficult areas to pinpoint, this matter could be dealt with by use of the prescribed independent counselling service to the staff team of prison TCs. In this scheme individual counselling sessions are offered to members of the team if existing arrangements have soured or staff members feel the need to consult externally to the team. Therapy managers, if they seek their own supervision, have a further place in which they can reflect and think through the clinical material of supervision that may be causing problems they cannot see themselves and will be better thought through outside the group supervision process itself.

Case example

On one occasion a therapist in a group steadily maintained that she was alright despite appearing to be in real difficulty with the members of the group. On my asking about the constant, aggressive challenges to her in the group, she reported being alright while not appearing so and appeared not to be able to acknowledge what the difficulties were, insisting on carrying on with the job. However, after a while she did become unable to continue doing the job and went off sick for a sustained period of time. This was clearly difficult for her and might have been avoided if an earlier decision had been made, by her or by me about how to resolve the difficulties. It may have been useful to add a co-therapist but there was none available or for a decision to have been made for her to stop conducting the group in acknowledgement that high levels of stress were making it unreasonable to continue.

Recuperative space: limited time as a therapist

Time may be needed by supervisees to talk through their responses and thoughts about many matters taking place in the therapy work they do. These may not coincide with what the supervisor thinks. Acknowledgement of and respect for such possible differences of view needs to be given by the supervisor to create the space that might be needed for the supervisee to think in their own time. Dependent on the level of training and experience it may be possible to run groups for only limited periods of time before becoming tired to the point of losing an ordinary ability to defend the self from incoming emotional demands or attacks and becoming unable to make interventions due to being repeatedly shut down by more aggressive members in the group. The effective time each therapist may have in a group as facilitator can be thought about as part of supervisory planning to safeguard against the tendency to staff groups at all costs and risk exhaustion or burnout or staff who cannot make the decision to stop before being overwhelmed by their work.

It may be necessary to advise withdrawal from the role of therapist if the task has become too stressful or destructive to either the supervisee or to the therapy group, and it may fall to the supervisor to make that decision, as part of their supervisory responsibility, to protect both supervisee and client group, rather than leave developments of an unhelpful kind unresolved for too long. Shame and a wish to do the job well regardless of personal difficulties may obscure real difficulty in coping that the supervisee finds it hard to acknowledge.

The idea of keeping a balance between the three elements outlined in this chapter: line-management, teaching and supportive-recuperative work in forensic supervision are aspirational aims to match the challenges of the forensic setting but also point the way towards safeguarding the health and wellbeing of both staff and Community members in the forensic clinical setting.

References

Andrews, D. and Bonta, J. (1998) *The Psychology of Criminal Conduct*, 2nd edn. Cincinnati, Ohio: Anderson Press.

Bottoms, A., Rex, S. and Robinson, G. (2004) *Alternatives to Prison: Options for an Insecure Society*. Cullompton: Willan.

Cullen, E., Jones, L. and Woodward, R. (1997) *Therapeutic Communities for Offenders*. Chichester: John Wiley & Sons.

Del Pozo, M. (1997) On the process of supervision in psychoanalytic psychotherapy. In B. Martindale, J.P. Vidit, M. Morner (eds.) *Supervision and its Vicissitudes*. London: Karnac Books Ltd.

Doehrman, M. (1976) Parallel processes in supervision and psychotherapy. *Bulletin of the Menninger Clinic, 40*, 71–79.

Downie, A. (2004) Thinking under fire. In D. Jones. *Working with Dangerous People: The Psychotherapy of Violence*. Oxford: Radcliffe Medical Press Ltd.

Driver, C. (2002) Internal states in the supervisory relationship. In C. Driver and E. Martin (eds) *Supervising Psychotherapy: Psychoanalytic and Psychodynamic Perspectives.* London: Sage Publications.

Fonagy, P. (2001) *Attachment Theory and Psychoanalysis.* New York: Otherress.

Fonagy, P. and Bateman, A. (2004) *Psychotherapy for Borderline Personality Disorder: Mentalization-based treatment.* New York: Oxford University Press.

Foulkes, S.H. (1990) *Selected Papers: Psychoanalysis and Group Analysis.* London: Karnac Books.

Fuller, G. (1995) Effects of institutional dynamics. In M. Sharpe (ed.) *The Third Eye: Supervision of Analytic Groups.* London: Routledge.

Grinberg, L. (1997) On Transference and Countertransference and the Technique of Supervision. In Martindale B., J.P. Vidit, M. Morner (eds) *Supervision and Its Vicissitudes.* London: Karnac Books Ltd.

Gunn, J., Cordess, C. and Cox, M. (2002) *Forensic Psychotherapy: Crime, Psychodynamics and the Offender Patient,* 3rd edn. London: Jessica Kingsley Publishers.

Hawkins, P. and Shohet, R. (1989) *Supervision in the Helping Professions.* Buckingham: Open University Press.

HM Prison (2004) Training, assessment and programme manuals for democratic therapeutic communities *What Works in Prison Units.* HMSO: London.

Langs, R. (1997) The framework of supervision in psychoanalytic psychotherapy. In Martindale, B, J.P. Vidit, M. Morner *Supervision and Its Vicissitudes.* London: Karnac Books Ltd.

Lewis, P. (1997) Context for change (whilst consigned and confined): A challenge for systemic thinking. In E. Cullen, L. Jones, and R. Woodward (eds) *Therapeutic Communities for Offenders.* Chichester: John Wiley & Sons.

Meloy, J. Reid (1992) *The Psychopathic Mind: Origins, Dynamics and Treatment.* New York: Jason Aronson Inc.

Morris, M. (2004) *Dangerous and Severe – Process, Programme and Person: Grendon's Work.* London: Jessica Kingsley Publishers.

Searles, H. (1986) The informational value of the supervisor's emotional experiences. In *Collected Papers on Schizophrenia and Related Subjects.* London: Maresfield Library, Karnac Books Ltd.

Welldon, E. and Wilson, P. (2005) Introduction to special issue: Group analysis in forensic settings. *Group Analysis, 38,* 355.

Widom, C. (1989) The cycle of violence. *Science, 244,* 160–166.

Yalom, I. (1995) *Theory and Practice of Group Psychotherapy,* 3rd edn. New York: Basic Books.

Chapter 9

Through-care, After-care: What Happens After Therapy?

Alan Miller

What happens after therapy in a prison therapeutic community (TC)? You move on, we would hope! This appears to be a reasonable assumption for those who have stayed the course, survived, bared their soul, learned about themselves and explored their hopes and fears. Moving on to a new life is easy to see if release is the next stage of sentence progression. At HMP Dovegate Therapeutic Community the release rate direct from the TC to the outside world has been approximately 5 per cent of the population per annum during the first 3 years of operation, leaving 95 per cent who will return to the Prison system to complete their sentence. This rate of release is similar to the release rate at HMP Grendon Therapeutic Community. How do TCs help those survive both the outside and the system, which often has had a profound influence in their offending? This chapter identifies and examines some of the issues for those moving on following therapy, whether to release into the community, to progression in the resettlement estate or to further imprisonment in mainstream prison.

Resettlement from a therapeutic community: A historical perspective

From HMP Grendon's opening in 1962 resettlement was seen as an important component to compliment therapy. A Welfare Officer and Psychiatric

Social Worker were appointed to make links between Grendon prisoner's families and other professional agencies with an emphasis on interaction with statutory and voluntary agencies in the community (Healy 2000).

Work lasted the whole day at Grendon and was also seen as an important factor in resettlement as it contributed towards the development of a work ethic. Prisoners were taken from work to attend groups in those early days. To reinforce this concept, D Wing became a pre-release hostel in 1969. This experiment, however, did not last long as there was no formal regime structure to this part of the programme. A prison officer at the time commented, 'They get themselves up in the morning and go to bed whatever time they like' (Parker 1970, p.98). Support in the community was also attempted early in Grendon's history when a psychiatric social worker from the establishment set up regular meetings for ex-Grendon residents in a London pub. This group developed into a more formal setup as they obtained a residential flat, which was initially staffed by the Psychiatric Social Worker and then by Grendon ex-prisoners *with* the Psychiatric Social Worker. Problems with after-care, indifference of the residents and the suspicion that the flat was a base for re-offending led to its demise. Not all early resettlement initiatives have ended in failure; the ability to maintain contact with the Prison following release has been part of Grendon's and now Dovegate's support strategy for those released into the community. This has proved to be a successful strategy in relapse prevention for a number of ex-residents.

The idea of a unit that would help with resettlement of the individual on release was resurrected in the early 1990s with the opening of the Pre-release and Pre-transfer Unit following a suggestion at a conference to develop local initiatives held at the Prison in 1992. The Units were set up above the hospital block of Grendon, with the Pre-release Unit capable of holding up to six category D (open-condition) prisoners in the immediate weeks prior to their release. However, on Monday 9 May 1994 the tabloid newspaper *The Sun* published a story entitled 'Jail Perverts Live in Luxury'. The leader for the article, 'Lags get posh flats and taxis to town', gave the scheme seriously adverse publicity by claiming that prisoners were living in luxury flats and that sex and drugs were freely available. The Governor at the time, Tim Newell, immediately contacted the Press Complaints Commission with the result that *The Sun* printed a retraction following investigation; however, the damage was already done. Not long afterwards the Home Secretary restricted home leave and temporary release for prisoners and a stricter regime was introduced at Grendon.

Contemporary issues

At the beginning of the new century there was a joint initiative between the Prison and Probation Inspectorates to undertake a thematic review of through-care, the result of which was the publication in 2001 of *Through the Prison Gate* (Great Britain, Her Majesty's Chief Inspector of Prisons for England and Wales 2001, p.12). This supplied a definition of resettlement as: 'A systematic and evidence-based process by which actions are taken to work with the offender in custody and on release, so that communities are better protected from harm and re-offending is significantly reduced. It encompasses the totality of work with prisoners, their families and significant others in partnership with statutory and voluntary agencies.' So the question should be: how does a prison TC address the business of protecting communities and reducing re-offending through the resettlement process?

Resettlement as a continuous process

Until recently the notion of resettlement was that this was something that happened towards the end of the sentencing process, however, it must be recognized that leaving the process until the end of the sentence is not sufficient. A far more sensible approach to through-care and resettlement is to begin the process as soon as the resident enters therapy and to recognize and address the many facets of through-care and after-care from the start.

Elements of the through-care process

A number of inter-dependent components make up the through-care process. The responsibility for each component lies with each specialist within the team but forms part of the overall therapeutic process as a whole.

Education, work and careers

In 2004 the National Offender Management Service (NOMS) was created to amalgamate the Prison Service and the Probation Service. Within that remit the Offenders' Learning and Skills Unit (OLSU), a partnership between the Department for Education and Skills and the Home Office, came into being to promote learning and work skills. In the OLSU's publication, *The Offenders' Learning Journey*, (OLSU 2005, p.1). They describe their vision as: 'That offenders, in prisons and supervised in the community, according to need, should have access to learning and skills which enables them to gain the skills and qualifications they need to hold down a job and have a positive role in society.'

The importance of this in the through-care of all prisoners including those volunteering for therapy is that the Government has recognized the importance of the links between education, work and a reduction in the rate of re-offending. For the prison TC this means that the provision of education is a requirement. There are a number of elements to this requirement. The key features of these requirements are:

1. the production of individual learning plans, which should follow the offender through their sentence

2. effective screening and assessment of needs in relation to education and employment

3. access to information, guidance and advice so that learning and development opportunities are comparable to those offered outside the criminal justice system in the community.

Basic and key skills are central to this strategy and include E learning and information and communication technologies.

At Dovegate TC each new resident has a basic skills and educational assessment within the first three weeks of arriving in the Assessment and Resettlement Unit. This provides the core strategy to the resident's individual learning plan. Work histories are taken and compiled, with a *curriculum vitae* produced for each resident. The CV and learning plan become the initial documentation in a Record of Achievement that follows the offender through the secure estate and into the Community. All residents are required to attend Educom (education and commerce) as part of the therapeutic compact. Those requiring basic skills education have a choice of education delivery through either Learn Direct, a computer-based learning system or by a specialist tutor. In both cases the use of peer group tutors (experienced residents) is strongly promoted to overcome the stigma that many educationally limited residents experience.

Specialist careers advice is available and residents are encouraged to develop business and information technology (IT) skills such as the European Computer Driving Licence (ECDL), word processing, spreadsheets, desktop publishing, marketing and business planning. The development of self-resource for employment is central to Dovegate TC's philosophy for its residents, many of whom may find difficulty getting well-paid employment because of their criminal history. For those who are academically able, a full range of courses from General Certificate in Secondary Education (GCSE) to Open University are available with visiting or telephone tutorial support available to each resident.

There are practical skill-based training opportunities available in horticulture, catering and ceramic design and production for those who do not want to follow a more academic pathway. All courses from basic skills literacy and numeracy to Open University and vocational qualifications from basic food hygiene to City and Guilds technical qualifications are certificated and are added to the Record of Achievement as they are gained; this reinforces the notion that lifelong education is the best way to gain and preserve employment. For those who will be released into the community, staff members trained by the National Association of Care and Resettlement for Offenders (NACRO) Prison Link Unit are also available to provide advice and information relating to housing and employment.

Families

The role of the family has always been central to the through-care work of the TC and plays an important role in Prison Service Order (PSO) 2300 Resettlement issued in 2001. However, one surprising demographic fact found at both Dovegate and Grendon is that less than one-third of each population is in an ongoing relationship whilst in therapy, suggesting that relationships are a problem area for the people we see in prison TCs.

In the early days of Grendon this was reflected in the information letter about the process of being in a TC, which was sent to the prisoner's next of kin when they first entered Grendon. An extra visit, 'a Grendon visit' was also available each month as an incentive to those who co-operated with the regime. In the early 1990s, family days were added to the therapeutic regime. The family day was conceived as a therapy-orientated occasion, with inmates organizing a number of formal presentations for the morning, a buffet lunch and an informal afternoon schedule designed to enable families to gain some understanding of the therapeutic process. HMP Dovegate Therapeutic Community has adopted this feature into its working arrangements and hosts two days per year, the same as Grendon.

Family involvement is an area that may be further expanded at some time in the future. If we consider the number of relationship difficulties experienced and spoken about by those in therapy it becomes clear that any opportunity to engage partners and family in the therapeutic process would be a useful addition to the overall therapy process.

A proposal currently being considered at Dovegate is the development of a Family Centre, where families, partners, children, parents and significant others can participate in work with the resident. Systemic family therapy may be run alongside the group work elements of the TC as other offence-related programmes have previously done.

Offence work

Offending behaviour programmes are also considered to be important to the through-care process, however for some there has been an uneasy co-existence between the cognitive-behavioural approaches of Offending Behavioural Programmes (OBPs) and the psychodynamic orientation of the TCs. TCs have always valued other programmes such as Reasoning and Rehabilitation (R&R) and the Sex Offender's Treatment Programme (SOTP) as complimentary to the overall therapeutic process.

Grendon in its existence has run stand-alone programmes, such as Social Skills, Image Breaking, Alternatives to Violence, Parenting Skills, Sex Education and Family Group Therapy to name a few. In the mid-1990s, Art Therapy, Psychodrama, Reasoning and Rehabilitation were introduced, with the SOTP being added in 1999. These latter two programmes are accredited with the Correctional Services Accreditation Panel (CSAP) and audited by the Offending Behaviour Programme's Unit (OBPU) based in HM Prison Service HQ in London.

Both establishments lost the R&R programme due to budget cutbacks in the Prison Service but the loss of the SOTP has been less straightforward. In 1990 the residents of Grendon were relocated to other prisons around the country whilst potentially very hazardous in-cell electrical installations were replaced. Immediately prior to this move, large numbers of sex offenders were placed on G Wing; their return prompted the development of Grendon's own sex offenders' programme in partnership with the National Society for the Protection and Care of Children (NSPCC). Another version of SOTP was bought in, this time from the USA; the programme was based on cognitive behavioural techniques and was called Psycho-Education. This remained until 1997 but was deemed too expensive by the prison management and a decision was made to replace it with the OBPU's accredited SOTP.

An internal debate followed about running one of the wings with a same offence population. This went against Grendon's tradition of having a heterogeneous mix of offences and offenders on each wing. The sex offenders stated that they felt safer doing SOTP in a homogenous environment with similar offenders. Externally there was debate over the Socratic delivery style of SOTP being incompatible with the more confrontational style of TC group therapy. Dovegate TC as part of its initial contract had psychodrama and both SOTP and R&R accredited programmes as co-lateral therapies. Although there was no specific community assigned to sex offenders as Grendon's G Wing, the argument over delivery styles emerged again. Dovegate TC eventually lost SOTP and R&R in a re-organization of delivery centres and cost considerations.

It would have been an interesting piece of research to see the combined effect, or 'double dose', of SOTP and small group therapy on re-offending when compared to SOTP alone. The general opinion, when asked of both staff members and inmates at Dovegate and Grendon, was that they were sad to have lost the SOTP as a programme as both establishments felt that the 'double dose' would have been a very effective strategy over time with this most controversial group of offenders. Despite the setbacks experienced in delivering accredited OBPs, the group of prison TCs remain committed to providing complimentary therapies as part of their overall strategy.

The Director of Therapy at HMP Send is very committed to developing an SOTP programme specifically for female sex offenders. Dovegate TC is developing programmes in relapse prevention, relationship management and a new style of anger management programme to be delivered in conjunction with a theatre group is being written. Grendon TC is resubmitting bids to run SOTP again.

Risk assessment

Continual risk assessment from the beginning of a custodial sentence to a period following release is another part of through-care and after-care, as it will determine the level of supervision and support required for each offender through the prison sentence and into the community. Risk and responsivity principles are highly relevant to therapy targets and co-lateral programmes available to residents of TCs. The notion of low-intensity treatment for low risk and more intensive therapy for high risk has been widely acknowledged in correctional services over a period of time (Andrews and Bonta 1994) and has a place in the TC.

The Offender Assessment System (OASys) is the risk predictor tool developed by the Home Office for the Probation and Prison Service. OASys is based on the social learning theory developed by Bandura (1973) and assesses actuarial and dynamic risk factors across a number of domains (Home Office 2001). Kemshall (2003, p.71) states: 'The tool's major contribution is in the area of criminogenic needs assessment and the targeting of offenders for accredited programmes of intervention in both prison and probation settings.'

In prison TCs OASys serves a triple function. First, it can identify if going to a TC should be a consideration in a prisoner's sentence plan (the word *consideration* is used as going to a prison TC is a voluntary agreement). Second, it can be used to set treatment and sentence plan targets for the person in therapy (in conjunction with the therapeutic assessment process). And finally, it can form the basis of the through-care and after-care plan by indicating further programmes to be completed and resettlement issues to be considered either on release or as progression through the prison system.

Other risk assessments such as HCR-20 *Assessing Risk for Violence: Version 2* (Webster *et al.* 1997) for the assessment of violence; *The Risk of Sexual Violence Protocol* (RSVP) (Hart *et al.* 2003) for the assessment of sexual violence and the *Spousal Assault Risk Assessment Guide* (SARA) (Kropp *et al.* 1999) for the assessment of domestic violence are useful tools in the through-care process. The dynamic risk factor component found in all of these assessments, whether it is substance misuse, employment preparation or cooperation with supervision, provide very good indicators as to what further work and support is necessary for the offender to complete their sentence and offers information and guidance about the level and type of supervision required on release.

New public protection initiatives such as the Multi Agency Public Protection Arrangements (MAPPA) apply the dynamics of risk assessment to supervision of offenders in the community by involving responsible agencies, for example Prison, Probation, Police, Social Services, Housing and Health in the decision making process. To further illustrate the concept, meetings of MAPPA boards occur both in prison and in the community prior to release and will help determine in what area the individual can or cannot live or visit, who the individual is allowed to contact and determine the level of supervision required by the probation service. If the individual has ongoing mental health problems the Board may determine minimum contact levels between the individual and the mental health services.

After-care

The processes involved in through-care have been described and these elements should be the same for all residents in therapy. As described earlier, there will be few prisoners in therapy released directly into the community. For those few who will be, there is a dedicated resettlement team to help with housing, employment and benefit needs. For the majority, Dovegate has developed a specific education programme for returning to mainstream prison and how to survive the experience; this we had termed *re-integration*.

Re-integration

Dovegate TC formed a committee to look at the problems of reintegration and initially identified the following issues:

- detaching from therapy and rejoining mainstream prison life

- maintaining gains that have been made in therapy
- finding appropriate support mechanisms
- managing expectations
- myths versus reality.

Residents coming to the end of therapy, those opting to leave therapy and those deselected from therapy were given questionnaires enquiring what information or skills they thought they required to survive the transition from therapy back to prison. Researchers from the University of Surrey (who currently hold the HMP Dovegate TC research contract) completed follow-up questionnaires for ex-Dovegate TC residents. The residents themselves confirmed the original brief, but to this was added the concept of bringing into the course someone who had successfully completed therapy in prison, finished their sentence and was living successfully in the community. This person could talk current residents through his experience and give them both hope and knowledge of the survival skills required for success.

From this beginning the reintegration course was born with the first one run in May 2004. The course content is a mixture of experiential and discussion groups, role-plays, relapse-prevention strategies and practical information. An ex-Grendon resident, who is now a practicing psychologist, was enlisted to reinforce the message of progression and release. Initial feedback from participants was very good, with the result that the reintegration course is a regular part of the Dovegate TC calendar. The course continues to evolve, with new additions such as the impact of continuous risk assessment, MAPPA and other initiatives being added to the core reintegration programme at the request of participants, and this demonstrates that the process of reintegration can be dynamic.

The future

What next? The number of therapeutic places available in the secure adult male estate has approximately doubled from around 240 at the beginning of 2001 to 480 as Dovegate and Blundeston TCs joined Grendon and Gartree TCs. The development of a women's facility at HMP Send in 2004 and the established Young Offender's TC at Aylesbury strongly suggest that prison TCs are becoming more accepted as an intervention for offending behaviour. To meet this expansion the newly formed NOMS need to consider the question: 'What happens after therapy?' in order to support those who have gone through the TC experience.

One way to achieve this would be to expand the linked progression scheme that currently exists between groups of prisons. Those who follow their sentence plan, establishment expectations and most importantly further reduce their criminogenic risk get increasing amounts of freedom in the secure conditions of the category C estate. A record of good discipline, taking responsibility and further risk reduction should lead to transfer to the open conditions of category D to complete resettlement work prior to release. A further extension of this arrangement would be for NOMS to fund TC follow-up and sponsor outreach workers to visit ex-TC residents through the prison and probation systems to offer support when required.

An alternative to this would be to set up *therapeutic link prisons*, for example; pre-therapy wings where those either identified of expressing a wish to join a TC could go to work on motivation and the application process. The next stage would be the TC itself, where the main work on change would be achieved. Those individuals deemed to have been successful would then progress to an identified post-therapy prison. This establishment would act as a bridge by offering similar levels of community responsibility to residents, without the requirement to participate in group therapy. Acceptance of responsibility, demonstrations of self-reliance and pro-social behaviour would result in a further progression to a resettlement prison prior to release.

The title of this chapter posed the question 'what happens after therapy?' To answer this question, the following aspects have been considered:

- What has happened in the past to those leaving therapy?
- What is happening to those leaving therapy today?
- What should happen to people leaving therapy in the future?

In the process of writing, I realized that all involved in prison TCs have a long way to go to work with endings, especially in relation to what happens after therapy. I consider this uncertain situation unsatisfactory as we all work in the area of attachment and loss and, like our clients, find it difficult to work with this area of pain and difficulty at times. In this I am reminded of the words of John Galsworthy, author of the *Forsyte Saga*: 'The beginnings and endings of all human undertakings are untidy' (Galsworthy [1933] 1968, p.9).

Finally, I conclude that our task as TC practitioners is to make the through-care process during and after therapy less untidy than the one we have today.

References

Andrews, D.A. and Bonta, J. (1994) *The Psychology of Criminal Conduct*, 2nd edn. Cincinnati, Ohio: Anderson.

Bandura, A. (1973) *Aggression: A Social Learning Analysis*. London: Prentice Hall.

Galsworthy, J. (1933) *Over the River*. First published by William Heinmann Ltd in Penguin Books 1968. Harmondsworth. Middlesex, England.

Great Britain. Her Majesty's Chief Inspector of Prisons for England and Wales (2001) *Through the Prison Gate: A Summary of HM Inspectors of Prisons and Probation Thematic Report*. Home Office, Inspectorate of Prisons for England and Wales. London.

Great Britain. Her Majesty's Government, Home Office (2001) *The Offender Assessment System: OASys*. London.

Great Britain. Her Majesty's Government, National Offender Management Service (NOMS) (2005) *The Offender's Learning Journey*. London, p.1.

Great Britain. Her Majesty's Prison Service (2001) Prison Service Order 2300, Resettlment. London.

Hart, S.D., Kropp, R.P. and Laws, R.D. (2003) *The Risk for Sexual Violence Protocol (RSVP)*. Vancouver: Simon Fraser University.

Healy, B. (2000) *Grendon Prison: The History of a Therapeutic Experiment 1939–2000*. HMP Leyhill: Her Majesty's Prison Service. England and Wales.

Kemshall, H. (2003) *Understanding Risk in Criminal Justice*. Maidenhead: Open University Press.

Kropp, R.P., Hart, S.D., Webster, C.D. and Eaves, D. (1999) *The Spousal Assault Risk Assessment Guide (SARA)*. Toronto: Multi Health Systems.

National Offender Management Service (2005) *Offenders Learning Journey. London*.

Parker, T. (1970) *The frying-pan: A prison and its prisoners*. London: Hutcheson and Co. Ltd.

The Sun (1994) *Jail Perverts Live in Luxury*. London: News Media International, 9 May.

Webster, C.D., Douglas, K., Eaves, D. and Hart, S.D. (1997) *HCR-20 Assessing Risk for Violence*. Version 2, Vancouver: Simon Fraser University.

Psychodynamic Aspects:
Inside Forensic Therapy

'We used to make a football out of a goat head': Working with Young Offenders in a Prison Therapeutic Community

Teresa Wood

Resident: When I first came to prison I didn't care, I didn't give a fuck, had plans to come out and still do crime, live the same lifestyle.

Staff: How did that fit with everyone else?

Resident: Perfectly.

Of principal importance in the treatment of young offenders is the recognition that treatment interventions should have the specific needs of young people as their foundation and the flexibility to adapt interventions to accommodate these needs. No therapeutic intervention will be effective in facilitating change unless based on this tenet. The primary symbolism contained in behaviour as a means of communication for young offenders often takes the place of language and so this chapter will focus on the staff role of teaching young offenders how to manage their behaviour and internalize behavioural control and the methods through which to facilitate this change.

The following key themes are relevant to this work.

Containment versus control

Adult offenders are likely to have some experience of how to conduct themselves in formal social situations. This is not necessarily the case for young offenders. Within the school system they have often failed to comply with rules that allow groups to function effectively. A lack of compliance in the classroom and failure to interact collaboratively with the majority of their peers in the less formal settings of unstructured leisure activity are common features of their educational history (Patterson 1986; Dishion *et al.* 1991). In addition, exposure to other formal or informal settings that would provide a template for how to behave within acceptable group norms has usually been limited. While it has been relatively easy to learn the formal disciplinary requirements of the prison setting, the TC can be more challenging with its emphasis on pro-social rules being generated by and policed by the Community itself. In keeping with this, most young offenders joining the Community will adopt the general unwritten prison rule of superficial compliance (Weinstock 1989). Thus, new residents will usually be polite and seek instruction from staff on how to behave in this new setting and try to find norms for behavioural compliance in the Unit. In meetings they may sit quietly and fail to participate in any constructive manner, possibly engage in non-verbal contact with other less engaged residents and respond in a startled way if asked to join any ongoing discussion. New residents struggle to understand what is expected of them in the community and will turn to peers for advice on how to 'play the system'. Often, in keeping with patterns outside prison, advice will be sought from peers most clearly seen as similar to themselves. Thus they may avoid being pro-active in seeking guidance from more established residents who appear to abide by unfamiliar rules: talking honestly in front of staff or working collaboratively with staff, and will instead seek advice from other residents who are less engaged in treatment.

As treatment progresses two things happen: senior residents become more familiar with new residents and their pathology and as a consequence become more willing to challenge this. Initially this takes place 'behind the scenes' in the absence of staff as to do so in the presence of staff would break an unwritten code of conduct: basic non-compliance with staff. Later, in response to more senior residents teaching them that the TC is not pre-occupied with superficial behaviour but instead intends to identify and address individuals' behavioural problems and offence-related risk factors, newer residents begin to test behavioural boundaries. It is at this point that less experienced prison staff members begin to question the efficacy of treatment and are at risk of re-asserting overly controlling behavioural boundaries. The issue of control versus containment comes to the forefront. This is largely played out between the representatives of the system, those with parental function, the staff members, and residents and takes the form of minor prison rule infringements, an increased tendency to act in an aggressive, provocative manner towards staff and as time progresses, an overt challenging of staff and their authority.

During this period staff must be able to subjugate their natural inclination to re-assert complete control in response to fears of losing their authority and being unsafe, and instead provide a containing environment (Bion 1962). Staff members need to be able to tolerate behavioural indiscretions that do not threaten the safety of others while at the same time not be overwhelmed by feelings of helplessness and impotence regarding their position. In doing both of these things the staff team model an ability to contain rather than control behaviour to the resident. Throughout the lives of most young offenders their behaviour has either been controlled or 'out of control' and as such there has been no experience of their potential destructiveness being able to be managed by themselves or by others in a way that has been able to be internalized. If staff respond to behavioural testing of boundaries by over-emphasizing control and authority the internal notion held by young prisoners of their being omnipotent and beyond control is reinforced and behavioural problems escalate in a desperate attempt by them to have the 'adults' take control of their behaviour.

While the exclusion of young offenders from treatment if they present a serious risk to others is necessary to protect the therapeutic integrity of the Community, this should not be necessary if the management of minor rule violations is managed appropriately. Young offenders' receptivity to firm, fair boundaries needs to be utilized sensitively in order for control to be maintained. Distinctions can be made between critical rules and minor rule violations that can be managed safely over time, in collaboration with staff members and peers. Behaviour that can be safely contained needs to be differentiated from that which cannot. Over time, collaborative management by staff members and residents together of less extreme behaviour serves to provide a template on which the Community can build to develop their abilities to safely contain themselves.

Action versus reaction

The tendency to react rather than think first then act is a natural response for staff with numerous pressures on their time and attention. However, it is important in working with young offenders in a TC to be proactive rather than reactive in interactions with residents. This is not to suggest that the underlying principle of democracy in TCs is undermined, rather that staff are aware that they are the model for the young offenders within the Community. Senior residents can set an example for others and teach others how to act within the Community. In times of crisis, residents often turn to staff for guidance on how to behave. If the staff and resident groups have established a strong Community ethos, approval from staff for decisions made and whether behaviour is acceptable will be sought. Young offenders need guidance to avoid their behaviour escalating and becoming either disruptive or unsafe. Staff should seek to proactively intervene to shape young offenders' behaviour towards desired social norms rather than wait to respond to rule breaking in a punitive manner. One young offender put it in this way: 'Good staff listen to you and not just give you nickings; they can sit and talk to you'. Reactive behaviour from staff leads to a circular dynamic in which young people receive no attention until their behaviour breaks behavioural boundaries and then they receive sanctions or negative attention when this happens. The psychological literature is clear that this behavioural style (from staff or parents) serves to reinforce behavioural difficulties in young people (Miller 1980; Patterson 1982).

Another major problem in reacting rather than acting is that it disempowers staff who if they respond to the tone set by young people are more liable to feel helpless to control difficult behaviour without resort to sanctions. Experience of how to intervene to shape young people's behaviour positively within the community is reinforced when a successful intervention generates positive feedback from residents and obvious behavioural change is shown. The increased confidence experienced by staff when they see this happening enables them to better contain young people within the community and to help them model other key community themes such as taking responsibility.

Accountability and responsibility

Within a Community, accountability is taught through staff modelling while genuine responsibility is taken through the free choice of the offender. Often staff members working with young offenders are tempted to teach the latter and fail to model the former. Individuals cannot meaningfully be told to take responsibility: at best this treatment approach will generate superficial compliance. At worst it may lead to the disempowerment of Community members and the subsequent failure of residents to take responsibility when it is within their emotional and psychological capacity to do so. Being able to take responsibility may take time and a significant proportion of young offenders will need considerable therapeutic input before they are sufficiently emotionally mature to do so.

Difficulties in accepting responsibility by those in the young offender age group are linked to internal vulnerability about whether they are perceived to be a good or bad person to themselves or to others. Public exposure of offences can lead to shaming and make it more difficult to access openness to change. While fear of formal sanctions as a result of problem behaviour is present, failure to take responsibility among young offenders may also be linked to a fear of social sanctions such as the fantasy that through taking responsibility they will be separated from their 'in-group': their peer group and friends. This holds true for the act of taking responsibility in challenging others in a pro-social way and in terms of taking responsibility and being held accountable for antisocial actions. Therefore, staff members working in TCs for young people must be attentive to residents who demonstrate responsibility by challenging others and consistently reinforcing such behaviour as valuable, however small the example, if they wish this culture to spread through the Community.

The behaviour of staff within a Community is constantly being monitored by young offenders and failure by staff to abide by the rules of the Community will be logged and used to challenge staff at a later date. Young offenders will generally choose to highlight the least therapeutic behaviour displayed by the staff team in public forums, particularly Community meetings, rather than the most useful, as this serves to deflect the focus of attention from themselves and places responsibility and accountability back with the staff team: a more comfortable position, but one that maintains a no-change dynamic. It is important that staff respond to such challenges by modelling a capacity to admit mistakes (Livesey 2001) while evidencing that this does not undermine their integrity as a person or render their view invalid. Through staff modelling an ability to take responsibility, young offenders are provided with an opportunity to learn that a willingness to be held responsible and accountable for one's actions only serves to engender increased respect from others. Also important may be the notion that being 'good' does not involve being perfect. This in turn frees up residents to take responsibility and be accountable for their own misdemeanours without fear that to do so will result in them being ostracized, rejected and perceived as worthless by peers or staff.

'Acting out' and projecting in

A notable feature of young offenders' behaviour is their habitual 'acting out' through antisocial and criminal behaviour, their internal emotional states that are otherwise experienced as intolerable. Violent and aggressive behaviour is frequently engaged in to release internal tensions (Bateman and

Holmes 1995). Other criminal activities such as acquisitive crime, although less clearly identifiable with negative emotions, may serve the same purpose. Through projecting fear or distress and vulnerability into others the young person, particularly in the company of peers, is able to feel strong and powerful in the moment, rather than helpless and worthless when measured by society's standards. With regard to the expression of emotion, and in many cases the internal acknowledgement of emotions, the young offender is generally comfortable with the expression or acknowledgement of one emotion, that of anger. Sadness, fear, guilt and other less 'macho' and potentially threatening emotions are hidden behind the more tolerable emotion of anger.

Within treatment the same dynamic persists. The majority of young offenders rarely spontaneously or voluntarily display other emotions. Whilst different personality types will display anger in different ways, some threatening violence, some being passively aggressive, some more subtly sadistic towards others, the attacking of others as a form of defence against experiencing feelings that would potentially overwhelm the young person is a regular feature of young offenders' behaviour in treatment. Aggressive, impulsive, unboundaried, and on occasion unsafe behaviours are consistently presented to the staff within the TC. The subtext offered by young offenders in their acting out behaviour is: if you can tolerate and contain my emotions perhaps it is possible for me to learn to do so (Winnicott 1965; Bion 1962). This places considerable demands on TC staff members, who must not only be able to tolerate the dominant emotions displayed, and often projected into themselves (Klein 1946), but also remain grounded and secure enough in themselves to be able to resonate emotionally with the emotions behind the presenting emotional expression whether this be anger, despair or other equally difficult to tolerate emotions (Gabbard and Wilkinson 1994; Money-Kyrle 1956). The natural tendency for all of us when faced with another's potentially threatening emotion is to respond in kind. In so doing the staff member activates their own fight-or-flight response, and comes to occupy the same internal emotional position as the young person (Ogden 1979). This only serves to heighten the young person's anxiety as if others cannot contain their emotions this gives a clear message that they are not containable.

'Acting out' behaviour is not only a testing of boundaries; it is also a request on the part of the young person to have their internal emotions acknowledged and responded to in a way that diminishes the power of these emotions. One young offender describes the overwhelming nature of such emotions in this way: 'But the surface is all just a mask which covers up a gloomy part and many unsolved issues. The deeper I think the more I burn, so sometimes I try not thinking but what would I be without any thoughts? Simply a corpse with a heartbeat?' Staff need to be able to tolerate the external expression of emotion by young offenders through their behaviour and the potentially vulnerable emotions these can generate in themselves. This does not mean that boundaries are avoided and young people not contained; it means that staff members try to be emotionally resilient enough to accept the projections of disturbed young people into their own internal emotional world and attempt to remain able to think and process these emotional states. This is not easy and it is helpful to be able to talk over such emotional demands with colleagues in supervision and develop a culture of support and understanding within the staff team about coping with projected emotional states.

Boundaries versus care

One of the primary ways in which staff can work effectively to ensure that they do not become prey to the projections of young people and helpless in response to 'acting out' behaviour is through establishing an appropriate balance between boundaries and care. All too often texts focus on the sum of all parts when considering this area, i.e. is a Community as a whole manifesting both containing boundaries and care? It is important in working with young people to understand that it is the internal emotional capacity and external behavioural capacity of each individual staff member working in the Community that is reflected in the Community culture. Young people need consistent boundaries and consistent care. Communities can, and do, operate successfully with different staff members holding more responsibility in one of these areas. However, an imbalance can potentially be exploited by young offenders in treatment. When certain staff members set boundaries and others break boundaries at best confusion ensues, and at worst manipulation and a potentially unsafe therapeutic environment can be generated. When some staff shun the 'caring' role and others take emotional responsibility for empathizing with and understanding young residents, staff may be at risk of overload and 'burnout' unless the sharing is more evenly distributed between colleagues (Freudenberger 1974). Other staff members may be unable to be effective in their work if they cannot resonate emotionally to a sufficient, good enough, degree with the young people in their care. It is the responsibility of each individual member of staff working in a TC for young people to maintain an internal balance of boundaries versus care that they can apply to contain the behaviour and emotions of the young people with whom they work. Ultimately, this cannot be taught in manualized form alone but may require personal development together with learning from the body of research work detailing effective techniques in the management of young people (Herbert 1987).

To clarify, TC staff working with young offenders must at any moment in time, like a good parent, be able to hold responsibility for boundary setting and be able to identify a young person's emotional needs. Again, described by a young offender in treatment: 'They [staff members] need to understand that there's been things in our lives that have affected us for us to make those mistakes, didn't have right guidance, role model to show us right and wrong way of life.' The extent to which boundary setting or care is used is dependent on the needs of each individual and interventions need to be informed by consideration of individual offenders' developmental stage and their treatment responsivity. Over-dependence on boundary setting as a method of dealing with challenging young people will impair the establishment of a therapeutic rapport with clients and in so doing undermine the staff members' therapeutic efficacy. An inability to set and maintain boundaries will lead to young people feeling unsafe and to escalation in behavioural problems.

As this chapter focuses on working with young offenders in a prison TC it is important to focus on the component of 'care' that tends to be marginalized, if not held as taboo within a prison environment, and the importance of this as a treatment tool. A genuine capacity for care on the part of staff members working in a therapeutic environment for young offenders is the most powerful treatment tool available to staff. The therapeutic relationship is the template on which all therapeutic interventions take place (Horvath *et al.* 1993; Horvath and Symonds 1991). One member of staff may contain an out-of-control young person with no physical harm experienced by the young person and another may not. If young people feel valued and validated for their positive potential they will use this as a foundation on which to control and contain their own and others' behaviour within the Community. Empathy is a two-way emotional exchange. Young people who have given no thought to their victims, through the capacity to care modelled by staff begin to consider what they have done to others. The notion of staff caring leads to young offenders starting to care about themselves and this can be the precursor to caring about others in a more global sense (Staub 1986). Without fail this is the therapeutic trajectory displayed in the TC. On the theme of learning empathy: 'At that time coming to prison didn't bother me, didn't realize what was important in my life and others. Now I'm fully aware of the consequences of my actions and things I do and I value my life more and everybody else's.' Behavioural compliance emanating from a desire to work collaboratively with others based on a value and respect for others is distinct from that brought about by consistent application of external boundaries (Kohlberg 1971). Whilst boundaries provide clear and necessary guidelines as to how to behave, care is the motivating factor in applying these and generalizing this compliance outside the treatment or prison environment. It is essential that staff members are able to model care as this is ultimately a primary treatment goal. If young offenders learn to care about others their capacity to offend against them will be more limited regardless of the presence or absence of external boundaries.

Expression versus repression

A further challenge for staff working with young offenders is to allow and encourage creative expression. A consistent theme in the lives of young offenders is that of crime as the only expressive outlet. While some may have latent talents in more creative pursuits such as art or music these have invariably been abandoned for the pursuit of a criminal lifestyle. A recent description has a creative, expressive power to it: 'I try to talk but feel like there's no one listening, I'm spittin' plenty of verbs, but feel like they're all empty words.' Young offenders in TCs generally need consistent and targeted encouragement to engage in creative pursuits. Activities such as making a video or designing a mural all require the sustained involvement and encouragement of staff if they are to be attempted and completed. In our experience once staff members cease to provide the creative momentum for such communal activities, the activities cease. Young offenders are fearful of expressing themselves creatively and need considerable support to overcome internal hurdles to doing so. Destructive activity is more readily taken up.

Once given permission to be creative, an exuberant outburst may be experienced and this can be shown in excitable, impulsive or chaotic behaviour. Thus, young people enjoying painting a mural may well be tempted to start painting each other. The challenge for staff is to draw the boundary for creative expression in such a way that enthusiasm and spontaneity are encouraged but behaviour remains contained and the overall task focus is maintained. Focusing a group of emotionally immature young people on an activity they are newly exposed to demands skills of staff more similar to those needed by a parent engaged in a creative activity with a toddler than an adolescent. Residents will look to staff to generate enthusiasm and only when encouragement is received give themselves permission to take risks in expressing and exposing themselves. In the absence of staff support, very few young offenders will be able to overcome their low self-esteem or the self-imposed rigid constraints on 'play' behaviour they impose on themselves.

Such factors have major resource implications. Young people need to be empowered to express themselves creatively as this is a potentially constructive outlet for their emotional expression. The importance of art and other complementary activities in a TC for young offenders should not be underestimated. The broadening of young peoples' expressive horizons and the harnessing of their creative expression into areas where they can achieve without harming others is a critical treatment intervention as 'it is only in being creative that the individual discovers the self' (Winnicott 1971, p.63). To learn to be creative as opposed to destructive is a skill directly rather than indirectly related to rehabilitating young offenders.

Staff as 'parents'

A theme running throughout this chapter has been that of the parallels between the role of TC staff and the role of a 'good enough' parent (Winnicott 1965). An absence of adequate parenting is a feature of almost all residents' lives (Loeber and Stouthamer-Loeber 1986; Farrington 1986) and relations with staff will be coloured by previous parental experiences. Thus, in the transference, staff who represent male authority figures may be obeyed more readily but equally tested more harshly once a therapeutic relationship is established: will they abandon the resident as their father did? Other staff members may be idealized and then, as treatment progresses, become recipients of residents' anger in the transference at parental figures who were unable to protect or nurture effectively. An overdependence on therapy group facilitators, who tend to be given the parental role, is manifest and other staff members may be rejected as untrustworthy or unskilled, or alternatively seen as surrogate siblings.

It is the role of TC staff to identify and understand such transference dynamics without adopting prescribed roles blindly in the here and now. Staff should be sensitive to the relationships between themselves and offenders and each other in relation to offenders and serve to utilize the strengths and weaknesses within these relationships to facilitate the therapeutic progress of residents. Staff must perform the function of good enough parents in all domains. They must implement boundaries, model pro-social behaviour, display care, help shape pro-social attitudes, develop young people's creativity and be able to relate to adolescent culture and use this capacity to influence the group culture in pro-social ways. Most importantly they must work to help young offenders take responsibility for their own behaviour by being willing, incrementally, to surrender their own institutional omnipotence.

Conclusion

TCs for young offenders challenge the cultural fabric of the Prison System as such work involves empowering young people to manage their own risk and dangerousness within institutions that traditionally rely on external controls and sanctions to ensure compliance and safety. Staff in such Communities become the interface between the harsh, punitive superego of the Prison System and the potentially out of control Id drives of the young offender. Consequently, the demands made on staff are immense and often appear insurmountable with the result that staff may reject the 'young' part of the offender and seek solace in the 'offender'. This is a recipe for therapeutic failure but can be avoided if staff consolidate their own ego functioning and in so doing model the functioning of a healthy adult to those in their care.

References

Bateman, A. and Holmes, J. (1995) Clinical dilemmas. In A. Bateman and J. Homes (eds) *Introduction to Psychoanalysis: Contemporary Theory and Practice.* London: Routledge.

Bion, W.R. (1962) *Learning from Experience.* New York: Basic Books.

Dishion, T.J., Patterson, G.R., Stoolmiller, M. and Skinner, M.L. (1991) Family, school, and behavioural antecedents to early adolescent involvement with antisocial peers. *Developmental Psychology, 27,* 172–180.

Farrington, D. (1986) Stepping stones to adult criminal careers. In D. Olweus, J. Block and M.R. Yarrow (eds) *Development of Antisocial and Prosocial Behaviour.* New York: Academic Press.

Freudenberger, H.J. (1974) Staff burnout. *Journal of Social Issues, 30,* 159–165.

Gabbard, G.O. and Wilkinson, S.M. (1994) *Management of Countertransference with Borderline Patients.* Washington, DC: American Psychiatric Press.

Herbert, M. (1987) *Behavioural Treatment of Children with Problems: A Practice Manual.* 2nd revised edn. London: Academic Press.

Horvath, A.O., Gaston, L., and Luborsky, L. (1993) The therapeutic alliance and its measures. In N. Miller, L. Luborsky, J. Barber, and J. Doherty (eds) *Handbook of Psychodynamic Psychotherapy: Theory and Research.* New York: Basic Books.

Horvath, A.O. and Symonds, B.D. (1991) Relation between working alliance and outcome in psychotherapy: A meta-analysis. *Journal of Counselling Psychology, 38,* 139–149.

Klein, M. (1946) Notes on some schizoid mechanisms. In M. Klein, P. Heimann, S. Isaacs and J. Riviere (eds) *Developments in Psychoanalysis.* London: Hogarth.

Kohlberg, L. (1971) From is to ought: How to commit the naturalistic fallacy and get away with it in the study of moral development. In T. Mischel (ed.) *Cognitive Development and Epistemology.* New York: Academic Press.

Livesey, W.J. (2001) A framework for an integrated approach to treatment. In W.J. Livesey (ed.) *A Handbook of Personality Disorders: Theory, Research and Treatment.* New York: Guilford.

Loeber, R. and Stouthamer-Loeber, M. (1986) Family factors as correlates and predictors of juvenile conduct problems and delinquency. In N. Morris and M. Tonry (eds) *Crime and Justice: An Annual Review of Research* Vol. 7. Chicago: University of Chicago Press.

Miller, K.L. (1980) *Principles of Everyday Behaviour Analysis*, 2nd edn. Montgomery, California: Brooks/Cole.

Money-Kyrle, R. (1956) Normal countertransference and some of its deviations. *International Journal of Psychoanalysis, 37*, 360–366.

Ogden, T. (1979). On projective identification. *International Journal of Psychoanalysis, 60*, 357–373.

Patterson, G.R. (1982) *Coercive Family Process*. Eugene, Oregon: Castalia.

Patterson, G.R. (1986) Performance models for antisocial boys. *American Psychologist, 41*, 432–444.

Staub, E. (1986) A conception of the determinants and development of altruism and aggression: motives, the self and the environment. In C. Zahn-Waxler, E.M. Cummings and R. Ianottis (eds) *Social and Biological Origins of Altruism and Aggression*. Cambridge: Cambridge University Press.

Weinstock, R. (1989) Treatment of antisocial and other personality disorders in a correctional setting. In R. Rosner and R.B. Harmon (eds) *Correctional Psychiatry*. New York: Plenum Press.

Winnicott, D.W. (1965) *The Maturational Processes and the Facilitating Environment*. London: International Universities Press.

Winnicott, D.W. (1971) *Playing and Reality*. London: Tavistock Publications.

Chapter 11

A Schema for the Transition from Cruel Object to Tender Object Relations Among Drug Users in a Prison Therapeutic Community

Ronald Doctor

This chapter discusses the psychodynamic processes involved in treating, within a psychotherapeutic community in the prison service, those offenders who show addictive behaviour in both criminality and drug abuse. The setting provides an intensive relationship experience in which the interaction between the inmates and staff members in the prison institution is mirrored in the TC in general, and in groups in particular. Using clinical material as direct examples of the transference addiction, it will be illustrated how the containing therapeutic environment allows prisoners the experience of new possibilities of ways of coping with anxiety, whereby the customary defences of cruelty and violence, when creatively challenged in the therapeutic groups, may be attenuated in favour of a more humane understanding of underlying conflicts.

Transference addiction has attracted less attention than other forms of transference, such as those of neurotic, psychotic or perverse states, perhaps, because it is not easy to define a special type of transference link in addicted patients, in whom psychological mechanisms are combined with the physio-pathological effects of the drugs. A peculiar difficulty with the addict is that if the drug taking is not checked, analysis becomes difficult, whereas if it is interfered with, analytical neutrality suffers.

Addiction can exist in a number of non-drug relationships, such as those with food, gambling, work and television; in fact, any human activity can bear the stamp of such behaviour and in a letter from Freud to his colleague Fliess (1897), Freud states that masturbation is the primal addiction for which all others are substitutes. In his book, Etchegoyen (1991) is of the opinion that the mental structure is the same in every case, but the clinical consequences are different. This is where the quantitative factors of the psychological conflict and the pharmacological action of the drug play a principal role.

We consider as an addict the patient who turns to alcohol and/or drugs as his main recourse in order to maintain a psychological balance and gain relief from anxiety and to obtain a feeling of pleasure and wellbeing. When the drug is used to counteract the negative effect that appears as its action ends, a vicious circle is formed, which is very important in the establishment of addiction. The addict's craving is, by definition, impossible to satisfy insofar as it does not arise from necessity but from greed.

The addict's sadomasochistic conflicts are fundamental and they are morally amplified by very strong aggressive impulses. Sadism and masochism exist not only in the unconscious of these patients but also quite openly in their conduct and they can be triggered not only by frustration, but also by envy. Rosenfeld (1965) highlights the addict's struggles against powerful anxieties surrounding homosexual tendencies, and has also linked the periods of taking and abstaining from the drug with the cycles of manic-depressive psychosis, together with the importance of narcissism and vulnerability to self-esteem.

I have been engaged, as Visiting Psychiatrist at a psychotherapeutic community centre, housed within a large London prison. The Unit is separate from the other wings of the prison and consists of a multi-disciplinary team. Whilst this admixture inevitably produces a certain tension, this can be constructively integrated within the therapeutic endeavour. There are various therapy groups comprising large community groups and small groups designated for more intensive work. Alongside the professionals (psychologists and probation officers) facilitating the groups, one or two prison officers will join the groups, often acting as co-therapists, even though their primary function is one of safeguarding security. Although the inmates are wary of their presence, in time, they develop some trust in officers respecting their confidentiality. Inmates who participate in the scheme have personally applied and are subsequently sent a questionnaire and interviewed to assess their suitability to think psychologically and their capacity for change. Prisoners must commit to a minimum of 18 months in the Unit and have to forego any parole privileges during that time, thereby indicating their motivation to change their behaviour.

It is striking how the nature of the prison building itself can be viewed as a concrete illustration of the psychological terrain held within. Thus, there is not only the physical difference between the outside world and the one inside, but there may also be remarkable physical contrast *within* the prison itself; for example, the drab and barren building, a legacy of incarceration and punishment, is in marked opposition to the unexpected find of the most ornate and elaborately adorned church, dedicated to the spiritual awareness of the prisoners. Perhaps this is a reflection of the extreme polarities in the prisoner's mind, of hope and salvation on the one hand, and psychic despair and death on the other. This is typical of many contradictions and contrasts that may be encountered in the prison system. Yet it is these very incongruities that encourage splitting and projective processes to take place in the organization, which can be of help in thinking about working in the prison itself. Currently, there is a debate about what to do with prisoners, whether to punish or help them and this reflects the duality in prison life itself. Both become split within the prison, with discipline losing its concerned aspect and compassion its firmness, resulting in an attitude of brutality versus pathetic compassion (Doctor 2001).

Perhaps the main obstacle to working as a psychotherapist in prison lies in the prison culture itself, a culture that is formed from entrenched attitudes adopted by the prisoner that dictate his relation to others. This self-same culture, one of macho bravado (with proud boasts of crimes committed), keeps prisoners emotionally ensnared and renders them unable, because they are unwilling, to express themselves. The fear, perhaps, is that to articulate their feelings could make them vulnerable and hence unable to function within the prison milieu, as there is no sympathy for weak prisoners. This amounts to a duplicity created by the prisoners, in an effort to deceive themselves. A prisoner is hard and lives by his wit, cunning and deception. Those on the receiving end are the prison officers. They too are engaged in a relentless struggle to preserve and defend their image, self-esteem and masculinity against the deception of the prisoners. In their efforts to do this, they must grossly over-respond to any slight to their esteem, or when being made a fool of by the prisoners. They must outsmart the prisoners by beating them at their own game of toughness. As a result, they are contemptuous of any displays of humane feelings of concern and gratitude.

By contrast, psychotherapists, psychologists and probation officers who are acting as receptacles for all the disowned feelings of frailty and tenderness are consequently regarded as a 'soft touch'. Thus on the one hand, psychotherapy is denigrated and undermined, while on the other hand it serves the purpose of being the receptacle for softness and to allay anxiety and guilt. One of the first experiences for the author in the prison was to hear and feel the antagonism from the prisoners, medical officers and prison staff towards the psycho-therapeutic community as a whole for being a waste of time, a soft option or a dumping ground for sex offenders, the weak and the cowardly.

This defensive organization of the prisoners, prison officers and psychotherapists serves a function: to separate or split the hard authority and power from the soft empathic tenderness towards others, thereby avoiding the anxiety and guilt of the criminal mind. Freud (1916) noted that it is not the weakness or lack of a superego but its overpowering strictness that is characteristic of the behaviour of the criminal person. The criminal feels a persecutory or oppressive guilt that is extremely harsh. Faced with such horrendous judgement or attack he can only conceive of defending himself by mounting an equally violent assault on some enemy and thus project his persecutory violence into the cruel justice system. This reaction to an internal enemy, self-condemning judge or superego entails actually finding an enemy to assault in the real world.

Clinical example

A clinical example of such a mind state arose during one of the group sessions with the prisoners. John, one of the members of the group, convicted for bank robbery, told of an episode during his adolescence. He spoke of his early life, which had involved being fostered at the age of 6 months, before returning to his mother and stepfather at the age of 2. His mother had re-married whilst John had been in care. John stated: 'I hate my mother. I feel like killing her. She never loved me. She tried to drown me.' The latter comment referred to an incident in John's childhood when he said his mother tried to choke him in the bath. He said he also loathed his stepfather who, he remembers, would lock him in his room, saying that John was not fit to associate with the rest of the family. He went on to talk of an incident involving his biological father, a railway worker, with whom he was still in fairly regular contact when growing up. John, aged 14 years, had run away from a children's home and gone to his father's house. The latter was unhappy with John's escapade, and arranged for his son's return. John, meanwhile, stole £120 from his father's wallet, met with friends and bought solvents, which they proceeded to sniff on board a train. When other passengers expressed concern and called the guard, John drew a knife and attempted to stab the complainant, a man. A tussle ensued, following which John and his friends were arrested by police. John described how his father was so angry with him at this time that he said he wished to have nothing further to do with him. John took this at face value and did not make contact again until he was informed of his father's imminent death and agreed to see him again. He said that subsequently he discovered that his father appeared to have forgiven him soon after the incident, as he had included John in his will.

John went on to describe his feelings towards his mother. He felt he wished to kill her and his stepfather. He complained bitterly that on her one visit to him in gaol that she had come with him (i.e. his step-father): '...She opened her arms, cried, tried to hug me, but I wasn't having any of it'. He said he wanted his stepfather to look him in the eye, but that he wouldn't, adding that if he had done so, it would have felt like a cue for John to 'smash his face in ... I really wanted to.'

I pointed out that it seemed that, whilst John's (biological) father appeared to have forgiven him, John himself was nursing a grudge against both his father and mother, whom he could not forgive. I wondered if John was truly aware of the degree of murderousness and hatred he could feel for his mother whilst at the same time wishing that he was loved by her. (John had commented earlier that he would be willing for his mother to visit again, but only if she came alone.) John reluctantly acknowledged the possibility.

Etchegoyen (1991) describes how 'transference of the drug addict fluctuates rapidly and continuously from love to hate, from tenderness to the most extreme violence. There is an oscillation between the primitive addiction to triumphant potency and criminality and the more human qualities of remorse and reparation.'

Thus, by converting violent beliefs into acts, the criminal gets a commensurate reaction and retaliation from others and this confirms his belief system. They retain their belief that they are the innocent victims of society's oppressive cruelty rather than accepting that cruelty is also within themselves. Were they to do this, persecutory guilt would give way to depressive guilt, which might be too much to bear. It is not uncommon for such extreme states of violent arousal to acquire an erotic or sexual charge, making the violence seem exciting and eventually compulsive, creating an addiction to a sadomasochistic relationship (Doctor 2003).

Another component of this, referred to by Rosenfeld (1965) is that the superego is, in effect, paralyzed by the drug addiction that is common to many criminals, and in some way thereby eliminates the superego's influence on the ego, which can be 'boundlessly magnified and will become intoxicated with its own perfection and self-sufficiency'. Rosenfeld maintains that there is in the addict a splitting of the internal object into the idealized and persecutory, and he considers that addicts generally have a structure similar to manic-depressive psychosis, in which the drug acts as a sort of artificial mania, protecting the addict from a depressive pain and from persecutory anxieties. He maintains that the addict's basic conflicts have to do with a fixation at the paranoid schizoid position in which the object is deeply split.

Clinical example

An example of this sadomasochistic relationship can, again, be illustrated clinically by an exchange that occurred during a prisoner's group session, when some members expressed their profound and ambivalent feelings towards one or other of the parental couple. Thus, Simon, in prison for importation of drugs, spoke of his alternate feelings of murderous rage towards, and need to acquire approval and forgiveness from, his mother. He described feeling that he had never been good enough for her and that she had never been able to make him feel loved or wanted. In the past, when they had had arguments, the pattern was often that of Simon 'storming off' and telling her to 'fuck off', followed by his telephoning an hour later asking if she was alright. He said he had bought many material things for his mother over the years, including cars and furniture, but that it didn't seem to change her attitude. He talked of feelings of jealousy about her close relationship with Simon's sister: 'They're always on the phone,' and contrasted this with the seemingly perfunctory conversations she allowed him: '...She can't wait to get me off the phone.' Simon added that, since his index conviction for importation of drugs, his mother had told the family she was ashamed of him, and he mentioned that her condemnation had not been to the same degree following a previous crime of armed robbery. Simon said that he often feels 'very angry' with his mother at times but still telephones the next day.

I commented that Simon was reporting how angry he could be with his mother, to the extent of hating her. I contrasted another prisoner's experience of good and helpful authority figures, such as the prison officials who tried to expedite a visit to a dying father, with Simon's experience of a harsh authority figure, and of the conflict in trying to reconcile the two perspectives. Simon, a longstanding member of the group, displayed puzzlement, anger and upset whilst recounting his experience, but appeared able to accept and consider the possibility of the nature of his unconscious responses to the situation and the transferential repetition produced in prison life.

In general, alcohol and drugs are for the addict an idealized object and, at the same time, a bad persecuting object. The addict always takes an extremely contradictory position with respect to his drug and the condition it causes in him, in which exaggerated idealization and the most violent rejection co-exist. The speed with which the drug changes, in the addict's mind, from an idealized object that protects from all possible pain, into a persecutory object that threatens the most cruel destruction, means that the addict tends to be comfortable only in a transference link that mirrors such fluidity, which fluctuates rapidly and continuously from love to hate, from tenderness to the most extreme violence.

The drug addict fears tender feelings because they imply dependence and emotional surrender and thus trigger an immediate reaction of destructive criminal hate, defending against pain and guilt and, ultimately, emptiness. Just as the addict's link with the drug is changeable and extreme, his transference to the analyst changes its nature and this is often accompanied by renewed drug taking and acting out. Etchegoyen (1991) goes on to state:

> By opposite and converging paths, transference addiction becomes a bond in which the therapist is both drug and anti-drug. The addict can only relate to the therapist when he "transforms" him into the drug and at the same time, the bond or healthy therapeutic dependence is misunderstood, mainly through envy, as a threat of the worst addiction. The transference conflict then leads continuously to the drug, and therein lies both the danger and the hope of the therapy of addiction. (pp.199–200)

These conflicts often cause a negative therapeutic reaction, which when severe becomes very difficult to deal with, all the more so when added to the pharmacological effect of the drug.

The analytic process develops from a mature and reciprocal bond of dependence between patient and analyst, which is called a *working alliance*. A distinctive feature of transference addiction is that analytical dependence tends to be converted into an addictive bond in such a way that the analytical relationship swings like a pendulum between dependence and addiction. It may be reasonable to expect that the addict will take the analyst's (good) attitude towards him for an addiction and in this sense we have to interpret that he (the patient) believes that the analyst depends on him as a drug. At the same time, if the patient receives the interpretation like a drug and not like something equivalent to the original object (the breast), the analyst's task will be to discriminate between the two types of relationship.

Clinical example

A clinical vignette serves to illustrate such conflict. A young, middle-class, public-school-educated male, in prison for serious drug dealing, related the following fantasy to a small group. He wanted to flood the town in which he lived with drugs, to turn all the youngsters into drug addicts and subsequently to withdraw all the drugs from the market, thereby causing all these addicts to be utterly dependent on him. This fantasy was acted out when, on one occasion, without explanation, he did not turn up for his session, leaving the group and analyst feeling useless, inadequate and defeated, in not knowing where he was or why he had not attended the group. He came at the eleventh hour to inform the group, to the latter's incredulity, that he had been visiting the prison medical officer, as he wanted someone to talk to. By suddenly absenting himself, without informing the group, he was ensuring that the group would become dependent on him, by virtue of his absence, and in this way, getting the group to shoulder what were his feelings of utter defeat and hopelessness, thus enacting the addict's conflict of potency and grandiosity versus his inadequacy. Through his envy and destructive attack on the group, he left them feeling worthless, but also curious about his esteem of the medical officer.

Melanie Klein (1934) noted that:

> one of the great problems about criminals which have always made them incomprehensible to society is their lack of natural human good feelings, which is only apparent to the casual observer. In psychoanalysis, where one reaches the deepest conflicts from which hatred and anxiety spring, one also finds love as well.

This apparent contradiction between their criminal behaviour and their more compassionate and caring feelings towards each other would be useful were it not for the baffling and chaotic scenarios that emerge (in large groups with their widespread projective processes), and which inhibit the more human feelings from developing.

Clinical example

The opportunity to allow outsiders into the Prison (and Unit) was not an unusual event and one that the inmates would normally welcome. The group was made up of about 15 inmates whose crimes were all serious offences against the person, and who introduced themselves to the visitors with a short account of what had brought them to prison. This is always a little disconcerting because it presents the prisoners as having some form of label, marked by the crime they committed, and little else. On this occasion, the visitors introduced themselves, and one of the group members, 'Andy' (a bank robber), asked the visitor about his accent, where it was from. Although the question was posed in a jocular way, it was fairly obvious that this was a mocking gesture, confirmed by the ripple of giggles that followed the comment. He answered nervously, 'Nowhere, in particular' in an effort to evade precise answers, and therefore humiliation. Another inmate, 'Bill' (a drug dealer), rose to the bait and coyly asked, 'How do you feel about being here?' and tacked onto this the question, 'Are you worried?', with a knowing grin as he did so. The reply from the visitor, 'Yes, I feel nervous, being new in a group is anxiety-provoking,' although it seemed too personalized, did at least help the group to be receptive to their own feelings. They reassured the junior doctors that they were not going to beat them up, which went some way to dissipating the tension. Seeing the presence of the two junior doctors aligned with me also provided a link that opened up the prisoners to a discussion (perhaps unconsciously) about the absence from many of their lives of a father figure.

'Dave', a bank robber, continued this theme in relation to himself as an absent father towards his girlfriend's children. He then moved on to express his anger about figures in authority. He said that he had anger towards people like social workers, the two visitors, and me:

> I could tell there was authority figures here today. There is a certain smell that comes with them, a fresh smell. Nothing personal, but I do not like people like yourselves, psychiatrists, social workers, and so forth – people who feel that they can control your life.

He went on to describe how he felt that most of his adult life, mainly spent in prison, stemmed from his hatred of authority.

'Don', who was serving time for fraud, interrupted by pointing out that Dave seemed to be lumping people together into slots – for example, psychiatrists and social workers – that seemed appropriate to their outer characteristic, but 'if the doctor's house was burgled, Dr Doctor could say that he does not like burglars and you would understand him saying that, while you feel that not all burglars are the same.'

I felt that Don was usurping my role as therapist (whilst also providing quite an insightful interpretation) and thereby trying to pass himself off as the authority. By aligning himself with me he tries to please and, as such, marks himself off from the group with his comments. As a result, my counter-transference was to feel stuck between two stools: to collude with his 'fraudulent', though insightful, perceptions or to challenge him.

I interpreted that the group's resentment towards authority and the new doctors, coupled with the need to put people into class divisions, was to hide their real feelings of sadness and loss in relation to their absent fathers. This theme of desertion was further resonated by me when accompanying, and aligning myself, with either the fraudulent prisoner masquerading as therapist or with the junior doctors. The prisoners had seen the two junior doctors and me entering the Unit and at the end of the group session would see us leave, abandoning them to the fraudulent therapist.

Dave continued by highlighting his intense anger over recent events regarding the separation from his children. He felt that nobody really cared about prisoners as individuals with their own problems. He continued by expressing irritation over the fact that only fellow prisoners seemed to care for each other and their problems and that those in the Community like social workers and psychiatrists were hypocrites. This led to a lengthy group discussion about concern for each other and whether the doctors really cared. Dave ended the session by stating that he felt that his expression of anger did help open the group up to discussion and to move beyond behaving artificially.

Each of the members of the group remains insecure, and even if he feels he is temporarily in favour he knows that the tables can be turned and that he may find himself a victim. Each member identifies with both victim and oppressor, and each is held in the same type of perverse grip. The grip gains its power from seduction and collusion on the one hand and from threats of violence on the other. However, I think that the group, within the prison, has the potential to provide a psychological home that enables the inmates to be more true to themselves and to draw strength from each other in a more authentic and humane way. They begin to explore the possibility of coming alive in a safe and generous world, rather than inhabiting a deadly world by hiding behind their deviant and fraudulent behaviour.

Conclusion

Most authors agree that drugs are, for the addict, an idealized object and at the same time a bad, persecuting object. The addict's fear is of tender and loving feelings, since they imply dependence and emotional surrender. Self-sufficiency is idealized and any hint of dependence triggers off an immediate defensive reaction of destructive criminal hate. The TC does offer some possibilities of working effectively as a psychotherapist within the Prison System and more importantly, of allowing prisoners the invaluable opportunity of accessing safely their more vulnerable and human sides, rather than having to rely on their accustomed criminal and deviant behaviour. It seems that this containing environment allows new possibilities of coping with the anxieties of both prisoner and prison officer, and of creatively challenging the automatic and habitual defences of sadomasochism, violence and power posturing within the therapeutic groups.

References

Doctor, R. (2001) Psychotherapy and the prisoner – impasse or progress? In J. Williams Saunders (ed.) *Life Within Hidden Worlds, Psychotherapy in Prisons.* London: Karnac Books.

Doctor, R. (2003) *Dangerous Patients: A Psychodynamic Approach to Risk Assessment and Management.* London: Karnac Books.

Etchegoyen, R.H. (1991) *The Fundamentals of Psychoanalytic Technique.* London: Karnac Books.

Freud, S. (1897) *The Complete Psychological Works of Sigmund Freud* (Standard edn.), Vol. 1. London: Hogarth Press.

Freud, S. (1916) *Some Character Types Met with in Psychoanalytic Work in, Criminals From a Sense of Guilt* (Standard edn.) Vol. 14.

Klein, M. (1934) *On Criminality in Love Guilt and Repatriation and Other Works,* London: Hogarth Press.

Rosenfeld, H. (1965) The psychopathology of drug addiction and alcoholism: a critical review of the psycho-analytical literature. In *Psychotic States: A Psychoanalytic Approach.* London: Karnac Books.

Chapter 12

Internal World, External Reality: From Fantasy to Reality in Violent Offending[1]

Liz McLure

This chapter describes attempts to link the internal world of those who have committed serious offences with the external world of the lives of those affected when fantasy becomes reality in offending. The role of fantasy and enactment are considered as a survival mechanism and as part of a process of developing a concept of self. The experience of a particular sequence of events in a small therapy group in one of the Communities at HMP Grendon, a therapeutic community (TC) prison, is used to explore this process.

In serious offending the outcome of the offence is often not what was intended. Fantasy does not continue uninterrupted as the reality of enacting fantasy dawns and the offender becomes aware of the consequences to the victim and to the self of the action done. This is not congruent with the original (unconscious) expectation: mastery, control and relief from unbearable emotional pain and turmoil. When a fantasy becomes reality it no longer

---

[1]   Written consent for the use of clinical material has been obtained from each individual prior to writing this chapter. Names and some facts have been changed to protect anonymity and the confidential nature of the material.

belongs in the mind of the individual, is no longer within their control and is subject to all the forces that constrain it: others, the Community and society at large. The loss of omnipotence in the fantasy has to be mourned like any other valued, albeit damaging asset. In the TC all aspects of the self are exposed. When the Community mirror is held up the individual can see himself and a new sense of knowing who and what 'I' am may develop. Myths held about oneself are dismantled. This journey is not without danger and the compulsion to repeat and use familiar antisocial defences highlights the need for the physical containment the prison walls offers, together with therapy group, Community boundaries and therapist integrity.

The internal world

Engaging with the fantasy world of those who have offended and working within these fantasies is a necessary process to understand the conflicts that maintain antisocial defensive reactions that hinder the capacity to lead a satisfying and peaceful life where intimacy with another is possible (Arlow 1998). To be able to immerse oneself in this process and to remain able to tolerate pain and madness is important (Searles 1979 in Campbell Le Fevre 1994) but not without danger to the therapist. All are acting and interacting in the dynamic interplay between each layer of the system. We reach in and then out again to touch upon a more objective reality to rediscover the split off or dissociated primitive feelings and anxieties to enable a more acceptable integration of our experiences. Fantasies emerge against the backdrop of the group and when aware of them we can acknowledge our thoughts and feelings towards an event in a more mature fashion.

The foundation matrix: what each individual brings to the group in terms of family history, experiences and ways of relating, is problematic. Most men were subject to early traumatic abuse or neglect and have internalized jointly the masochism of the victim and the brutal sadism of the aggressor. Threats to m(other) and self were real. Many of these men had to accommodate mothers who were themselves unable to cope or manage their feelings and violently projected their masochistic, self-sacrificing tendencies into their infants (Hopkins 1992; Wilson 2000). Experiences of being loved, cared for, feeling secure, being treated with compassion and being comforted and reassured when in crisis were minimal in the lives of the men in the group described. The role of the therapist in maintaining a safe space to think and to model and engender these deficient experiences is crucial. Being able to be hard on the behaviours, soft on the person and not respond with abuse offers a maxim for success (McLure 2004). To collude with abusive behaviours that maintain a destructive defensive pattern is not good for the individual, likewise to allow oneself as therapist to be a victim is soul destroying and counterproductive. The internal victim–perpetrator–victim pattern needs to be broken.

In the prison setting there is a fear of talking about one's fantasy life. Men have to bear the pain and trauma of already having acted on their fantasies for the rest of their lives. There is resistance to reveal further thoughts, the fear that, 'if you know how mad/bad/dangerous I think I am you will keep me locked up forever', remains a real hindrance to openness. Men have to risk going against the grain and 'grassing themselves up' to be able to explore their underlying unconscious conflicts. They fear learning how to contain the unmanageable and unbearable feelings without being overwhelmed due to a lack of trust. Many were betrayed as boys (Gartner 1999) and had no experience of being able to depend on others. The need–fear of engaging with the group and the process itself creates anxieties (Campbell Le Fevre 1994; Voorhoeve and van Putte 1994).

Primitive material that is not in total awareness or is preverbal requires the therapist to tune into the communication at all levels in the group to 'capture the psychotic elements that are truly "mute" and outside the realms of secondary process' (Bion cited in Ganzarain 1991). What is being said in the here and now? What is triggering a reaction in others? What is being projected out into the Community? How am I feeling and how am I being pulled to respond in the transference? What is the perceived threat to existence? As each layer of defence is stripped away the fragile core self of men in therapy is at risk of overexposure and there may be risk of more desperate measures being utilized to defend against such fears of exposure or disintegration.

Each new event, incident or piece of information alters the knowledge, attitudes and beliefs about every previously known situation. Some memories may be screen memories (Arlow in Blum et al 1988) and when viewed from different perspectives in the group threaten the myths and fantasies that maintain symptomatology and perverse behaviour. The chaos and confusion caused by having to take apart and reconfigure life's experiences and accept new reality may cause great anxiety (Lewin 1995).

Bearing witness to each other's narratives can be traumatic as resonance with personal experience may be powerful. This may threaten those with weak defences who are prone to enter places of psychic retreat in which almost all anxieties are avoided. Such retreat may also cloud reality to such an extent that personal behaviour and its consequences for others is also taken into retreat and if not addressed therapy is in danger of becoming out of touch with reality.

> Masochistic pleading for love when hurt may readily merge with sadistic coercion and reactions to narcissistic injury of narcissistic entitlement, rage, and demands for vindication and vengeance. In extreme form, with massive projection, these reactions regressively become paranoid fantasies of grievance, persecution, and revenge. Omnipotence and invulnerability are asserted to protect against traumatic helplessness and further narcissistic injury and to assure control over dangerous impulses and objects. (Blum 1980, p.349)

The individual in the state described may find little option than to become a perpetrator who inflicts his pain upon others. If there is a sufficient degree of ego-syntonic perverse pleasure in administering pain and suffering to others to ward off emotional pain, a therapeutic impasse can result, the group is abused and this is both difficult to sit with and will, if unyielding, be an obstacle to analysis. A pathological narcissistic personality organization may persist in which flight from the pain of both the depressive and paranoid-schizoid positions and any movement between them persists and renders therapeutic movement void (Mishan and Bateman 1994). A game of beat the therapy before it gets you begins and the systematic destruction of whatever is experienced as good and valuable gathers pace. Whatever sympathetic feeling the analyst had for the patient is systematically destroyed in this situation (Kernberg 1975 cited in Cohen 2002). Telling lies to cover lies to distort the truth and avoid the reality of a situation is an example of this. It presents as a negative therapeutic reaction and all are forced to engage in the fantasy like puppets in a game, open to the manipulation and control of the one who wishes to destroy and break down whoever has threatened his vulnerable core-self.

External threat

'Family Days' occur twice a year. These trigger huge anxiety as the men sit together with their families on the Wing. They face the wrongs done to each other in the hope of mending the broken ties in their relationships. This is a day fraught with difficulty. Falling into old familiar patterns and roles is hard to resist: 'When talking to mum I'm eight years old again'. If the men have been able to work through their childhood difficulties and have let go of their rage and fear, they can be more objective about the reality of their parents' relationships and begin to understand and to a degree accept why they behaved the way they did. They can have a mature adult relationship with them and can easily assimilate the 'outside' family with the 'inside' family in a healthy relationship based on honesty, truth and trust. If there is no change and they cling to unconscious revenge fantasies they cannot tolerate the coming together of the outside and inside and panic sets in. If they have not been open and honest with either 'family' the anxiety triggers attempts at control. In the individual who still believes himself to be subject to Mother's emotional world or was consumed by her, keeping the inside private and the outside out is a real struggle. Attempts to manipulate and control my feelings and behaviours (the symbolic mother) start to emerge. Compound this with an internalized bully of a father and these attempts can become sadistic and brutal. In the family where secrets and lies form the basis of relationships, the truth is seen as dangerous. Conscious awareness that the fantasy of omnipotent control is not effective, especially with me, and by extension with Mother, results in the emergence of repressed rage and fear. Fantasy and reality clash and control is lost. The fear and rage resonates in the group and massive projection hits its mark as the relaxation of the boundaries on this day leaves everyone vulnerable.

In the following vignette one central character is discussed in relation to the others as he emerged as the 'patient' at this time. Some pertinent information on those who got tied into his difficulty is provided to give a glimpse of the complexity of identifications, communications and resonance at all levels in the group.

Lenny

Lenny has been with the group for over a year. He has always been in trouble and whenever there is a fight or a disturbance he is there, either as the causal figure or as the one who tries to deflect the damage in order to protect. One of his early memories was the terrifying experience of being used by his mother as a human shield to prevent his father from stabbing her. Her emotional pain was forced into Lenny and the fear of death was in his face in the form of his father. The situation was played down. His father lied, manipulated and cheated his mother and Lenny identified with him in order to survive. Witnessing, experiencing or perpetrating violations, keeping secrets and telling lies became a set pattern. He became a self-styled one-man vigilante and created trouble in order to win the battle to become a hero, in his eyes, and regain control all over again. His escapades became more serious and he became known for the wrong reasons, was isolated and unpopular, and suffered from anxiety. He got involved in a fracas outside a club. He was beaten up and humiliated by the local hard man in front of others and could not let this rest. He fantasized about getting his own back and regaining his 'status' in the community. In reality he was new to this town and had no status. He donned his 'rambo kit', stalked his victim and stabbed him in the back. Lenny knew that he was in more trouble now and his fantasy of status and recognition and usurping the 'big guy's' position would not follow his actions. He was arrested shortly afterwards and initially lied, saying that it was self-defence: in his mind it was, he was saving himself, but in reality he had instigated the whole scenario and had killed someone who represented all the bullies he had ever known including a part of himself.

Vignette

In the days following family day Lenny was furious with me. He had invited me to sit with his family but could not control his mother's questions to me. He had spilled the beans and told his mum something about himself that she did not know. She was very distressed and blamed herself for not noticing his plight. He blamed me for her upset. His fantasy of us all having a 'fun' time together in the 'perfect family' had not played out. It turned out that he had kept secrets and told mum lies and my presence threatened his false image of himself. He had no protection from her emotions. They wounded him and added to his pain. He also felt humiliated by her public display of emotion. In the next group meeting after Family Day, he proceeded to seek revenge for this insult and loss of control by attacking me and halting the group attempts to share experiences of the day. The intimacy of the group was shattered; we were now under siege. In his omnipotent state Lenny was determined to 'murder the reality' of their experiences (Chasseguet Smirgel 1988 cited in Norvick and Norvick 1991). He would not allow others to speak of their emotions and feelings and was unwilling to share the space with them. The rage that surfaced from this domination became murderous and was expressed through an engagement with Ross.

Lenny and Ross had a love–hate relationship right from their first meeting. They represented a malignant mirror for each other and their competition and rivalry was constant in every group. Ross had suffered from early neglect and rejection from his mother, his stepmother was critical and scolding and father took her side and meted out physical punishment. Ross used to lie and manipulate in an attempt to control his predicament and had recently given this up. He too was doing life for murder but feared his own rage and was easily wound up by Lenny. Each time Ross spoke Lenny got in on the act or rubbished him. His fury with me deflected into a challenge of Ross for his behaviour on Family Day. Ross got into an argument with someone who in his neediness demanded 'special chips' when Ross was busy cooking for over 80 people. Ross had offered his services to the community as he had no visitors – his family disowned him after his offence. He was sitting on his feelings of abandonment and envy of others, like Lenny, who had family. Ross got most of the time and attention from the group much to Lenny's disgust and he took further revenge on all of us by giving terrible feedback to the Community and saying how useless and unsupportive the group was of him.

Dan, the longest serving group member, who had status and respect, is normally quite contained but lost his temper later and volleyed off at Lenny after the feedback session. He knew the pain and distress he inflicted on others when, in a psychotic state filled with hatred, he had tried to kill his own family; he has spent years repairing the damage he caused and healing his fractured self. He was now defending the group family and took great offence at this attack. He told someone else that he felt like 'stabbing Lenny up', an old fantasy now expressed. Lenny heard about this from another when out on the garden party. This fed his persecutory anxiety. Lenny knew of Dan's capabilities and fantasies. He thought he was serious, and as knives are carried in other prisons to him the threat was real. At the next group meeting, Lenny told us that he had smuggled a piece of fence post that he fashioned like a knife back onto the Wing. He had intended to stab Dan up. Fortunately Dan had not known this, had contained himself and explained to Lenny why he felt the way he did and made the threat on his return. Lenny was disarmed by Dan's words and said that he later destroyed the piece of wood.

No one knew for sure if this was another fantasy or if he had indeed brought a weapon onto the Wing. We had to treat this as a real breach of security as this presented a potential risk to the whole Community. It is worth noting that my fantasies regarding what could happen were stimulated by Lenny's disclosure, a common occurrence in therapy work (Weiss 1998). Lenny was tearful when it was pointed out to him that he had recreated a family scene here, creating havoc and blaming others for the disruption and distress caused in his attempt to manage and control others. His violent projections into others resulted in a replay of his offence. Their identification with his projections completed the cycle. Lenny knew that this disclosure would place him up for his commitment in the Community and he could be voted out for his actions. Together we wondered if he had deliberately set himself up for further public humiliation.

Billy, who lost his mother because she could not give up her drug addiction and was thrown out of the home by his father when he was a baby, was visibly distressed. He did not want to be in his father's position and reject someone for unacceptable behaviour; for him this loss and subsequent events damaged him. He said he felt like Lenny's victim here. Lenny then told us that he did not want to believe how close he had come to killing someone again and how dangerous his actions were in this company. It was clear that revenge fantasies run constantly in his mind, the planned attack was already there in response to a perceived threat. The group were dismayed and angry to discover that a respected member of staff was also compromised for not finding a 'weapon' on Lenny when searched.

Knowing all this I was now in the position of having to spill the beans and report this breach to halt this abuse, to report the one who betrayed the trust of the group and was continuing to stab us in the back with his attacks on others. Lenny could ill afford to have this on his record but he had to face the consequences of his actions. It was hard to feel any warmth and compassion towards him when we were being abused in this way. He certainly had not thought of the potential damage to Dan or the group. This traumatic event was a gift to the group, a complete re-enactment of an index offence triggered by anxiety and fear of truth being known and family myths being shattered. It was a rich opportunity for identification, insight and the experience of victim empathy. I felt a sense of shame, had I failed Lenny? There was a period of jocular ridicule of me in the community and I was made to feel responsible for his actions. I took an emotional beating and had to bear this discomfort. Lenny got his revenge on me after all. He had used his power to try and manipulate others to crush my individuality, my dignity and capacity to feel deeply and think rationally, a phenomenon described as *soul murder* (Shengold 1997). This was Lenny's experience of his parents' relationship, mother crushed by father and his experience of his father crushing him. If I had got lost in the madness of this it would have resulted in a repetition of the maternal failure under pressure rather than provide the opportunity for the corrective emotional experience where recovery and repair becomes possible (Winnicott 1958).

In the next group several reported dreams of near-death experiences and frightening situations. They talked of how they try to hide their emotions particularly towards their mothers, who could not hold their distress. To break down in front of a woman presented them with a serious threat to their manhood. Loss of control of situations was not something they liked at all. Knives were introduced as weapons early in most of their lives, giving a false sense of potency and protection against feelings of inadequacy. They talked of being forced to eat things that don't agree with you. They had a belly full of threats and violence. Ross was in a positive frame, perhaps enjoying seeing Lenny having to face up to the consequences of his actions. He reported that all his fantasies were of a sexual nature, all he wanted was a 'shag'. When asked what this would give him right now he said 'it's not just the sex, it's the warmth and closeness with another'. In this group we went from fear, threat of death, mistrust of mothers, loss of potency and helplessness to knives sex, pleasure and intimacy. Family Day and subsequent events represented the symbolic penetration of the group and had taken us through the threat of annihilation in the primal scene towards a new sense of hope and life.

The group took time to recover from this incident although the hostility and the memory of such a powerful attack left them wary of Lenny. It was impossible to know what he had learned from this experience and if his behaviour would change as a result. Was he able to empathize with those he hurt and develop remorse for his actions or was he still trapped in his narcissistic pattern of offending?

References

Arlow, J. (1988) In H. Blum, Y. Kramer, A. Richards *et al.* (eds) (1988) *Fantasy, Myth, and Reality.* Connecticut: International Universities Press, Inc.

Blum, H. (1980) Paranoia and beating fantasy: An inquiry into the psychoanalytic theory of paranoia. *Journal of the American Psychoanalytic Association, 28,* 331–361.

Campbell LeFevre, D. (1994) The power of countertransference in groups for the severely mentally ill. *Group Analysis, 27,* 441–447.

Cohen, D. (2002) Transference and countertransference states in the analysis of pathological narcissism. *Psychoanalytic Review, 89,* October, 631–651.

Ganzarain, R. (1991) Extra-analytic contacts: Fantasy and reality. *International Journal of Psycho-Analysis, 72,* 131–140.

Gartner, R.B. (1999) *Betrayed as Boys: Psychodynamic Treatment of Sexually Abused Men.* New York: Guilford Press.

Hopkins, S. (1992) Countertransference and containment in a patient with a psychotic mother. *Psychoanalytic Psychotherapy, 6,* 89–106.

Lewin, K. and Shein, E. (1995) *Kurt Lewin's Change Theory in the Field and in the Classroom.* Notes towards a model of managed learning. www.solonline.org/res/wp/10006.html

McLure, L. (2004) Working with the unbearable. In D. Jones (ed.) *Working with Dangerous People. The Psychotherapy of Violence.* Oxford: Radcliffe Medical Press Ltd.

Mishan, J. and Bateman, A. (1994) Group-analytic therapy of borderline patients in a day hospital setting. *Group Analysis, 27,* 483–495.

Novick, J. and Novick, K. (1991) Some comments on masochism and the delusion of omnipotence from a developmental perspective. *Journal of the American Psychoanalytic Association, 39,* 307–331.

Shengold, L. (1997) Child abuse and deprivation; soul murder. *Journal of the American Psychoanalytic Association, 27,* 533–559.

Voorhoeve, J. and Floor, C.A. van Putte (1994) Parallel process in supervision when working with psychotic patients. *Group Analysis, 27, 459–466.*

Weiss, J. (1998) Some reflections on countertransference in the treatment of criminals. *Psychiatry, 61,* Summer, 172–179.

Wilson, N. (2000) A psychoanalytic contribution to psychic vampirism: A case vignette. *The American Journal of Psychoanalysis, 60,* 177–186.

Winnicott, D. (1958) *Collected Papers: Through Paediatrics to Psycho-analysis.* New York: Basic Books.

Chapter 13

Changing a Life Sentence into a Life

Judy Mackenzie

The little knot of civilian staff sat tensely in the Community meeting room. The door was shut. All the prisoners were in their cells. Along the corridor burly men in riot gear were waiting for the signal to go. It was supposed to be an assessment meeting where the various applicants for the therapeutic community (TC) were being considered. Nobody could concentrate. Every ear was cocked for the sound of shouting and possibly violence. After what seemed like an age, during which much was said and nothing remembered, the door opened and an officer put his head into the room. 'It's alright', he said, 'he walked down'. There was a collective sigh of relief. Violence had been avoided, no weapon had been found, there was no struggle or loss of dignity. Nevertheless, this incident was out of the ordinary.

A man sits sobbing. There are two members of staff present: neither speaks. The sobs continue. These are not the sobs of the vocalized sorrow of an adult, they are the gasping, choking, inarticulate, heaving cries of an abandoned child. I glance at my colleague. He looks wordlessly back at me. The desolate individual in front of us has lived over 30 years on this earth, but the person before us is around four years old. There is nothing to do but hold the space in which to allow him to break his heart again, but this time in conscious reality. He has been telling us about his early years when his beloved father left home, to be replaced by a brutal man who systematically beat him while his mother looked the other way. Without warning the scene has shifted from an adult relating a tragic story, to a child re-experiencing the repressed pent-up rage and desolation that had nowhere to go at that time. It has nowhere to go now except into awareness, there to be shared, held and integrated. This child had taken that rage and turned it into systematic comfort thoughts of revenge, which resulted in increasingly sadistic fantasies of doing harm to others. Ultimately they were acted upon and he is serving life for a particularly sadistic murder. This is not an unusual occurrence.

The group of eight men and two staff members is silent but deeply attentive. Jazz, a large black, intimidating looking man with a long history of excessive violence, has been speaking slowly of his journey to the point where he is now. He looks round at the rapt faces of the others. 'Although I have another 12 years to do before I can even think of getting out of prison', he says, 'for the first time I can remember, I know I am free'. This is a special occurrence.

TC members everywhere will recognize similar scenarios. These three occurrences came from Gartree Therapeutic Community (GTC). This is a small TC with 23 bed spaces, in an all-lifer prison, taking first- and second-stage life-sentenced prisoners. Its motto, 'changing a life sentence into a life', forms the title of this chapter.

All of the residents are adult men and all are serving life sentences. They are relatively near the start of their sentence, having completed only three or four years at most. The GTC differs from other prison TCs that prefer to take life sentence prisoners towards the end of their sentence. The rationale for this: taking them towards the end of their time, comes from the Grendon reconviction study (Marshall 1997), which found that the mode of leaving influences reconviction rates, i.e. transfer back to the general prison estate is associated with less positive outcomes than release direct to the outside community. However, life-sentenced prisoners are practically never released from the high-security estate direct to the community and only exceptionally are they transferred to open conditions. Thus nearly all will return to the mainstream prison population.

Most life sentences, at the time of writing, are mandatory – that is they have been passed for the offence of murder. There are also discretionary life sentences for serious offences such as rape and arson, custody for life and detention at Her Majesty's Pleasure: a separate system of sentencing to life for those who have committed an offence of murder whilst under the age of 21. There are also new automatic 'two strikes and you're out' life sentences. These are for two or more serious offences of physical or sexual violence or arson and they tend to have shorter tariffs, sometimes as short as 2 years. However the majority of prisoners on the GTC have long tariffs and the offence is usually murder. Thus one 30-year-old man still has 20 years left to serve before he reaches his tariff date.

Tariff is the minimum number of years that an inmate must serve in prison before there is any possibility of release to the community. After the tariff date has passed, the prisoner must present sufficient evidence to the Parole Board to convince them that he is no longer a risk to society. Then he can be released on life license. The conditions of a life license mean that at any time, should his supervising officer have any doubts about his continued safety to the community, he can be recalled to prison again.

Why offer therapy and why at this stage?

The GTC believes that every individual has value and that underneath all the defences of a life-sentenced prisoner is a human being who is redeemable and that redemption of the offender is perhaps the only way of truly repaying the victim. This contrasts with the talion law of revenge repudiated by Mahatma Gandhi, who pointed out that 'An eye for an eye makes the whole world blind'.

More pragmatically, a significant improvement in adjustment to prison following therapy completion will enable a prisoner to access more courses, facilities and training opportunities than he otherwise might do, due to innate resistance to the system. It makes sense, therefore, to maximize the length of 'co-operative' time. Equally well the chances of release on tariff by having sufficiently reduced risk will be greater the more interventions they have been able to access. Research to confirm this clinical impression has yet to be conducted. There are, however, other reasons for making the therapy intervention early in sentence, rather than late. The first reaction of a prisoner on receiving a life sentence is shock. When this wears off the impact of both the sentence, and more especially its cause, which is still most frequently the taking of a life, is so great that it is very often met with a period of denial and acting out. A 21-year-old automatic life-sentenced prisoner described it in this way: 'I couldn't believe it! Life! My first and main thought was "escape". After that "kick off, fuck up, make as much trouble as possible. What did I have to lose"' Underlying this of course is fear, grief and loss. Expectations of what others already in prison may be like can be frightening. A 26-year-old new Community member put it in this way:

> When I knew I was coming to a life sentence prison I was terrified. I knew it would be full of murderers, alright I killed someone, but that was a mistake, but I thought they'd all have, like red eyes, be real monsters.

This is often the point of contact with the GTC. At this stage a man's motivation is not likely to be for practical gain: parole, good reports, earlier release and so on, because any benefit in this field is likely to be too far away to have any realistic motivating power. It is questions such as 'How did I become who I am?' One man really did ask me 'What made me the monster I am today'? Is there any point? Is there any hope? Guilt and shame, especially where the victim has been a loved and intimate partner, are often prime movers.

Thus it is often at the point where the extent of loss is finally beginning to sink home that they will apply to us. This stage, typically three to four years post sentence, is characterized by grieving, which goes hand in hand with an almost complete absence of self-esteem. 'When I first came here I hated myself; I felt I didn't deserve to live. The only reason I didn't take my own life was for the sake of the other members of my family who are still alive'. By any account this would be a waste of several lives. This statement was made towards the end of his therapy by a young man who had killed his father. The significant members of his family were his grandmother, the victim's mother, and his sister. Both of these had come to terms with the offence and forgiven the offender.

Time spent on the GTC is typically between two and three years. At the stage of arrival raw feelings of grief and remorse are still fresh and accessible and have not had the chance to be clouded by learned expressions from programmes.

Even so, three years is a long time in therapy and given the existential nature driving the offence of murder it is not surprising that attachment theory and the interpersonal schools of psychodynamic theory underpin much of our practice. Listening to, attempting to understand and beginning to think about changing involve an interactive approach to our work that often goes to the depths: 'No one – not the dying, not the outcast, not the mighty – transcends the need for human contact' (Yalom 2005, p.21).

Underlying this bedrock of more in-depth thinking and attempts to understand are the four principles of democratization, communality, permissiveness and reality confrontation (Rapoport 1960). Only after these two aspects of therapeutic culture and structure are established and men come to trust each other and the staff, can attention be focussed on criminogenic need, offending behaviour and risk assessment, as demanded by the prison TC accreditation programme.

This is not to imply that risk does not matter. Indeed its assessment, management and reduction are essential aspects of any individual's work on the GTC. However, these elements need to be built on solid ground. In this sense the theoretical foundation for the Community is a magnification of how the

GTC believes an individual changes in such a way that his risk will ultimately be reduced. The primary focus, therefore, is moving from the I-It position to I-You, the I-Thou of Buber (Buber 1958). Once established, the Self and the Other are no longer seen as objects, the individual is free to make real choices in his life, even within the confines of a prison. He can then add the skills necessary for contented social functioning and positive work in family relationships in the future. Thus the individual's primary relationship with himself and with others as people, as opposed to merely objects for self-gratification, is crucial to his ability to function healthily in the future.

A prisoner can learn all about his risk factors, he can demonstrate that he no longer loses his temper when provoked, he can show he is not impulsive, he can control his greed, and he can learn to speak well in social situations. However, if he has not learned to come into relationship with himself, and thereby into relationship with others, he will offend again in some way, whether or not this is in respect of the Law. Whilst it may seem a luxury, the extended time on the GTC is crucial. It allows the foundations of the personality to be repaired as solidly as possible without the constraints of too much 'window dressing'. Once there is a core concept of 'myself in relationship to the world', there is a working model for every eventuality.

With this in mind, a successful period on the GTC should result in a prisoner's ability to gain more from offending behaviour programmes that are available later in the prison, should they still be required and to make better use of vocational and educational opportunities. Thus a prisoner may leave the GTC with some risk factors apparently still outstanding. These can be targeted by programmes specifically designed for that purpose later on in the sentence. The majority however are found not to need further offence-focused intervention other than 'booster' types of revision courses.

The extended period early in the sentence also allows sufficient attention to be paid to the leaving process and separation without the disruptive effect of parole dates and establishment moves. As the majority of residents have had difficulties with early attachment, discharge into a 'local community', i.e. the main prison that houses the GTC, makes follow-up much easier. There are regular ex-members nights and leavers groups: every leaver has a sponsor who meets regularly with him; there is an open invitation to return to the Community meeting should there be difficulties. Ex-members are also invited to open and social events. It is expected that separation will be difficult, activating as it does early core wounds. We expect the return of difficult symptomatology for a short period immediately prior to discharge.

Somewhere in here also is squeezed, between the therapeutic work on the personality, and the reactivating trauma of separation, the possibility of discovering a 'passion', a way of combining absorbing interest with relationship. This will hold the prisoner over the next 10–20 years, which are after all a period of life, not a period when life is placed on hold. 'I don't care about parole, I'm not in a position to even begin thinking about it, I'm here to learn about myself and how I can make a life over the next 18 years', said a 27-year-old man. It is the challenge to the 'wasted years' that persuades us that intervention at this early stage is worthwhile. Anecdotally it is confirmed by a Principal Probation Officer:

> You can always tell the people who have come from GTC; not only do they engage with the prison, but they are more insightful, more aware of their offending behaviour and generally much easier to get on with than other prisoners.

Research due to be published in 2007 will show that the fall in antisocial acts, as measured by adjudications, continues to further improve over stays of 24–36 months. Also that unlike the Grendon findings (Shine and Morris 2000), there does not seem to be a negative effect with early drop out, i.e. improvement occurs even in those who have only stayed between 6 and 12 months (Charters in press). When the GTC has given presentations this fact has been the topic of some debate. If therapeutic communities (TCs) are still 'counter-culture', how can an apparently successful stay result in a better adaptation to an environment such as a prison? Should not the Culture of Enquiry mean less uniformity and pliability? Well yes! Certainly with young prisoners, the successful learning of how to think for themselves often placed them at odds with the rest of the institution. This seemed, however, to enable them to resist the pull of their peers on release and resulted in a concomitant reduction in re-offending (Mackenzie 1985). One possible reason for the different effect of the GTC is in the emphasis placed on the relational aspects of therapy. The prisoners who are in therapy no longer have to live up to an image for their own defence or to impress others, and they have a variety of alternative responses to difficult and potentially explosive situations.

Not every story glows with success of course. The internal journey is extremely difficult, costing, as T.S. Eliot wrote in Little Gidding, 'not less than everything'. Some of the people who leave early have misunderstood the true cost of membership of the GTC, believing it to be a programme like any other. Just at the brink of attachment, they realize what is being required of them and at this point they panic and go.

The other reason for early drop out, in particular with automatic life-sentenced prisoners, is, paradoxically, the moment when they realize the possibility of hope. This is the stage when a man now does have something to lose. Here is the point where courage and the support of the group become essential. Paul, for example, overcame enormous personal resistance, which included testing the staff to the utmost, with anger and threats in order to finally feel safe enough to share his multiple losses with the group. His negative attitude dropped, he began to reveal more and was able to spend time with staff on an informal basis. However, at the point of his first parole hearing, realizing that reports were positive in their recommendation, suggesting that he was already close to being able to return to the outside world, he panicked and chose to terminate therapy abruptly, as far as possible rubbishing all the work that he had previously done. Paul had avoidant, dependent, and paranoid features in his personality profile, and it is likely that these contributed significantly to his fear of engagement and failure to internalize hope (Yalom 2005).

Over 75 per cent of prisoners on the GTC have one or more personality disorders as measured by the PDQ-4 or the International Personality of Disorder Examination (IPDE) (Davies in press). Normally a combination of schizoid, schizotypal and paranoid features are difficult to work with, particularly in a system that depends so much on observation and report writing as well as on the concept of offence paralleling, which is so much part of the offensive against criminogenic factors in TCs in prisons.

Jim, for example, was convinced for eight months that the green central heating light in the ceiling was a microphone. As he worked with us, as expected, his distress concomitantly increased and so did his obsessional symptoms. As with other interventions, people usually get 'worse' before they get 'better'. Ultimately he was able to confess to his group his anxieties. He was surprised to discover first that many other people had entertained the same suspicion, and second that he was allowed to check out the panel himself and discover the exact source and reason for the light. After 12 months Jim has addressed the Family Open Day with confidence and has allowed himself to be pleased with his performance. It is even possible to joke with him about his 'paranoia'.

So what are lifers like? Well, at least at the end of therapy they reveal themselves to be funny, affectionate, talented and empathic. They are also grumpy, bad tempered, depressed and moody, like anyone else in fact. Daily they restore faith in human nature in their courage and tenacity in overcoming their personal and inter-personal difficulties.

There are many ways of measuring the outcome of successful therapy completion. For me the answer lies not in the psychometric tests or any other rating scale. It is the clear change in people's faces, from hostile, frowning, narrow-eyed glares, with hunched shoulders and the avoidance of too-close contact; figures become straighter, features relax, eyes open and emotion is clearly displayed. These people have gone from being, in their own eyes and the eyes of society, the lowest of the low, to recognizing the eternal truth that we are all as one and we share a common humanity.

Rob (age 38) is having a second try on the GTC having been removed ignominiously from therapy the first time around. In his application to reapply he said, 'I have been inside since I was 16. Please don't give up on me even though I have not always been able to keep faith with you'. Rob is now an active and middle-stage member of the Community. He has been helped by his best friend, who is now Chairman and who brings his own particular style of management to the Community. This friend used to maintain his anti-authority and delinquent approach to every aspect of the Community. He has now practically completed therapy, certainly in understanding his offending behaviour. He is one of the few who will certainly take the next step to finding something with which to engage his passion. Some of the formative years of his life will be spent in prison (15 more years), but he no longer sees his life as without value, but is actively looking for a way to 'put something back'.

He is truly engaged in the GTC motto, 'changing a life sentence into a life'.

References

Buber, M. (1958) *I and Thou* (2nd edn) Edinburgh: Clark T and T.

Charters, E. (in press) *Gartree Therapeutic Communities Statistics*. 2005.

Day, J. (in press) *Gartree Therapeutic Communities Statistics*. 2006.

Mackenzie, J. (1985) *Glen Parva Follow-up Reconviction Rate*. Personal Communication.

Marshall, P. (1997) *A reconviction study of HMP Grendon Therapeutic Community*. Research Findings No. 53, London: Home Office Research and Statistics Directorate.

Marshall, P. and Newton, M. (2000) Psychological variables as dynamic risk factors among residents in a prison therapeutic community. In J. Shine and M. Morris. *A Compilation of Grendon Research*. HMP Leyhill: Prison Service Press.

Rapoport, R. (1960) *The Community as Doctor. New Perspectives on a Therapeutic Community*. London: Tavistock Publications.

Shine, J. and Morris, M. (2000) Addressing criminogenic needs in a prison therapeutic community. *Therapeutic Communities, 21*, 197–219.

Yalom, I. (2005) *The Theory and Practice of Group Psychotherapy*, 5th edn. New York: Basic Books.

Chapter 14

Repeating Patterns: Sexual Abuse, Sexualized Internal Working Models and Sexual Offending

Michael Parker

Some research indications

Much of the evidence from research about the link between sexual abuse and sexual offending clarifies that experience of sexual abuse of itself does not lead to a sexually offending career in any certain causal way: in one example, 'The simple answer to the question of how childhood sexual abuse contributes to adult sexual offending, is that we do not know' (Grubin 1998). However research does uncover the fact that sexual offenders present strikingly high rates of personally experienced sexual abuse across different population studies that seem to require some explanation. Research in this area began early and a little-cited figure from East and de Hubert's report noted that in their study period (1934–1938), 'About 60 per cent of the homosexuals [they studied in prison for offences of exhibitionism, sadistic/masochistic practices and perversions] had a history of seduction in childhood or about puberty by a much older youth or man' (East and De Hubert 1939, pp.151–152). We are more certain that the experience is seldom an indifferent one and in Baker and Duncan's (1985) study 51 per cent of abused children reported feeling harmed by the experience. Some who have been sexually abused go on to commit violent, not sexual offences (Widom and Ames 1994). Some do not offend at all but were found in one community study in the USA to develop anxiety disorders, alcohol abuse and dependence and antisocial behaviour (MacMillan *et al.* 2001) In an Australian study 16 per cent of 657 men and 50 per cent of 132 women reported being sexually abused before the age of 16 and abuse was associated with a history of psychiatric treatment and suicide attempts (Butler *et al.* 2001). One study found the effect size of abuse 'small' in a college student sample (Rind *et al.* 1998, p.31) but few studies indicate little effect at all from abuse and more often abuse seems to signal wider problems in relationship and family life that when combined with abuse become 'additive' as pathogens (Merrill *et al.* 2000).

Widom and Morris (1997) found 'Substantial under-reporting of sexual abuse' (p.45) in their research on court substantiated cases of child sexual abuse in which some of their sample had forgotten the abuse they had suffered despite its occurrence being recorded in transcripts of court proceedings. From their research, they concluded that the most important factor in research seemed to be how to ask the kinds of questions that would give valid answers in an area so prone to under-reporting compounded by such factors as shame and fear of ridicule or ostracism.

Does the term *sexual abuse* need to be qualified? Will there be the same effect on an individual's internalized attachment patterning and later behaviour for someone who has experienced an isolated sexual assault but who has a basically sound family and relationship life as for someone who has been subjected to years of forced sexual abuse and who has been in many care homes and has no stable or consistent relationship life? It seems that wide-ranging use of the term *sexual abuse* may be describing a phenomenon that is not comparable in experiential terms between one individual and another if the manner of perpetration and the length of time abuse has been perpetrated are taken into consideration and other factors are added to the picture, such as the number and strength of alternative pro-social relationships that may have had an influence.

Bearing these ideas in mind, it is notable that the co-occurrence of sexual abuse and sexual offending in a high proportion of male sexual offenders' personal histories appears consistently in the literature across populations. Additionally, rates of sexual abuse in male sexual offenders are very much higher than rates found in the general population. Two general population studies found one child in 6000 (0.02%) had been sexually abused during the study year (Mrazek *et al.* 1983) and using a wider, non-physical contact definition of abuse, Baker and Duncan (1985) found 12 per cent of females and 8 per cent of male children had been exposed to abuse as children.

In contrast, in the USA 17 per cent of a cohort of 1440 male prisoners had experienced sexually inappropriate behaviour or abuse at a time when reporting this form of abuse was much less common (Gebhard *et al.* 1965). In Canada 11.4 per cent from a cohort of 604 male federal inmates reported sexual abuse and 40 of the group of 69 (58%) men who had been sexually abused committed sexual crimes. Despite these figures, the authors concluded that there was still a problem in under-reporting child sexual abuse among men but that 'Being a victim of sexual abuse increased the odds of committing sexual abuse against strangers fivefold and within the family eightfold' (Dutton and Hart 1992, p.135). More recently in a cohort of 301 male prisoners in the USA, 26 per cent of the sexual offender group reported sexual abuse in childhood against 14 per cent of the violent offender group (Widom and Ames 1994).

What is not so readily articulated in the research on sexual abuse and sexual offending is to what extent such factors as the length of time exposed to perpetration; the context and manner in which abuse takes place or the use of force involved in perpetration may be influential in the development of an offending or other outcome, or in contributing to an attachment pattern that may become sexualized in proportion to the exposure of sexualized behaviour experienced. There is a suggestion of what may be important in Skuse's research on a cohort of 224 former male victims of sexual abuse in which 26 were found to have subsequently committed sexual offences. This cannot account for those not caught, but the risk factors his team identified for later offending included: material neglect; lack of supervision and sexual abuse by a female person. This victim–abuser group had also more frequently witnessed intrafamilial violence (Salter *et al.* 2003).

What was striking in a small qualitative study of 12 men who had both offended sexually and been exposed to childhood sexual abuse was that 83 per cent of this sample had experienced sexualization of a key care-giving relationship that was prolonged and influential in childhood involving penetrative sexual acts to orgasm of the perpetrator (Parker 2004). These were not chance or one-off events but in each case prolonged and repeated patterns of behaviour that had an effect on the victim that was still clearly evident and unwelcome to think about to the research subjects at interview. Abuse was not the only form of difficulty experienced by these men and there were absences of care, sexualized care, violent or neglectful forms of problematic behaviour in their antecedent histories that made sexual abuse part of a much wider picture of difficulty and disruption. While small, this sample appears to have some trend similarities to the sexual offender populations noted earlier. What researchers find may depend on what questions they ask (Goldman and Padayachi 2000) and so, careful semi-structured questionnaire interviews may be required to provide direct answers to the difficult and elusive questions in this field such as: 'Why do some who have been abused offend and others not' and 'What influences such outcomes?'

This chapter attempts to look at the possible dynamic interplay at work in the co-occurrence of sexual offending and experience of unwanted and traumatic sexual abuse in the same person and how an offending outcome may be influenced by what become sexualized attachment styles and arguably, sexualized internal working models. Some examples may help clarify these thoughts.

Examples from therapy in a prison setting

The examples described are composites containing aspects of real events and people only. Names and key identifying events and facts have been changed to preserve the anonymity of both the victims and perpetrators involved. It is hoped the effects of abuse made clear in therapy remain true in the examples described.

Andrew

Andrew's aggressive and violent father had subjected him over many years to frequent and savage beatings. This was a family secret and otherwise the father was a 'pillar of the community'. A teacher at school had taken an interest in Andrew and knew his father. After establishing the confidence of the father and the boy he subjected him, age 9, to anal penetrative sexual abuse for a year and a half using rounded objects from a woodwork class and his own penis and did so using the threat that he would tell his father, who, he assured him, would not believe him and would only be likely to give him further beatings if he were to tell him what he had done. What stood out in this account was the extent to which Andrew felt used as an object for the sexual gratification of the teacher and forced by a form of blackmail to keep silent about the abusive activity he experienced. It stopped only after the boy had the courage to refuse to return despite threats. It was not discussed and the teacher remained a figure in his life within the local community whom he could not altogether avoid for many years.

It was difficult to find alternative, redeeming attachment experiences in his life: his mother was 'alright' but in fear of his father and was described as 'distant' and sometimes, he reported, 'bitingly critical and angry with him'. Andrew's crime was to rape a boy who looked very like himself. He was aware of this and of the fact that on the day of his offence he had been angry, preoccupied, unable to rid himself of thoughts of revenge and stated that he knew all day that he felt he had to go out and find a victim. He was able to describe a powerful sense of rage that would not go away and which seemed to focus itself in the act of rape. There was some closeness of fit in the personal experience of abuse received and the enactment of abuse committed.

Revisiting the scene of trauma in reverse, the offender appears able through perpetration to be in control of the act of forced sex but rather than being repeated for the enjoyable quality of the experience the repetition seemed to be connected with a wish or need to rid the self of disturbing reminders of the past. In this case the offender raised the question to his therapy team: 'Was I trying to kill off a part of me or that part of me that had been abused to get it out of my head?' There is no exact answer to this question but exploration in the service of understanding why such a crime has been committed and what might motivate it in order not to act on impulse in future formed work in therapy. Such acts had been committed before and so work in therapy attempted to find alternative sources of relief for rage and anxiety felt and to change this pattern of behaviour away from repetition of what seemed to be a known and familiar pattern.

Jim

Jim had been subject to severe beatings from his father, who was away a lot, and had what was described as an angry, avoidant and critical relationship with his mother, in which he never felt he knew how to 'get it right'. This same criticism was also levelled at the father but he was seldom there to receive it. Jim was regularly criticized and never felt he did anything right for his mother. He would have liked his mother to stop the beatings but she could not do so as she received severe beatings herself and was described as being terrified of his father. He had difficulties in relationships in general and in sexual relationships in particular, and none had lasted more than a year and a half. All but one of seven relationships had become violent: Jim became violent to his partners when they would not do as he wanted and began to be critical of him. He felt he was no longer in control of himself or the relationship and became physically and sexually violent. While not in a relationship, he sexually attacked a woman in the street at night and when she did not submit to his attack he became enraged because of her kicking and screaming at him. There was no rape but he tried to kill her and she escaped when a passer-by called the police. He was identified and prosecuted for a sexually aggravated assault and given a prison sentence.

In therapy he described a strong image of the incident in which he had become most enraged and lost control, doing most damage in his attack, he said, at the point at which the kicking he was receiving was like the kicking he had so often received from his father and mother, and that this had provoked him into completely losing control of himself. His intent to rape remained, however, in his version of events. What seemed clear was that he would have raped the woman whether or not she had kicked and tried to resist him. Arguably, she had interrupted his enactment of reversal and wish to control in this scene in which he once more felt himself in a repetition of his own prior physical attack. Some form of repetition in his thinking seems to have taken place that triggered his loss of control and cued his thinking to past experiences of being kicked and beaten.

It was important to understand these trigger points in therapy and work on emotional responses that were still activated by this kind of recall or by others' perceived critical or controlling behaviour towards him that happened in the prison wing in which he lived and which was drawn into therapy for exploration. This was highlighted in order to try to reduce the impact of such cues and his response to them, and to find other pro-social emotional and thinking-through responses within therapy when behaviour within the Unit echoed such offence-paralleling behaviour. For example, his need to be in control of the report his woman Probation Officer was engaged in writing for him and exactly what was contained in it. Efforts were made in therapy to work with this live current example of a need to control a woman through to a different outcome in which, in place of absolute control he could try something closer to a collaborative approach to working with a woman. Theoretically, this modelling of a different behavioural style in therapy, if sufficiently internalized, serves as a model for future more pro-social behaviour on release from prison. Sufficient practice in this different behaviour will be likely to be needed before it can become understood and internalized.

Sam

One of the most difficult dynamics to speak about in men appears to be sexual abuse by their mother. In those instances in which this has been reported it was in almost every case not spoken about to anyone until therapy had begun. This leaves the emotional and cognitive impact of such acts to the victim to digest psychologically and emotionally alone. Growing up in the Island of Malta and starting to go to sea at the age of ten with his father, Sam was, after several years, able to outline in therapy that his mother had initiated a full sexual relationship with him when he was about age

13–15, 17 months after the father had left home when he was 11. When his father was at home he had been a heavy drinker, violent and frequently engaged in affairs with other women. This seemed to draw the mother and son closer together. He sensed the abuse was wrong but it was the only expression of care he thought he had at that time. He was not permitted to speak about his father, whom he had liked, because of his mother's remaining anger at him for his father's behaviour. He described feeling confused between a sense of enjoyment and great anxiety concerning the abusive experience. His mother sought comfort in him but later, at age 15, when he began to reciprocate advances to his mother, she denied fiercely that any such thing had ever happened in seeming shock and realization at what had happened. Shortly after he raised this subject with her, she withdrew from him suddenly and became pointedly unavailable, sexually and emotionally, took up with a new male partner and Sam had to leave home hurriedly to fend for himself at 15, seeking a bed wherever he could find one. He had never spoken about this experience for 29 years and felt a powerful confusion between the comfort of the sexual contact and feeling ashamed at having this experience.

After many years of difficulty in relationships he aggressively raped a woman older than himself when she had shown an interest in him and begun to become friendly with him. He was aware that his mother had denied what had taken place forcefully and that there seemed to be something in the fact that his offence was committed on an older woman but had never spoken with anyone about it. He made the link himself, thinking that it was no coincidence his victim was old enough to be his mother but was not sure why. Rage at not having had a satisfactory childhood, for not being protected, for being abandoned so suddenly accompanied by total denial of what had been his experience of his mother until then all appeared as themes in the therapy group but understanding was interwoven with retreat, hatred of the memories and attack of the understanding and thinking process that emerged in talking about these events. He remained in therapy working on issues connected with his anger and hatred of his mother, sense of being abandoned and let down and powerful shame at what had happened. He attended the Sex Offender's Treatment Programme (SOTP) in conjunction with his work in the TC, which provided a dual and powerful approach to the therapy process.

Repetition compulsion in sexual offending

What appears to have taken place in the examples above is that a more extensive and prolonged sexual abuse history has made an emotional and behavioural impact on the victim. After more serious and prolonged abuse, a learned sexualized attachment style appears to become adopted, but intermittently, not necessarily exclusively. However, a more complex pattern seems evident in the examples than simple attachment including care, love and support. A sexualized attachment style seems to take precedence over other ordinary attachment or relationship features and cognitive distortions and sexually styled internal working models develop in response to prolonged experience of sexual abuse and form a socially learned pattern. In turn this pattern appears linked with rage, retaliatory wishes and often a clear sense of making the other, the victim, 'experience what I have experienced', in one man's words to me one day, in the abusive scene, and a broader sense of getting even as if wiping the self clean of hateful, disturbing or indigestible feeling states of mind seems to take place. Campbell and colleagues view the victim's relationship with the perpetrator as 'based on identification with the aggressor as a means of turning the traumatic passive experience into an active one as the perpetrator.' They continue that if rage and aggression cannot be safely expressed 'they become sexualized as a means of allowing their modified and covert expression' (Campbell *et al.* 2001, p.490).

It seems unlikely that there is any simple explanation for the cognitive and emotional thinking that takes place in the preparatory stages of sexual violence or assault but the narratives from therapy, in reverse, and given after the event, may lend degrees of understanding to the construction of a sexually abusive attachment style as a form of modelled and learned behaviour, albeit perverse, which needs to be unlearned in therapy and alternative, equally satisfying relationship styles formed, practised and re-enforced. Concluding their research review on the sexual abuse of male children, Watkins and Bentovim noted the key factors contributing to a perpetrator outcome as being 'a combination of sexualization and externalizing responses' (Watkins and Bentovim 1992, p.232) and so a capacity to deal internally with what has become traumatic will be important to help prevent the automatic externalizing response and will form a goal in therapy together with thinking, practice and experience of other, non-sexualized relationship styles within the TC.

When care and attachment have become fused sexually, particularly when care is contingent upon the sexual gratification of the carer and is not forthcoming without it, the exchange of any real care and concern is absent. This absence of other non-sexualized or good enough ordinary care-giving aspects of relationship life seems to be important in itself but also helps pave the way for protest, discontent or anger to be vented through the most known form in this scenario: sexual behaviour, rather than through other expressions of anger or discontent. The task in therapy is to help find alternative, normative sources of outlet for anger, rage, shame, humiliation and any retaliatory thinking and feeling evident and for new ways of behaving and coping to be practised on the Wing in non-sexualized ways and in current prison relationships with peers and staff in order to underpin and anchor the process of change.

Stoller (1986) writes of sexual perversion as eroticized hatred which becomes akin to an act of violence, losing the loving, nurturing, reciprocal and warm characteristics of healthy sexual relating. The discharge of a whole range of emotions appears to have become routed through the sexual act itself, which may be disliked, feel repulsive after the act has been committed or even hated but includes some attraction and sadistic pleasure in what seems to be a return to what is known. Ordinary, containing and reciprocal aspects of a sexual relationship seem to be largely absent in many of the histories of sexual offenders. The sexual act has replaced care and concern in such a way that given and received expressions of ordinary affection and emotion may have been quite alien. A search for love and care through sex alone, when repeated in the denuded form learned in abuse, repeats the abusive and sexualized styles learned into future relationships, unless challenged, as social learning theory suggests.

Avoiding such repetition requires consistent and steady focus in therapy on current behaviour on the Wing and comment on it, bringing attitudes, thinking patterns and fantasies that may reinforce sexualized thinking into therapy for exploration and feedback and active provision of a range of alternative, ordinary, healthy relationship styles and work and educational achievement to give real alternative social experiences in readiness for release. One of the most important tasks for staff, through ongoing training and supervision, is to be able to identify and think actively about the targets in therapy in relation to behaviour as it emerges in the Community and remain able to comment on it in a constructive manner without being seduced, conditioned or otherwise drawn in to their own projective counter-identification: the staff contribution to acting-out. In one situation a therapist had become convinced that the right course of action with a man who had committed carefully planned kidnap and sexual assault, but not dealt with his targets in therapy at all convincingly, was to allow herself to become his therapist on release from prison and without letting the staff team know of this important piece of information emerging in the therapy group, set about loosely planning to arrange this. There were clear dangers, unnoticed by her, but of such concern to other members of the therapy group that they felt they had to come and let the wider staff team know of this plan. This course of action – possible repetition of past offending behaviour by an offender coupled with staff unconcern when venturing into a potentially dangerous course of action – may correspond to Grinberg's second form of projective counter-identification. This forms an unintended situation but nevertheless one in which,

> [t]he emotional response may be quite independent from the analyst's own emotions and…in certain cases, the analyst may have the feeling of being no longer his own self and of unavoidably becoming transformed into the object which the patient, unconsciously, wanted him to be (id, ego, or some internal object). (Grinberg 1962, pp.436–437)

The situation described could have become one in which the offender re-enacted his offence with careful precision and the therapist became victim in the drama without realizing it. Acting into the dynamics projected by residents of forensic TCs may incline staff members to states of certainty and sureness about their course of action and render them unaware of any discomfort, seduction or non-therapeutic course of action until it is too late. It may be best to try to remain open-minded as a therapist in the forensic setting about what to do and what to think, be wary of any gathering certainty and, by remaining accountable to the team as a whole, allow the staff team in supervision to retain a key steering role in an area of work so powerfully driven by unconscious and projective dynamics as inevitable but problematic forms of communication.

References

Baker, A. and Duncan, S. (1985) Child sexual abuse: A study of prevalence in Great Britain. *Child Abuse and Neglect, 9,* 457–464.

Butler, T., Donovan, B., Fleming, J., Levy, M. and Kaldor, J. (2001) Childhood sexual abuse among male and female prisoners. *Australian and New Zealand Journal of Public Health, 23,* 377–384.

Campbell, D., Glasser, A., Leitch, I. and Farrelly, S. (2001) Cycle of child sexual abuse: links between being a victim and becoming a perpetrator. *British Journal of Psychiatry, 179,* 482–494.

Dutton, D. and Hart, S. (1992) Evidence for long-term specific effects of childhood sexual abuse and neglect on criminal behaviour in men. *International Journal of Offender Therapy and Comparative Criminology, 36,* 129–137.

East, W.N. and de Hubert, W.H. (1939) *The psychological treatment of crime.* London: HMSO

Gebhard, P., Gagnon, J., Pomeroy, W. and Christensen, C. (1965) *Sex Offenders: An Analysis of Types.* New York: Harper Row.

Goldman, J. and Padayachi, U. (2000) Some methodological problems in estimating incidence and prevalence in child sexual abuse research. *The Journal of Sex Research, 37,* 305–314.

Grinberg, L. (1962) On a specific aspect of countertransference due to the patient's projective identification. *The International Journal of Psycho-Analysis,* London: Hogarth Press.

Grubin, D. (1998) *Sex Offending Against Children: Understanding the Risk.* Police Research Series Paper 99, London: Home Office, Research, Development and Statistics Directorate.

McMillan, H., Fleming, J., Streiner, D., *et al.* (2001) Childhood abuse and lifetime psychopathology in a community sample. *American Journal of Psychiatry, 158,* 1878–1883.

Merrill, L., Thomsen, C., Gold, S.R. and Milner, J. (2000) Childhood abuse and premilitary sexual assault in male navy recruits. *Journal of Consulting and Clinical Psychology, 69,* 252–261.

Mrazek, P., Lynch, M. and Bentovim, A. (1983) Sexual abuse of children in the United Kingdom. *Child Abuse and Neglect, 7,* 147–153.

Parker, M. (2004) Violence, sexual offending and sexual abuse: Are they linked? A Qualitative Research Study. In D. Jones (ed.) *Working with Dangerous People: The Psychotherapy of Violence.* Oxford: Radcliffe Medical Press Ltd.

Rind, B., Tromovitch, P. and Bauserman, R. (1998) A meta-analytic examination of assumed properties of child sexual abuse using college samples. *Psychological Bulletin, 124,* 22–53.

Salter, D., McMillan, D., Richards, M., *et al.* (2003) Development of sexually abusive behaviour in sexually victimised males: a longitudinal study. *The Lancet, 361,* 471–476.

Stoller, R. (1986) *Perversion: The Erotic Form of Hatred* (Reprinted). London: Karnac Books Ltd.

Watkins, W. and Bentovim, A. (1992) The sexual abuse of male children and adolescents: A review of current research. *Journal of Child Psychology and Psychiatry, 33,* 197–248.

Widom, C. and Ames, M. (1994) Criminal consequences of childhood sexual victimisation. *Child Abuse and Neglect, 18,* 303–318.

Widom, C. and Morris, S. (1997) Accuracy of adult recollections of childhood sexual abuse. *Psychological Assessment, 9,* 34–46.

Managing the Therapeutic Community

Chapter 15

Governing Grendon Prison's Therapeutic Communities: The Big Spin

Peter Bennett

There is no manual, qualification or course that provides a complete introduction to the task of being Governor of a therapeutic prison. Grendon is a
prison after all, albeit one of a very special kind and as such is regarded by
senior Prison Service officials as an appropriate posting for a Governor, but it
has not always been so. Up until the mid-1980s Grendon was managed by a
medical superintendent. Thereafter, a Governor was appointed in charge,
supported by a senior medical officer as Director of Therapy, accountable to
the Governor. For many of Grendon's staff, this alteration was regarded as an
erosion of the Medical Officer's authority within the therapeutic communities (TCs), threatening the integrity and continuity of the therapy. It is not
surprising that the Governor and the Director of Therapy have not always
seen eye to eye. Indeed, at times they have not been on speaking terms. Two
of them communicated with each other by longwinded memoranda: I keep
these documents locked away, reminders of how debilitating conflict can be
and of the need for senior managers to broach positively managerial,
professional and ideological differences.

The beginning

For my own part, I had long been an admirer of Grendon and was delighted to be appointed as its Governor in 2002. Although I had no practical experience of group therapy or indeed any professional qualifications in therapy, I had taken an interest over the years and had a reasonable grasp of the workings of TCs. But even so, I had seriously underestimated the culture shock that came with becoming Governor of Grendon Therapeutic Community.

I had appreciated how in practical and conceptual terms TCs did not fit nicely in a Prison Service context. Grendon is designated a prison and yet some of its staff and inmates distance themselves from the Prison Service, or the 'system', as they see it. Governors are regarded suspiciously as agents of the new managerialism with its inevitable focus on performance targets at the expense of therapy, overriding the authority and clinical competence of therapists.

There is nothing new about this debate, or indeed about the disputes, tensions and conflicts that excite it. Following the Fresh Start initiative nearly 20 years ago there were similar fears that the unique identity of Grendon would be lost and that it would inevitably become no different to conventional category B prisons (Genders and Player 1995). And yet even though I was fully aware of internal conflicts at Grendon and conscious of the Governor's controversial position at the apex, I was nevertheless ill-prepared for the opposition and outright hostility that I was to encounter on my arrival. I soon began to feel with considerable justification that I was an interloper, an unwelcome intruder apparently sent to erode further Grendon's therapeutic core.

The 'unwelcoming', as I experienced it, was exacerbated by the fact that the TC was experiencing one of its periodic bouts of insecurity brought on by the escape of three prisoners. Concerns were rekindled that Grendon would be converted into a 'system' prison. Moreover, several months had elapsed without a substantive Governor. Conflicts thrived, kindled by uncertainties about a successor. The Director of Therapy was reluctant to leave until both a Governor and his own successor had been appointed. But even more ominous, my arrival coincided with a highly disruptive security search which, for many Grendonites, provided conclusive evidence that Grendon's very survival as a therapeutic prison was at stake.

Given Grendon's reputation in some eyes as a jewel in the crown of the Prison Service, along with its often alleged vulnerability as an endangered species in an environment that allegedly threatens to inundate it in a tide of standards, audits and performance targets, it is not surprising that the 'secular' Governor should have been cast in a negative light. It is fitting therefore that I should have an opportunity to present my part in this volatile context, not least because of my influential role in brokering the unique place of Grendon in the wider Prison Service. Rather than explain this in structural terms, I describe an event that occurred at the start of my tenure that demonstrates my initial difficulties coming to grips with a TC prison. I am prepared to acknowledge my naivety at the time, as well as the naivety of the most diehard Grendonites.

It all happened within a week of my arrival. I write 'happened' as if the search, later dubbed the Big Spin, had come to pass purely by chance, or at least as a result of events that had nothing to do with me. But I have been reminded often enough that there is no such thing as chance in psychotherapy. Every flinch, gesture, cough, grimace or apparently careless slip of the tongue betrays cavernous meaning and intent, and more often than not, once sifted through the filters of psychodynamic perception, allegedly reveals a darker side, in this case the ulterior, or at best naïve, motives of the intruder. In the eyes of my detractors at the time, any attempt by me as the incoming Governor to deny responsibility for such a flurry of oppressive measures was either a sign of managerial doublespeak, in which case it was inexcusable, or else of ignorance, in which case it was a matter of who was manipulating the Governor.

Interpretations of what actually happened, and why, are many and varied, as are the motives imputed to the various actors in this high drama, including my own. But whatever one's take on this defining moment in Grendon's recent history, there was a general consensus during, and in the immediate aftermath, that the Big Spin didn't just happen but was inextricably linked to my arrival as the new Governor. Theories were rife but differed according to my alleged degree of involvement. In some accounts, I was the active instigator, a system Governor who had made no attempt to understand Grendon and merely wished to manage it as if it were just like any other prison. In other accounts, I was a passive instrument, a puppet manipulated by a senior group of operational managers that sought to lock power in the operational line at the expense of a vulnerable therapeutic tradition. Even more sinister, I could have been an agent specially appointed by the powers that be to overturn the heresy of psychodynamic therapy, a Cromwell, mobilizing a new model army of shaven-headed Ironsides, sent to dissolve a tradition and its carriers – those cavalier therapists – that had doggedly kept alive the flame of rehabilitation.

I arrived as Governor of Grendon and Springhill on a Wednesday in mid-September 2002. Because of the difficulties posed by managing two very different prisons, as well as the distinctive managerial approach I anticipated I would need for Grendon, I planned to follow an intensive two-week induction programme, meeting key personnel and attending meetings, before taking over from the Deputy Governor, who had been in charge for 7 months during a gubernorial interregnum. After three informative and uneventful days, I travelled home to Nottinghamshire for the weekend and returned on Sunday afternoon to attend a ceremony at Springhill, an open prison also governed by the Governor of Grendon. The event was an annual celebration of the installation of a Buddha image. The circumstances of the inauguration of a Buddhist shrine at Springhill had all the characteristics of a story from the ancient Pali Canon. It transpired that some 12 years ago a prisoner had shown great devotion by persuading the authorities and the venerable Buddhist Chaplain to have a specially consecrated Buddha imported from Thailand and installed on a plinth set in a grove adjacent to Springhill Hall and overlooking Aylesbury Vale. The prisoner had shown great enterprise, recalling the pious deeds of Gautama Buddha's early followers. Fearing that the almost life-size seated Buddha might be stolen or knocked unceremoniously from its plinth, he had filled the hollow image with concrete, thereby rendering nigh impossible its theft or ignominious treatment. Thereafter, every year, Buddhist monks, Thai cooks, guests and prisoners have attended a candlelit ceremony, partaken of a sacred feast, and joined in a circumambulation of the image.

Attendance at the ceremony was a moving moment for me and I was particularly grateful for a decision to delay the event – risking the onset of darker and chillier autumn evenings – so that I, as the new Governor of Grendon and Springhill, could attend.

The 'big spin'

But the auspicious beginning was soon to turn sour. Just as the guests were arriving, the Duty Governor approached me in a state of some consternation. It was clear he had some bad news to deliver and had great difficulty in coming to the point. It transpired that there had been an incident at Grendon prison the day before which in Prison Service terminology comes under the category of a reportable incident known as a 'missing tool'. For those unfamiliar with operational practice it is perhaps difficult to appreciate why a Governor should be brought bolt upright by an event that would be a mild inconvenience to a plumber or carpenter. It is not so much that a useful instrument has been mislaid. Rather it is that the tool, following its loss, could be appropriated by a prisoner to perpetrate a wide range of misdemeanours varying from assault to suicide, murder, or even, Heaven forbid, escape. What is more, and by a strange inverted logic, what was so alarming about this incident was not that the tool was missing, but that it had been found, and found, alarmingly, in the possession of an inmate. And if that is not sufficiently confusing, the tool had neither been lost nor found because Wing staff had known all along that it was in the possession of a prisoner.

Pressing the Duty Governor to divulge the nature of the offending tool, he revealed it to be an electric drill of the kind used by countless hobbyists, but normally proscribed in prison cells. What is more, it was unregistered, uninscribed and with no corresponding niche in a secure tool cabinet, and which could, in the wrong hands and circumstances, fulfil the thereafter oft-repeated simile, of 'slicing through bars like a knife through butter'.

Obsessiveness is a useful trait for security staff – it's all about meticulous attention to detail and dogged pursuit of procedures. But security staff can be overly punctilious at times. They might exaggerate the dangers of certain items allowed in a prisoner's possession. Buddhist prisoners have long endured this irritation. Their incense sticks are purported to be convenient means of masking the whiff of cannabis; their little Buddha images can be used to conceal drugs, or even, given the Buddha's pointed coiffure, rendered in the hard metal of an image, can be used to stab someone. I cannot help but imagine the philosophical conundrum which Gautama Buddha might have faced given such a circumstance. Not only would he have been dismayed by the idea of an image of himself being worshipped, but also, and perhaps even worse, that his likeness might be even thought to perpetrate acts of bloody violence.

There is a certain comfort for a Governor in the knowledge that security staff members suspect everything and everyone. After all, prisoners must be kept in custody and the Governor carries a serious responsibility in preventing escape and injury to others. I'd rather encourage caution and decide myself when and where rules should be relaxed and reasonable risks taken. But in this case their concern was justified.

The explanation, preferred by many inmates and staff at Grendon, that the inmate in possession of the drill simply wanted it to pursue his in-cell hobby of carving Faberge-like eggs was in all likelihood true, but it is just not enough to argue that this did not amount to a serious lapse in security. Although I subsequently believed that he was innocent, and was indeed trusted implicitly by some Wing staff members, 20 years of experience have left me in no doubts as to the potential misuse of tools among prisoners whose escape would be highly embarrassing and considered dangerous for the public. Whatever the prisoner's motives, the Home Secretary would have been pleased to know that one of his Governors was blessed with sufficient good sense to know that there are those who would use a drill for purposes other than inscribing Faberge eggs. I had no doubts from the outset that a culture that allowed this to happen in a category B prison, despite the values of trust, individual responsibility and respect that are intrinsic to Grendon, was vulnerable to abuse by the few who might prefer escape to the undeniably hard labour of therapy behind bars. The discovery of the drill posed serious questions about security at Grendon and called for a response that would ensure that in future no other tools could fall so easily into the possession of inmates.

What is notable on this occasion, however, is that the nature of the response had already been decided, without my knowledge. The following Monday morning, so the Duty Governor informed me, prisoners would be locked up and a full search of all areas and prisoners would be conducted using all available staff and dogs.

It would be untruthful if I were to say that I was not a wee bit miffed that I had not been consulted, albeit I could put it down to the fact that I was still on induction and therefore not fully operational. Nevertheless, I could have decided even at that stage on a different course of action. But as an experienced Governor I had no qualms about overseeing a full search of the establishment. After all, I was taking on a prison that had, some 12 months earlier, allowed three category B inmates to escape from the sports field. A damming report had followed and I was well aware that security at Grendon was vulnerable, indeed that many staff had opposed attempts to improve physical and procedural security on the grounds that therapy, properly conducted, provided its own dynamic security based on trust and a knowledge of what was going on gleaned from the close relationships enjoyed by staff and inmates. An increased and overt display of security could destroy this delicate modus vivendi. Moreover, I was also aware that Grendon had suffered from a lack of established leadership for some time. The previous Governor had left before he had time to respond fully to the recommendations arising from the investigation into the escape and the Deputy Governor, who made great progress in managing a flyaway budget and implementing new staffing systems, could not be expected to provide the permanent lead of an officially acknowledged Governor in charge. Grendon, as I realized at the time from my own observations and reading of reports, investigations and briefings by key Prison Service staff members, was wanting in terms of its security, lacked clear direction and was riven by conflicting views as to its role and purpose as well as who should wield authority in the management of a unique therapeutic prison.

Given my assessment, I had no problems with the decision to instigate a full search. I also knew enough about Grendon to realize that this would not secure my popularity, but unpopularity seemed a small price to pay when set against the threat to Grendon's future from within – a prison that seemed to me to be tearing itself apart, exacerbated by the cavalier attitude of some staff, who seemed to consider themselves independent of Prison Service authority, and the threat from a Prison Service that could not and would not tolerate a security time bomb, no matter that Grendon was special. I knew that Grendon's future as a therapeutic Category B prison was in jeopardy and was dismayed that some influential staff could not, and would not, foresee this eventuality.

But decisions and their accompanying actions invariably have unintended outcomes. The day following the Buddha ceremony at Springhill, the planned search of Grendon duly got underway, beginning its transformation into what finally, and retrospectively, was dubbed by prisoners 'The Big Spin'.

Spin is prison slang for a search. But it was also a word of the moment, associated with New Labour politics and, as applied to the search at Grendon, was indeed a pregnant metaphor. Moreover, whereas spin can be tightly managed, shaped by the will of the spinner, it can also go awry, spin out of control. Whatever, there is an ambiguity that underlies the event at Grendon.

As I wandered around Grendon during the three days of the search, I could not have anticipated the intensity of the drama I had or had not allowed to be unleashed. My recollections are fragmentary, reflecting the varying observations and commentaries of a search in progress, as well as the panoply of emotional outbursts expressed by participants and residents.

By spinning out of control, I mean that a search originally instigated as a means of finding illicit items in possession, in particular those that might aid escape, should spiral into an opportunity by some staff, who were presumably less sensitive to the delicate nature of therapy, to clear inmate cells of excess possessions and furniture they had accumulated, indeed been allowed to accumulate, over months and years, even though officially they had exceeded the limits of what in the Prison Service is known efficiently as volumetric control. A prisoner's valued and scarce possessions are restricted to the three dimensions of an official box in the interests of economy, practicality and security.

What a prisoner regards as valuable, furnishing his intimate space in a cell, may not be appreciated by those of us who enjoy the privilege of household clutter. Prisoners can be as capricious as magpies, collecting bits and pieces that stand out in a spartan environment, expressing individuality where individuality is constantly threatened. It is, therefore, helpful if prison staff members can appreciate the profound feelings of humiliation and insecurity that can arise if a prisoner feels that his cell, his personal space and possessions, have been violated. And it is out of this sense of violation, a feeling that staff have exceeded their authority, gone over the top, that humiliation is felt and distrust is expressed, supported by those staff who alike feel that a special relationship of trust, so carefully nurtured over long periods of therapy, has been breached. In their opposition, some inmates complained that Grendon had become just like the system that is just like any other prison. That which was special had been lost.

Viewed in another way, however, it could be argued that prisoners had taken too much advantage of those staff members who were willing to turn a blind eye to almost anything. As the search proceeded, one skip after another was piled high with literally everything but the kitchen sinks. The Grendon magpies had, in their enthusiasm, decorated their nests with cupboards, shelves, wall hangings and makeshift modcons that would have left them with little room to sleep. It didn't make for good housekeeping, let alone good security.

Responses

But it is the case that the original purpose of the search, to discover any illicit items, had become for some staff an opportunity to have a mass clearout and that, contrary to any principles of consultation that purported to exist at Grendon, few people were consulted. Indeed, many inmates and staff had good reason to suspect that the whole and sole purpose of the exercise was to use the 'discovery' of the drill as an excuse to put inmates back in their place as prisoners in a 'system' prison. The winter of the 2002–2003 edition of the prisoner magazine *Feedback* dramatically says it all: 'over a few dark days in September Grendon was locked down as teams of officers conducted a search of cells. It sent shockwaves through the community'. Prisoners complained bitterly, 'we were invaded ... my cell was completely trashed – there was no clear set procedure – items were lost or kept on the whim of individuals – we were intruded upon unnecessarily – total disregard for our property and feelings – why couldn't they have explained it? – out of order – it seems to be connected to the new Governor – security took it as a big joke – I feel that I was raped and believe it was payback by security – a reminder of the system – it seemed to be reverting to the system'. And, perhaps most tellingly, '12 years ago Grendon was run differently – there was more interaction and there were more therapists – there's a conflict between therapy and security'. Such comments were typical and cannot be dismissed cynically as the whining of an inmate population who bemoaned the passing of a golden age of therapeutic liberality and excess. But nor can they be interpreted simply as the innocent outbursts of a violated minority.

The subsequent debate

In truth, the aftermath and the ensuing debate were more intense than the search itself. The Big Spin, it transpired, stirred up and made manifest all the emotions, conflicts, fault lines and divergent views that imbued the dynamics of Grendon. For me, the search and its aftermath became an epiphany, a dissection revealing momentarily the entrails of a diseased organism. This was a high drama in which I found myself to be one of the leading players cast in open conflict with those who perceived themselves as defending a tradition under threat. It was also a playing out of the stereotypical conflicts between therapy and security and more specifically of where authority and power should ultimately lie, in the therapeutic or operational line. In retrospect, it was this conflict, made vividly manifest in the search, that had to be addressed if Grendon was to move forward.

The opposition by prisoners was also expressed by those staff who found themselves diametrically opposed to the way the search had been conducted. One therapist, also interviewed in *Feedback*, and attracting a cult-like following, expressed his outrage in terms that invite interpretation. He described himself ruefully as 'the last of the Medical Officer therapists', described the Big Spin as 'damaging relationships and dynamic security' – in the name of 'security' and offered professional advice to the new Governor that 'if he wants to help Grendon survive he needs to learn to resist spin over substance'.

His view of the event was one of a topsy-turvy world where operational incompetents presided over the demise of medical therapists or, in his words, where 'the lunatics have taken over the asylum'.

Some three years on, many lessons have been learned and I would not wish to repeat the clumsiness of that search. The Big Spin revealed ancient fault lines, particularly the uneasy friction between operational authority and therapeutic, clinical and medical authority. Conflicts had to be resolved or tamed if progress was to be made. I was to learn ways and means of overcoming traditional rivalries by developing procedures characterized by consultation and working together. Others had to learn that although dynamic security was crucial to the workings of a prison TC, it nevertheless needed careful management and refinement; otherwise it might provide no more than a false sense of security. It seems to be a matter of getting the balance right and 'having custody, care and control in harmony' rather than being at war with each other (Home Office 1995). Dynamic security alone had not prevented the escape of three prisoners. Grendon has come a long way in developing a symbiosis between security and therapy, for the most part encouraged by the positive working relationship practised by the Governor and the new Director of Therapeutic Communities. But that is another chapter.

References

Genders, E. and Player, E. (1995) *Grendon: A Study of a Therapeutic Prison*. Oxford: Clarendon Press.

Home Office (1995) *Review of Prison Service Security in England and Wales and the Escape from Parkhurst Prison on Tuesday 3rd January 1995 [The Learmont Inquiry]*. London: HMSO.

Chapter 16

Directing Therapy in the Prison Democratic Therapeutic Community

Mark Morris

There is a distinction between delivering therapy as a therapist and directing therapy as a manager and all mental health and criminal justice workers with a rehabilitative task are involved in the management of their caseload, their group and their programme. The struggles of a large therapeutic community (TC) to make its way, to survive and prosper in a changing environment, are the same as the micromanagement of everyday therapeutic practice. Secondly, there is a much more specific clinical issue regarding the pathology of the patients/prisoners being treated and their interaction with the organization within which they are contained.

In management discourse and gossip, different managers are often judged on the basis of their 'effectiveness'. Managerial 'effectiveness' seems basically about whether or not they can actually get things done. Working with personality disordered patients I am constantly and repeatedly struck by how 'effective' those with personality disorders are at getting things done. On the one hand this 'effectiveness' is about personal tragedy, saying exactly the wrong most hurtful thing in a moment of rage in a valued relationship that is irrevocably damaged as a result, being violent to a beloved child with its obvious deleterious consequences as well as the inner anguish and turmoil this may eventually bring about.

On the other hand this frightening 'effectiveness' operates at an organizational level, distorting and potentially collapsing the structures created for treatment. The main stage on which personality disorder pathology plays is in care-giving relationships. The organization treating the patient becomes the abusive parent, the rejecting partner, the ungrateful child. Patients engage with and try to destroy their treatment as they have destroyed (and been destroyed by) their families. This is why the issue of therapeutic management is a central clinical issue.

While it seems grandiose to refer to 'four pillars of therapeutic management', the issues that are discussed later do seem to me to have central importance in the therapy management task. These issues are first leadership, which includes a clear sense of vision and direction, as well as an understanding of the basis of authority and its legitimacy. Second, there is an important ambassadorial role, developing and harvesting networks, and identifying environmental opportunities and threats. Third, there is the issue of research and development, and fourth, I believe there is a 'gladiatorial' element in the role. To protect what is good at times, you have to fight.

Leadership

The management literature on leadership seems to generate more heat than light. In relation to the leadership role in a TC treatment service, however, there are some things that the leader has to do. The most important of these is having a clear vision of the task. In relation to Grendon, this involves a clear and intimate sense of the clinical problems on the therapeutic factory floor, and about how the structure of the therapy responds to and manages these on the one hand. On the other, there needs to be a clear sense of the external environment, of the political and supra-organizational issues that surround the Unit.

For example, in Grendon, there is an intricate and delicate method for managing violence or intimidation that occurs while in treatment. The process includes both the protagonists facing the Community, and the details of the fight being discussed and investigated, including the antecedents and attitudes leading up to it, and any other Community dynamics that may have contributed. Once the facts have been thoroughly established, there may be a vote on whether a violent act has been committed, with the knowledge that a violent act is against the Grendon rules, and should automatically result in discharge. If it is concluded that a violent act has been committed, then there is a second discussion about whether the individual's commitment to therapy is in doubt. If so it is likely that the individual will be discharged, as it means that they have lost the confidence of the Community that they are motivated to change. If not, their continued stay lies in the hands of the staff group members, who will come to a decision. This process of exploration and establishment of accountability is often the most crucial part of an individual's treatment, establishing in real-time issues of responsibility, self-control, culpability and responsibility, and of understanding, remorse and forgiveness.

The result of this process is a steady stream of prisoners who need to be transferred out of Grendon. This issue is managed by front-loading it to the admission stage. Admission to Grendon is dependent on the governor of the sending establishment agreeing to transfer the inmate back if required. Amongst sending prisons, Grendon's 'sale or return' policy engenders negative comment, in a cultural setting where if a prison agrees to accept an inmate, they should then put up with them, come what may. The leadership task is to have a clear vision of the overall process that underlies the fact that prisoners on occasion need to be transferred out, and for that clear vision of the overall process to act as a compass in maintaining the unpopular 'sale or return' policy.

The leadership task has been likened to being the captain of a ship. By having a thorough knowledge of the ship and its crew, the captain can judge the best course through stormy waters. No one else has the same knowledge of the ship, and no one with the knowledge of the ship has the view from the bridge of the perils and challenges ahead. The leadership task takes place at the intersecting point between the external environment and the internal, and the best chance of success requires the combination of knowledge of both. The choppy seas and possible courses and ports of call are threats and opportunities. The task is to anticipate, chart and follow a course that avoids as many as possible of the threats while taking advantage of as many as possible of the opportunities, and most important of all, accurately distinguishing between the two.

Leadership, authority and legitimacy

The second leadership task concerns having a clear understanding of the legitimacy of the leadership role authority – in the metaphor of the ship, understanding how effective the rudder is. Over the last 15 years or so, there has been a developing culture of managerialism, initially in the private, and then in the public sector. Managerialism proposes that there are generalizable managerial competencies that are applicable to all organizations. Simply stated, a professional manager might run a hospital better than a professional doctor. In TCs, as in other settings, increasingly, the professional or clinical staff work to a more generic manager. In prisons, the general prison manager is a prison governor, who as captain might see his Director of Therapy as his first officer.

It seems to be a reasonable generalization to suggest that the majority of prisoners have issues with authority. A frightening number have been abused by a parental authority when they were vulnerable children, or subsequently abused by the structures of the State charged with their protection in children's homes and other settings. The symptom of breaking the Law, of violence and theft can often be understood as a dialectic about authority, 'fighting the power', undermining the authority of wealth by stealing, creating the feeling one has authority by spending the haul.

A TC is a treatment setting that facilitates communication through Community and group meetings. In this setting, the differentiation of roles between residents and staff is starkly visible. In the example above, the prisoners discuss and explore the facts and implications of the alleged act of violence or intimidation, then recommend whether the individual should be discharged from the Community. And then the staff members have a meeting at which they decide whether or not the prisoners' conclusion and recommendations will be followed.

Because of these issues, a TC setting is a managerial goldfish bowl, where the nature of the authority is discussed, where the quality of the decisions made is discussed, where the legitimacy of the authority structure is discussed and so on. In such a setting, it is vitally important that a Director has a very clear sense of her or his authority and its limits, and of the legitimacy of that authority, and its limits. In Grendon, some of the challenges to the legitimacy of the Director of Therapy have included whether or not the post holder is a doctor, a psychiatrist, an individual or group psychotherapist, a former Grendon Community therapist and so on. For each parameter, arguments have been made that not having these qualifications or experiences undermines the post holder's legitimacy. All of these may be true and if the rudder of legitimate authority is limited, it is best to be aware of this, in order to use it most effectively.

Where does this leave the debate between the generic manager/prison governor and the Director of Therapy? The answer is in terms of differential legitimacy. The generic manager has little legitimacy in the clinical realm and likewise the clinician has little legitimacy in the prison management realm. Working together, both have as full a knowledge as possible of the ship, its company and of the choppy seas outside. Pulling together, this combined rudder can be quite effective. Combining the aspects of prison management and therapeutic leadership enhances and legitimizes this joint approach to authority across the organization.

Clinical leadership and supervision

As with leadership, there is much literature about supervision both as a management task and as a psychodynamic process. Supervision of key staff in a therapeutic organization combines these two functions. First, there is the basic psychodynamic supervisory task in which the staff member describes the clinical situation and the supervisor identifies dynamic issues affecting the staff member's thinking about it. The Community members have agreed that a particular prisoner has committed an act of violence, but that his commitment to therapy is intact, so argue that he should stay. The staff group feel he should go, with the exception of the supervisee, who in discussion it emerges, is hooked into a perpetual 'last chance' scenario with this particular prisoner, linked to the prisoner's rescuing stepfather. With some insight into this dynamic, the staff member can become more objective in his or her clinical decision making.

The second supervisory function is to enable the staff member to share in the vision of the organization, of its task and strengths, and of its direction in the environment that comprise the leadership vision described earlier. Articulating the vision and direction of the organization will put in context any organizational changes and tensions that the staff member may be struggling with, as well as being able to see the significance of their own contribution in the wider picture of the organizational effort.

Ambassadorial activities

Aside from the obvious ambassadorial function, namely to represent the organization and to lobby on its behalf in different settings, ambassadorial activities have two other related functions, the developing and harvesting of networks. The TC as an organization will be situated in several different environments; for example, Grendon is a prison close to other prisons nationally with a similar function, or other category B security prisons, and the different sets of colleagues formed through daily work generate valuable but different networks of professionals. However, Grendon is also a colleague alongside other TCs, alongside other secure personality disorder treatment units, and so on.

These networks can be harvested in three ways.

1. *For the gathering of intelligence.* The quality of managerial decisions made on the bridge of the ship is only as good as the

information on which they are based. Networks provide information and the different networks providing different dimensions of information together build up a fuller picture of the environment. One colleague may have heard about a Government policy paper that has been published, and another may have an idea about what the implications may be.

2.   *Networks provide 'technology' information that contributes to research and development.* A colleague prison may have developed a room-searching technique that is more effective; a colleague personality disorder service may have a new battery of assessment testing that is particularly discerning. Identifying and then keeping up with best practice relies heavily on the use of networks.

3.   *To establish and maintain a group of extra-organizational managerial colleagues.* Having a leadership role in an organization can at times be rather lonely, for example having made an unpopular decision that with one's own perspective on the ship's bridge with the benefit of the radar screens seems the obvious and only choice, but which seems perverse to other shipmates. The leadership of a TC does bring with it a particular set of challenges that are difficult to articulate, but which all those who have led such organizations are familiar with, and it is useful to know where these colleagues are for advice and support if required.

Research and development

There is a curious timelessness about TCs. The communities in Grendon, some started in 1962, may be the oldest continuous TCs and small groups that there are in prison, with a continuous history and culture built up over decades. It is a truism that the 'feel' of the Community, the 'feel' of the work with its debates and challenges, its presentation of impossible situations and their eventual resolution are probably exactly the same in 2005 as they were in 1965. The technology underlying group psychoanalysis applied in a Community setting that adds social and behavioural therapeutic elements is timeless. However, this cannot be said for the environment outside.

Not only does society develop and change technologically, but its political, social and environmental attitudes change. Grendon began in a wave of optimism and medicalization of dealing with the problem of psychopathy. In the 1970s the criminal justice 'rehabilitative ideal' collapsed; in the 1980s and 1990s positivist empirical psychology-based 'what works' psychological treatments were the currency. Into the new millennium we seem to be in a 'post what works' era with the recognition that high PCLR scoring psychopaths, deemed untreatable in cognitive psycho-educational programmes cannot be ignored, ushering in an era of Dangerous and Severe Personality Disorder (DSPD) treatments. For each of these eras, the basic and unchanging TC technology product has had to re-conceptualize itself. For example, in the late 1980s pulling together an empirical evidence base to demonstrate its effectiveness; in the 1990s, interpreting its work into the 'what works' language; then into the new millennium, understanding its work in relation to DSPD and high-scoring psychopaths.

In addition to the developmental work of translation of the mechanism of the TC, there is also the need to develop the TC itself in response to changes in the external environment. Following the Wolf Report that set out specialized management arrangements for long-term and lifer prisoners, these had to be incorporated into Grendon's structure, leading to much debate and cries that it would distort the basic therapeutic frame. The same response followed the introduction of the 'incentives and earned privileges' scheme introduced into the UK Prisons Service in the 1990s, and the enhanced security and searching procedures following the Fallon enquiry. It took creative thinking and innovation to make these schemes work in the TC environment. The concern often is that these external requirements for development will degrade and dilute the treatment process, but on the contrary, they seem to enhance it. Whether this is simply because it becomes a focus for debate, negotiation and compromise that prisoners and staff get together about, or whether these enhancements in prison practice then combined with the TC for the treatment of prisoners augments the total treatment efficacy is not clear, but Research and Development work needs to be done, and its direction is a central aspect of the therapy directorial role.

The gladiatorial role

There is something rather counter intuitive about the idea that suited managers might be engaging in hand-to-hand mortal combat in their quiet panelled boardrooms. In the process of coming to a decision about the strategy that an organization will follow, there will be heated and at times acrimonious debates and following this, there will be heated and acrimonious debate with those at head office, and those in the organization justifying and arguing for the strategy that has been decided upon. Because of the 'goldfish bowl' management culture, where debate and enquiry are encouraged, TC managers cannot engage in underhand, manipulative or coercive tactics to get their changes through or accepted, or if they do, these will inevitably be found out, and they are likely to be confronted with their duplicity. As a result, the fight when push comes to shove is hand-to-hand, simple, bloody intellectual debate.

The issues for debate are twofold. First, that a head office manager directs that there should be some change that the unit management resist because it would undermine the therapy. One example was that Grendon should have a single central kitchen as this saves money. The Grendon view was that the TCs have individual kitchens and food preparation and serving as a central part of Community activity and that this provides realistic, Community-based work as part of the treatment process for residents. In this case, the fight is the prevention of and resistance to a change imposed from above that would undermine the core therapeutic task. The second is where a change is agreed by the Grendon management team, for example, the tightening of searching procedures and that individual Communities, staff or residents contest that they will damage therapy, and so resist it.

Clearly, the content of these two debates is similar, what changes are and are not damaging to the core therapeutic task, however the form is somewhat different: on the one hand resisting the will of a more senior manager, on the other directing a subordinate. Because of the goldfish bowl culture of management, subordinates have to be argued with rather than directed, during which any chinks in the manager's logic will be exposed, as will anything other than an honest account. Occasionally, the only logic is the directorial, namely that the structural authority has to have its way. It is, of course, much easier if managerial decisions are the right ones, so they remain legitimate and coherent under the intense scrutiny to which they will be put.

In some ways, the process of enacting change with subordinates in a TC just becomes part of the general discourse along with debate about day-to-day issues. However, with supraordinate management, it is somewhat different. Whereas the managers within the TC have learned to welcome the diversity of opinions and debate that in the end enhance the quality of strategy, supraordinate managers do not always have the same attitude, finding the challenging of and interrogation of decisions something of a surprise. There is often a 'risking one's career' feel in these debates with supra-ordinate managers, but the same process as with subordinates holds true, namely that it is legitimate to scrutinize and energetically argue one's position, recognizing that one might be overcome by the simpler logic of structural authority, doing what you're told, and then working to minimize the expected deleterious effects on the therapeutic work.

Conclusion

In this chapter I have described some of the underpinning themes involved in having a directorial role in a TC setting, arguing that themes can probably be found at a range of different levels from the chief executive of the NHS and his ministerial masters, to the psychologist managing their individual patient. I have suggested that there is a leadership role, involving having a clear vision of the task and the developmental direction in response to internal resources, and the external environment, and that the legitimacy of the leadership role needs to be established, for example in relation to the clinical leadership task. I have described the importance and benefits of network building, of Research and Development and described a 'gladiatorial' role in arguing for the vision and values one has while recognizing and respecting the framework of structural authority.

Finally, it is important to re-emphasize the crucial therapeutic importance of the way that one exercises authority for the prisoner client group. Their primary model of authority will often have been abusive, as victim and perpetrators. If the Director and staff team can make prisoners in therapy aware of the possibility of a benign, authority, a 'good enough', a non- or minimally abusive authority that can be internalized, then this may be the most important therapeutic lesson they can learn.

Chapter 17

Symbiosis: Therapeutic Communities within Non-therapeutic Community Organizations

Roland Woodward

This chapter is about sharing and partnership and so, of course, it is about envy, rivalry and the constant struggle to overcome intergroup anxiety. It is about how a therapeutic community (TC) can thrive in an organization which may have apparently very different functions or values than the TC. The experiences that I draw on in exploring this process come from the setting up of the 23-bed TC for life-sentenced prisoners at HMP Gartree (GTC) in 1992, and the designing, building and opening of the 200-bed TC at HMP Dovegate (DTC) in 2001. In the first case, the GTC became part of an established prison with a long and distinguished history. Dovegate TC opened six months after the main 600-bed prison on a brand new site. The GTC took over a small unit, which had a history of being a vulnerable prisoners unit, so there were a lot of ghosts as well as history. The DTC is a multiple site, with four communities of 40 beds, an assessment unit and a high-intensity programme unit, both of 20 beds. The DTC is a separate and distinct area within Dovegate but shares central services, so not only does it have to face the challenge of symbiosis but also sibling rivalry. Some would suggest that this was not only amongst itself but also with its larger but almost equally young, partner.

Symbiosis between organizational subsystems

Symbiosis is about the association of two different organisms living attached to each other or one within the other. It is a living together and a co-operation between persons: in this case, between different milieu or regimes. The definition *symbiosis* implies mutual benefit to partners that this is different from the relationship between host and a parasite. Unfortunately, the experience of setting up TCs within an existing organization has shown me that, psychologically, symbiosis has to be achieved by overcoming and working through all the impediments that a perceived 'host and parasite' relationship brings with it.

For an organization to find within itself a part that does not operate in the dominant organizational culture and requires resources that it insists on using in what feels like an unaccountable way, presents a shocking and difficult scenario. The realization that there is something different within itself is profoundly threatening, even when the organization has been involved in creating that new part of itself. The reality of the experience is, as usual, very different from the intellectual understanding during the planning and creation stages of development. This is vividly demonstrated by the creation of TCs in the prison setting. Barbara Rawlings (1998) defines many of the difficulties that are to be found in this situation. Similarly, the study of HMP Grendon by Genders and Player (1995) details the philosophical and practical differences between the operation of a TC prison and the general prison ethos. The reality that the TC is not living off the host and that a collaborative partnership benefits all concerned is not always immediately apparent or necessarily true. TCs, particularly in prisons, can be resource heavy.

The fact that TCs are vulnerable to the process of symbiosis breaking down and regressing to the 'host' turning on its 'parasite' is witnessed in the special edition of the *Prison Service Journal* in 1997 dedicated to TCs. Included in this collection of papers is Judy McKenzie's (1997) obituary for the TC at HMYOI Glen Parva. It is a sobering fact that since that edition, the TC at HMP Wormwood Scrubs, The Max Glatt centre and Albatross House at HMYOI Feltham have also closed. It is true that new TCs have risen but they often epitomize the difficulties of doing so within the organizational culture. A brief example is the way in which the first TC for women in the British Prison System was created at West Hill at HMP Winchester and before this could even reach infancy was transferred wholesale to HMP

Send, where it now strives to thrive in an organization that had its TC thrust upon it.

For the person or group of individuals setting out to create a TC in an existing organization there are some crucial issues to address:

1. the inevitable hostility of the organization, as manifested by lack of services, labelling of staff, resistance by managers

2. structural incompatibility

3. ignorance about the function and purpose of a TC

4. vulnerability of long-term survival

5. operating landscape

6. moral arrogance ('we are obviously worthwhile').

All those people who have been responsible for the leadership of a TC understand the perilous balancing act to be undertaken. On one side there is the desire to make manifest the democratic principles needed in the daily life of the TC. On the other hand there are responsibilities expected of the organization. For the responsible manager of a TC there is no democratic sharing of the responsibility when the organization is required to account for the TC. This may take many forms from staff competence to the cold hard fact of the bottom line. If an investigation finds significant failures of the TC it is the manager that bears the consequences. If the budget is over spent or the contribution to the profit line is missed it is once again the manager who is held accountable. This holding of the balance is often onerous. As Birtles *et al.* (2004, p.97) note: 'Leading in a new organization carries particular responsibilities, including the importance of ensuring the organization supports the growth of a culture of learning. This involves leaders at times taking risks.' Where the decision is made to follow best therapeutic practice it may clash with the organizational interest. As noted in Hemmings and Woodward (2004), when shareholders in an organization become anxious about cash flow they can exert great pressure on TC managers.

The day-to-day difficulty of being a manager of a TC is no different than being a manager in any organization. All the literature relating to managing change, motivating and leading staff apply to the TC manager. Whether one is influenced by Tom Peters (1992) Liberation Management; Lundin and Christensen's 'FISH' (2001) or Johnson's 'Who stole my Cheese' (1999), there remains a special realm that is unique to the TC. The TC manager/ leader has to be able to:

1. contain the anxiety of the managers and staff, of both the TC and the organization

2. guide the team continually to make conscious the inevitably unfolding unconscious processes that evolve through enactment in the TC

3. be the translator of the 'TC tongue' to the rest of the organization.

The following sections look at what each of these means in the day-to-day reality of organizational life, with containment being the major one.

Containment

For the TC manager the host/partner organization is an immense source of anxiety, if it is clear that there are differences in task and values. Even when the organization promotes and supports therapeutic work this can still be the case. Hinshelwood (2001) provides a good analysis of how the unconscious process of the individual is the driving force in the complex interaction between the elements in institutions. The organization projects an assortment of anxieties onto the TC that are focussed on the TC manager. The TC presents to the organization a hidden part of itself. It permits the expression of the fears, anxieties and angers that have echoes within all the other areas of the organization. The organization has difficulty understanding how this can be tolerated and encouraged, and feels itself uncomfortable. Campling (2004) points out that it is much easier to project onto an individual who is not well known or understood and this is true for a part of an establishment such as a TC, which is deliberately speaking of the unmentionable. Like Harry Potter the TC dares to talk openly of Voldermort whilst others would prefer to talk about 'you know who'.

The confidential nature of the way in which the work is done in a TC means that despite its democracy, the TC appears anything but transparent. This has several effects. First, it raises fantasies about what is going on and more to the point what is going on inside itself. The general organization outside the TC glimpses only moments of TC life and usually those moments are potentially contentious. When the anxiety of the TC spills out beyond its boundaries the alarm and anxiety caused tends to be catastrophized and create a disproportionate amount of anxiety outside the TC. Within the fantasies that are created are contained many of the unconscious fears and anxieties of the organization more widely. There may also be resentment, envy and anger generated by such fantasies.

It is possible for organizations to develop 'secondary phobic responses' to TCs. Some people who develop phobias also develop a secondary phobic response that involves a response to the awareness of the anxiety response to the primary phobic object. Organizations can do the same. If a TC gives the organization cause for concern it can become oversensitive to its responses to the TC, which triggers a phobic response to the TC whenever it detects anxieties connected with it. The definition of a phobia is that it is a response not grounded in reality.

Organizations may attempt to regulate the TC through what Shur (1994) calls bureaucratization. In this process residents (patients) become sources of information through which administrations believe they are able to monitor and control the organizational process. Shur contends that this invariably interferes with the therapeutic process. The TC manager needs to identify this process and to have in place a set of information gathering tools that can be used to demonstrate the therapeutic efficacy of the TC within the framework of choice. This can offset some of the demands created by an anxious organization regarding what the TC is doing.

Most TCs when encountered appear to give a sense of intimacy and high level of sharing that is not available to any but those in the TC. It is a form of exclusiveness found in the intimacy of intense relationships. This often produces jealousy and envy in people and in organizations. Consider the feelings aroused in colleagues when it becomes clear that two of them have fallen in love. All sorts of concerns are voiced and debates about how this will affect work and relationships in the team. The exclusivity of the relationship is a powerful stimulus to those around in the same environment or interpersonal network.

This position is a perilous one for the TC manager. On one hand the person is striving to contain or mop up the spillage within the TC and at the same time trying to provide a rational containment for the anxieties in the organization. Contiguously the TC manager is haunted by the fear that failure to do either will lead to the TC disintegrating, or its invasion by an organization that can no longer tolerate its own anxiety about the TC. If the organization reaches a point where it believes its own survival to be threatened it will act to eradicate that threat. All TCs are ultimately dependent on the organization in which they are embedded. The organization can choose not to support the TC and withdraw resources and services, although more commonly, I suspect, the process is more subtle. The organization will decide that the TC no longer provides a service that is either required or compatible with the organization's view of the current 'landscape'. The result is a cessation or conversion of services, which means the TC withers or is eradicated.

The position of the TC is made easier in the long term if the TC staff team and residents are guided towards the realization that the relationship between themselves and the wider organization is a central issue in their day-to-day life. The focus needs to be on the legitimacy of the organizational partner's needs and the responsibility of the TC to act in accordance with these needs as appropriate. Like any other relationship in life the relationship with the wider organization will only change if the TC team change their behaviour towards their partner and accept their responsibility for their role in the relationship. TC staff teams and residents often expect that in some mysterious way the organization knows what a TC is about and that this learning has somehow taken place through organizational osmosis. Whilst the TC wants to maintain its confidentiality and the privacy of a 'safe space', it needs also to be open to scrutiny and inquisitiveness. In this process the TC team needs to be able to recognize its responsibility to provide knowledge about itself in a proactive way. It also has to realize that, because the people that constitute the organization change, it needs to repeat this as part of the relationship over time. Although this is a frustration it is necessary. I have lost count of how often I have inwardly thought 'Oh no, I've not got to explain this all over again. Don't they ever learn?' It is at this point that I recall the counsel of one of the first group therapists I worked with in a TC. Whilst complaining in frustration about the fact that people took so long to 'get it' he calmly said 'It's good practice for raising children. You just have to keep saying the same thing until they understand it'. I soon learnt that the same applies to organizations. Of course it helps if you can find new ways of saying it. It's more stimulating for everybody and more likely to find receptive ears.

The crucial point in this is that organizations do not exist as an entity in their own right. An organization is people fulfilling roles with a common aim. Of course those people bring with them their humanity and it is this that has to be remembered and related to. An individual carrying out their role, while requiring a tough line to be taken may have no relish for the task and be feeling very uncomfortable. In fact the individual may agree with the position of the other person (TC manager) but is constrained to carry out the demands of the role. Recognition of this and a response that signals this enables dialogue and action that avoids the worse excesses of the defence mechanisms used to keep personal distress at bay. Being able to hold the balance between professional role performance and the acknowledgement of the other's emotional needs is one of the priority skills of any TC manager.

In essence the containment of anxiety is related to the ability to build a relationship in which there is a mutual recognition of each party's needs, both as a person and as an authority carrier in the organization. In an atmosphere of mature adult exploration and enquiry ways can be found to deal with both sides' anxieties. The key is whether all the staff and managers involved can be guided to understanding that the relationship between them is no different from any other interpersonal relationship and requires the same sensitivity. In this sense it is crucial to ensure that the process is seen and understood as people interacting, not 'them or it out to get us, because they are ignorant, vengeful or jealous.'

One important mechanism to put in place to help contain the anxieties of both the TC managers and the organization managers is an independent group of advisors. By setting up such a group a third body enters into the dynamic as a referee. In all relationships, no matter how good, there are times of unreasonableness where one side's anxieties overrun their ability to enter into a mature exploration of reality. I know we all like to think that we are mature and adult but every so often the doors to what we have hidden away inside ourselves get opened by someone either accidentally or purposefully. It is in that moment we discover that someone else has a key as well as us. At those times we regress, we become defensive and prey to all the defence mechanisms that are known. When this happens there needs to be a body of people who are mutually recognized as being expert and experienced in the field who can provide an objective view or interpretation of what is going on. It is immensely comforting to have people to who you can go and ask 'Is it me or am I right about this?' For both parties to have access to this intervention means that consultation can take place and conversations outside of the immediate relationship between TC manager and organization can be had. Taking an outside view has often enabled me to return to a difficult series of discussions in which I have been able break the deadlock or repair the damage by returning to a reasonable stance. Sometimes a simple admission that it was me who had not understood why something was being proposed and the importance of it in a wider context has been enough to move the process on significantly. On the other hand I have on occasions been encouraged to stand firm in an argument having been independently reassured that I was not being unreasonable and that the principles for which I was arguing were necessary and legitimate.

One very important function of such a group is to provide a sense of continuity and support to new managers coming into the arena. Organizations churn their managers at quite a high rate, as do some TCs. Organizational managers coming across a TC for the first time are often ignorant about them and are generally interested both from a management and a personal point of view. For them to have a group to whom they can turn for clarification in the early stages is invaluable. They do not have to rely on the TC manager's word that everything is 'just brilliant' and that there 'are no problems at all'. They can check their feelings and observations out. Very often this provides the reassurance that although what they are seeing and hearing is different from what they usually experience it is healthy within the TC culture and should be seen as a sign of health. This function should not be under-rated. In the prison environment the snapshots that are often the first experiences for new organizational managers arouse huge anxieties as it is often very different from their previous experiences. *Residents*, a label that in itself grates against the terms 'prisoner' and 'inmate', are often observed leading activities, setting agendas, challenging staff and generally not appearing to be 'good inmates keeping a clean and tidy cell'. In this situation new managers will almost inevitably experience anxiety and scepticism. I am sure this experience exists in other contexts such as medical and educational settings. Having a sounding board to check these anxieties out is good for everyone. It also applies to new Directors of Therapy who inevitably come with their own views of what a TC should be. At times these can get in the way, especially if their previous experience was in a different environment, e.g. moving from the National Health Service to the Prison Service.

Making conscious the unconscious process

As managers, staff and residents we live and breathe the unconscious process; our struggle is to make it manifest and available for understanding. The literature describes work, Hinshelwood (1999) and Shur (1994), which looks at this aspect of organizational life. By its very nature even though we all know we are up to our necks in it all the time it is the most elusive aspect of TC work. Simultaneously being part of and yet observer of the process appears to confound us continually. The outcome of this is that we trip over it with regularity. The managers of TCs need to be always trying to find ways of making sure that someone attends to the processes involved. Delegating particular staff members to holding this role in situations such as meetings and planning sessions helps but the crucial factor is providing time for the process to be the focus of the work in hand. This is easy in the TC setting, it is our work, but it is not so easy when interacting with the organization. The more time I devote to trying to think of ways of doing this, the more I continue to return to the basic solution of providing time dedicated to the purpose, either with or without a facilitator from outside the team. Perhaps this particular 'basic' is at the core of the TC process for staff. The task for a TC manager is to try and encourage the same process to take place within the wider organization, however the organization needs to be able to engage in the process and for that it needs the language of the process.

Translating the TC tongue to the rest of the organization

This is a slow process and requires someone who can speak both languages to be able to interpret what is going on. The staff team of the TC, if they are making the effort to understand their relationship to the organization, will have access to the language that the organization is using. It is up to the TC team to explore how the TC process can best be explained in their particular context. There is a set of values that underpins the work of all TCs and it is necessary for staff teams to be clear about what those values are and whether they match those of the wider organization. Very often significant progress can be made when it is possible to find congruency between the values of the TC and the wider organization. In the prison situation, for example, the difference in values relating to respect and to responsibility are far less than would be expected. How those values get expressed is often more related to the organizational practicalities than the management's value systems. It is clearly difficult to provide the same levels of responsibility to a large prison population than a relatively small group within it.

Being in the right place to have the right conversations is critical. As a TC manager it is crucial that the voice of the TC is heard when discussions take place about service delivery and policy. The TC has a great deal to contribute to this process but the real opportunity is to be able to demonstrate that the things the TC talks about all the time have relevance to the wider organization. Good managers know that how people feel about things affects the outcome; what they sometimes do not know is the unconscious process that accompanies this. The TC manager has the chance to explore this with them and by doing so indirectly demonstrates how the TC operates.

The way the TC talks about itself and the literature that it produces needs to be thought about carefully, not just for the receiving audience but also for the organization. The host organization needs to be acknowledged for its contribution to the TC and in language that makes it plain that the TC views the organization as a partner. This acknowledgement helps foster symbiosis rather than a view that the TC is a grudging parasite that privately thinks the whole organization would be better off if it was run by the TC. This is where the chapter started: it is steady and continuous partnership between the TC and its host organization that needs to be sought and cultivated.

Conclusion

The experience of starting and maintaining a TC in a host organization, be it in a prison, a hospital or any other organization, requires vision and energy but above all it requires a long-term view. In this view must be a belief in the process of partnership and true symbiosis coupled with the resolve to apply the TC values to that relationship. It is crucial that the central tenets of democracy and the exploration of the process be the underlying foundation. The search and exploration of the process engenders new meaning. For the individual in a TC this means a change of life through the TC and in an organization it means mutual benefit through growth, enrichment and diversity.

References

Birtles, J., Newrith, C., Brown, I. *et al.* (2004) Leadership in a new therapeutic community: Learning to regulate the temperature. *Therapeutic Communities, 25*, 85–99.

Campling, P. (2004) A psychoanalytic understanding or what goes wrong: the importance of projection. In P. Campling, S. Davies and G. Farquharson (eds) *From Toxic Institutions to Therapeutic Environments*. London: Gaskell.

Genders, E. and Player, E. (1995) *Grendon: A Study of a Therapeutic Prison*. Oxford: Clarendon Press.

Hemmings, M. and Woodward, R. (2004) The new individual and the new Therapeutic Community: Some parallels. *Therapeutic Communities, 25*, 100–110.

Hinshelwood, R.D. (2001) *Thinking about Institutions*. London: Jessica Kingsley Publishers.

Johnson, S. (1999) *Who Stole my Cheese?* London: Vermilion.

Lundin, S., Paul, H. and Christensen, J. (2002) *Fish*. London: Coronet Books.

McKenzie, J. (1997) Glen Parva Therapeutic Community: An Obituary. *Prison Service Journal, 111*, p.26.

Peters, T. (1992) *Liberation Management*. London: Macmillan.

Rawlings, B. (1998) The therapeutic community in the prison: Problems in maintaining therapeutic integrity. *Therapeutic Communities, 19*, 281–294.

Shur, R. (1994) *Counter-transference Enactment*. New Jersey, London: Jason Aronson Inc, Northvale.

Chapter 18

Security and Dynamic Security in a Therapeutic Community Prison

Kevin Leggett and Brian Hirons

In this chapter, we discuss issues surrounding the management of security in a prison that operates a democratic therapeutic community (TC) regime throughout. The subject of security has attracted very little attention in the literature but is an essential component of prison operational procedure. This may not always be easy to achieve and we call upon our first-hand experience of work in security in a therapy setting to highlight the tensions that can exist, and be overcome, between the principles of therapy and the requirements of security.

On 1 April 1993 HM Prison Service for England and Wales became an executive agency of the Home Office. The Framework Document that accompanied the implementation of agency status outlined the Prison Service's Statement of Purpose (HM Prison Service 1993):

> Her Majesty's Prison Service serves the public by keeping in custody those committed by the courts.

> Our duty is to look after them with humanity and help them lead law-abiding and purposeful lives in custody and after release.

Grendon is a secure prison accommodating up to 235 category B and C prisoners. The vast majority of the population is category B. More than half of the population is serving a life sentence. TCs gained status as accredited regimes with the What Works in Prisons Unit (now NOMS) in March 2004 that have been proved to help reduce re-offending (Marshall 1997; Taylor 2000). However, such total regimes are always located within the wider prison context and are reliant on the support of the establishment and the way security is managed and carried out to function effectively.

The basic principles of the democratic TC allow the residents, through their agreed meeting and decision making structure, to influence and change the way in which they interact within set boundaries. In a prison environment, the areas over which the Community can have legitimate influence are significantly reduced because of security restraints, some of which are mandatory. Unless sensitively managed, this can lead to conflict between the TC and those responsible for maintaining security.

There are three main aspects to security within a prison setting: physical, procedural and dynamic.

Physical security includes all those elements of the built environment that are designed to manage movement and prevent escape (a perimeter wall or fence with razor wire, a secure entry point to the establishment, locks, gates and secure accommodation). Despite the fact that these may be seen to be oppressive and unduly restrictive to the Communities, they are generally accepted as being an inevitable part of security. All of the residents have been in other prisons prior to transfer into the TC and so tend to accept the physical security, though not unreservedly. Changes to the physical environment excite strong responses, often with the comment that Grendon is becoming just like any other prison.

In any establishment the maintenance of effective and consistent security procedures is a constant issue for managers. *Procedural security* consists of a wide range of measures aimed at ensuring control of the population, including searching, monitoring of phone calls, drug testing and control of all movements. All of these can be seen by prisoners as invasive procedures and are especially so within a TC, where efforts are made to foster respect and trust for all participants.

Dynamic security. Ian Dunbar, a former Director of Inmate Administration, coined the phrase *dynamic security* in 1985, in the wake of the prison riots and disturbances of the 1970s and 1980s. The phrase captured a practical way in which prisons could be managed safely as well as decently. Dynamic security, he argued, was found 'when relationship and individualism come together in planned (and purposeful) activity, whether in a high or low security setting, the result is a relaxed and better ordered prison'

(Dunbar 1985, p.35). The stress he made was on ensuring that staff and prisoners were treated as individuals; staff member–prisoner relationships were characterized by fairness and decency and that there was sufficient purposeful and meaningful activity to occupy prisoners, bounded by effective security. It is neither a procedure nor a physical restraint. Developed over the years, dynamic security is essentially a way of working that relies on the traditional strengths of prison staff: developing relationships with prisoners, keeping them occupied, establishing trust and effective communication and therefore 'knowing what is going on'.

Good relationships with prisoners will mean that prisoners talk to staff members. In the course of such exchanges information will be given and received. Prisoners will let staff know what is going on thereby contributing to good intelligence and effective decision making in responding to prisoner needs, as well as maintaining good order and discipline. Prisoners are less likely to be disruptive if they regard officers as fair, reasonable and trustworthy. At the same time staff members must maintain their authority and their difference. By becoming too close to prisoners, staff members may also become vulnerable to conditioning. They should be 'friendly but not friends' with prisoners. Given that the Prison Service expects staff to maintain good relationships with prisoners, it is important that managers make clear what they expect of staff in order to avoid good relationships spilling over into inappropriate relationships. When the relationship between prison officer and prisoner is well balanced, then staff members are able to glean information from prisoners that will indicate what has or is about to happen within the prison, thereby demonstrating that effective dynamic security is the most valuable and unobtrusive form of control.

The status quo: separation

In early 2001, when we arrived at Grendon Prison, we had a clear impression that many staff members and prisoners regarded the Communities as being part of but separate from the Prison Service. Indeed, the Prison Service was referred to locally as the system. Any person who talked about a security issue that was perceived to have a possible impact on the current work at Grendon was referred to as having 'his or her system head on'. Such language was often deliberately used by some staff members and residents to point out that the person making such comments did not really understand the work of a TC in a prison setting and that he or she should think again before doing anything that would endanger the therapeutic process. This, borne of an understandable fear that what was good for the Prison Service wasn't necessarily good for Grendon, helped to strengthen the view that

Grendon was so different that many security principles and procedures need not apply, indeed could damage therapy. The therapeutic argument against security was potent and persuasive, reinforced by some charismatic and influential managers within the Communities. In our view, however, it had a downside, for it led to staff becoming complacent about security procedures and conditioned some staff members into thinking that security was a lesser priority or indeed that therapy encompassed dynamic security. Security was seen by some as a threat to Grendon. There was a genuine belief that dynamic security was incredibly effective at Grendon and that this meant that procedural security, including searching, did not require the same degree of emphasis that it required in other category B prisons. But a subsequent event was to prove otherwise.

In September 2001, three prisoners escaped from Grendon sports field. The escape was traumatic, not least because of the loss of confidence it caused. Why had staff not known about this through their dynamic security? Why had staff not been tipped off that the escape was going to take place? Surely more people knew what was going on than those who had escaped? Within 18 hours of their escape, all three prisoners had been recaptured, mainly as a result of the Police acting on the intelligence received from the remaining prisoners at Grendon. Dynamic security had worked, but only after the event. The sports field was taken out of action until it could be made more secure. But there were more important issues to address. Dynamic security had failed.

Following this incident, we set about the difficult task of rebuilding the security framework in Grendon while at the same time ensuring that it was fully integrated within the therapeutic processes. This was not going to be an easy task. Over the years the relationship between security and therapy staff members had been damaged to the point where there was very little meaningful interaction between the two groups. Some of the staff members who had previously struggled with therapy had been conveniently moved to the Security department. This meant that security staff members were generally regarded as having little or no understanding of the work undertaken in the Communities. Prison managers had encouraged the creation of two separate groups, one that helped deliver therapy and the other that purported to maintain a secure environment in which therapy could safely flourish.

This split seemed to dominate almost every meeting. Whatever issues were being discussed, someone would raise a criticism of this or that security measure, thereby diverting discussion away from the matter at hand. It was clear that the prison, and indeed the TCs, could not function effectively or move on until this matter had been resolved.

Resolution begins with what is widely acknowledged by all staff members at Grendon: security and therapy are not irreconcilable. Indeed, the core business of therapy is better delivered within a safe and secure environment. Within TC groups, prisoners will need to feel safe enough so that they can share with their group details of their offending and also challenge the behaviour of other Community members. The latter type of behaviour could be seen by some as 'grassing'. Sometimes the subject of conversations relating to the offending behaviour of a Community member may be highly emotive, particularly if the crimes and feelings being discussed involve offences of a sexual nature. Divulging innermost feelings and detailed information about criminal activity can leave individuals feeling very vulnerable. They need to know that the therapeutic context and process is safe and that fellow Community members will support them during their therapy.

We were very much aware that in order to achieve an environment in which therapy and security could work together, some significant changes would have to be carefully managed. The existing security managers had become disillusioned and ineffective. Some had accepted the position that they could no longer influence the therapeutic environment and basically managed their function through correspondence. When they had challenged an issue, fellow staff members had responded by arguing that therapy was absolute and that security could be unnecessarily destructive. It appeared that they had accepted the position that security as practised in the Prison Service would have only a minor part to play within a therapeutic environment and would always occupy a separate box to therapy. In our view, the security function was conditioned and neutralized by the persuasive and constant objections to its work by influential staff members involved in delivering therapy. This left the security staff demoralized and very negative.

What was clear was that any changes to the work of the Security department, especially those involving interactions with the Communities, would have to be handled very carefully and sensitively. One of the first steps that had to be taken was to re-energize the security department by changing some of the staff members. Once the security staff members understood and agreed with what we were trying to achieve, the next step was to develop trust between the Security department and the TCs. This was made more difficult by the fact that as the Security department had not shared much information with the Communities and had worked in isolation in the past, there was a perception that security officers had become very secretive. Whenever actions by members of the Security department had been challenged, they had responded by explaining that security matters were not for open discussion. This also worked against the grain of the spirit of openness required in a therapeutic context.

Initiating change

In order to have effective dynamic security, the Security department needs to have information to evaluate and process as intelligence. The Security department at Grendon had been starved of information because of the lack of trust and understanding that existed between it and the Communities. It was clear that this issue needed to be addressed as a matter of urgency. The Security department needed to be seen as part of the TC and the Communities needed to extend their therapeutic boundaries beyond the physical limits of the Wing. Each Community was assigned a security liaison officer (SLO) who was a member of staff from the Security department. The main purpose of the SLO was to help to develop effective relationships between the two functions, to improve communications. Staff members of the Communities had been hurt by the escape. Their trust in individuals had been damaged. Dynamic security, in which so much faith had been placed, had failed. Not only were the Communities starving the Security department of relevant information, but also the Security department was not routinely giving feedback on intelligence. This had rendered the exchange of information minimal and ineffective. It was by improving the exchange of information, or 'intelligence cycle' as we call it, that would lead to a much more effective process of 'working together', the latter motto having been coined by the new Governor and new Director of Therapeutic Communities, who together demonstrated the new spirit of cooperation.

As a result of the Security Liaison Officers working with the Communities and the Security department beginning to share its intelligence, the number of Security Information Reports (SIRs) received by them more than doubled in the first year. Figure 18.1 shows this change.

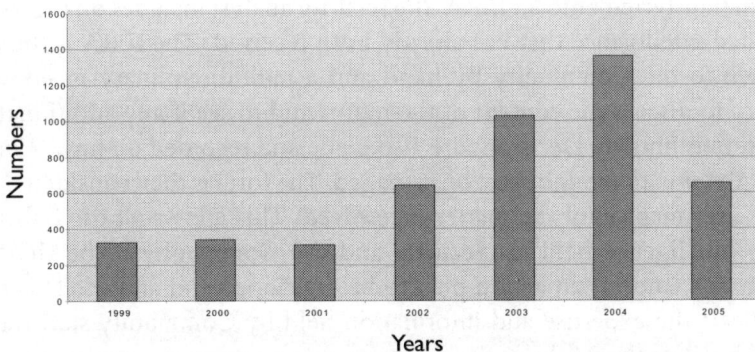

Figure 18.1 Number of SIRs from 1999 to June 2005.

From separation to co-operation

Although this could be seen as a significant improvement in relations, the level of trust remained delicate. The extension of the Community boundaries to include Security was being judged on a day-by-day basis. But the relationship between the Communities and Security became more trusting and there was a noticeable increase in the quantity and quality of information that staff were prepared to divulge and share with the Security department. One report contained information from a member of staff that during a therapy group a resident had divulged that he was having sexual fantasies about raping a female member of staff. The Community felt that they could contain and work with this individual. But the Security department needed further information if it was to be reassured. What if he should act out his fantasies? Clearly, the Governor has responsibility for the safety of his staff. And yet by informing staff members about his fantasies the prisoner was also acknowledging issues that could be dealt with in therapy. In any other establishment the prisoner would have been segregated from the general population and transferred to another establishment as soon as possible. Indeed, there has always been an operational override at Grendon whereby the Governor can transfer a prisoner if he is of sufficient concern, even if the therapeutic managers feel that he should remain. But this option is rarely used. Rather, the way ahead for all concerned is best established through a meaningful dialogue between those involved and those responsible for security. In order to do this, we developed the Intelligence-led Risk Assessment (ILRA).

The ILRA is raised by the Security department following the receipt of a SIR that identifies an issue that could present a significant risk to the security of the establishment or to an individual or group. The related SIR is normally submitted by an individual and contains perhaps only a small piece of what could become a bigger picture, as yet unknown. Once this information has been transferred onto an ILRA, the security analyst includes on the form any related intelligence that has already been received. The ILRA is then taken down to the Community by hand and a multidisciplinary meeting takes place to discuss the content of the report and to see if any additional information is known. Decisions are also made and recorded on how Wing staff feel the situation might best be managed. The form is then considered to be a live document until the matter is resolved. This allows all the information and intelligence held by Security and the Community to be shared and recorded, and for an action plan to be developed and agreed. This process respects the expertise and information held by Community staff members and involves them fully in the risk management process, a process that would have previously been solely managed by security without the help of Wing staff.

The use of the ILRAs at Grendon has been a significant tool in developing trust between departments and creating a better mutual understanding. Since its introduction in 2003, 99 have been completed. Figure 18.2 shows the changes.

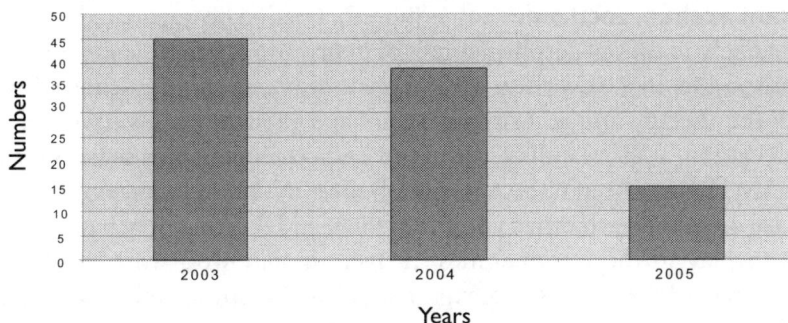

Figure 18.2 *Number of ILRAs from 2003 to June 2005.*

Restructuring communications

Prisons tend to be very much operationally focused at senior management level and this was no exception at Grendon. Some of the senior managers had been promoted *in situ* and so had a detailed understanding of the work undertaken within the Communities. But the rest had been transferred in from other establishments. Senior Management Team meetings tended to focus on operational elements and themes rather than on therapy issues, the latter being discussed at a senior level by a meeting chaired by the then Director of Therapy. In effect, these two separate meetings, chaired by the Governor and the other by the Director of Therapy, perpetuated old divisions and hindered working together. As a result of restructuring the senior meetings in the prison, the Governor and new Director of Therapeutic Communities agreed that the Governor would chair the Operational Policy and Therapy Policy Meetings. Senior operational managers and therapists attended both meetings. Operational matters that had an impact on therapy were now discussed by all representatives. Therapy and security were therefore considered as joint issues rather than as two separate and competing functions within the prison.

Conclusion

In order for TCs to operate effectively and to flourish, members must feel safe and able to disclose all aspects of their offending behaviour without fear of retribution in the form of bullying, intimidation or physical violence. Sparks *et al.* (1996) essentially argue that prisons can only be governed by the consent of the governed: the prisoner group. Consent tended to follow, they found, when staff–prisoner relationships were characterized by fairness, due process and justice. When this characterized the daily interactions of a prison, good order, something that had to be negotiated daily, was more likely to follow despite degrees of deprivation and difficulty inevitable in prison life. In a TC prison environment, this can only be achieved when both the therapy and security managers and their functions have a shared appreciation, understanding, trust and respect, interacting sensitively and effectively. They need to be open and honest in their relationship, prepared to take on board each other's points of view and feel that they have an equal part to play in the Communities. In fact all staff who work in Grendon should regard themselves as being involved in therapy as well as feeling part of the wider community that is Grendon Prison.

During 2004, Her Majesty's Chief Inspector of Prisons conducted a full announced inspection of Grendon Prison. The subsequent report made the following comments with regard to the relationship that they found existed between therapy and security (HMCIP 2004):

> In particular, there has always been an inherent tension between security and therapy and three escapes in 2001 required a re-balancing towards the former. This inspection provides ample evidence that the balance has been achieved and that Grendon has an important contribution to make. (p.3)

> Prisoners were also impressively open with staff about potential security and control problems. Grendon epitomized what could be achieved in terms of dynamic security: that is, security based on intelligence and communication. (p.4)

We do not believe that a utopia has been created at Grendon. Issues still arise in which security and therapy experience friction. But issues are discussed openly and sensitively. People try to understand each other's positions. We believe that we have come a long way. Both sides now value each other's input into the work at Grendon Prison and realize that they could not work effectively without each other. Security and therapy are not bound up in inevitable, perpetual and negative conflict. Indeed, their working together will secure Grendon's future and its continued effectiveness in changing lives.

References

Dunbar, I. (1985) *A Sense of Direction.* London: HMSO.

HM Prison Service (1993) *National Framework for the Throughcare of Offenders in Custody to the Completion of Supervision in the Community.* London: Home Office Publications.

HMCIP (2004) *Report on a Full Announced Inspection of HM Prison Grendon 1–5 March 2004.* London: Her Majesty's Chief Inspector of Prisons.

Marshall, P. (1997) *A Reconviction Study of HMP Grendon Therapeutic Community.* London: Research Findings 53, Home Office Research Development and Statistics Directorate.

Sparks, R., Bottoms, A. and Hay, W. (1996) *Prisons and the Problem of Order.* Oxford: Clarendon Studies in Criminology.

Taylor, R. (2000) *A Seven Year Reconviction Study of Grendon Therapeutic Community.* London: Research Findings, Home Office Research Development and Statistics Directorate.

Audit and Experience

Chapter 19

Therapy from the Inside:
Experiences from Therapy

Men and women users'
experiences of therapy

The following four accounts, two from women and two from men, who have been through therapy in therapeutic communities (TCs) in prison are included to enable them to give an account of therapy in their own words. These are broadly positive, albeit difficult and emotionally painful experiences of therapy told with a powerful honesty and an incisive depth of insight. Doubtless there are other accounts that could be given. There are men and women I have worked with who feel therapy has not helped and it has been hard to see what benefit they may have gained or whether they may have reduced their risk of re-offending by trying it. Negative views undoubtedly exist and there should be no pretence that experience in a TC is helpful to everyone. Such accounts are not represented here as the book intends to highlight those areas in which therapy might work or be useful in changing men's and women's lives and behaviour, and to articulate what it is that might make this happen. The accounts included in this chapter have been chosen because the writers have had sufficient time in therapy both to understand the process and to be able to articulate it in a way that might be of use to others considering whether or not to spend time in a TC. One thing standing out in the women's accounts is that the TC experience was only part of a broader spectrum of collected inputs that helped and time in individual therapy in one account and dealing more specifically with drug-related issues in the other also played an important part in the change process.

These accounts are written in such a way that they retain the confidentiality of the writer while keeping the essence of what each author wanted to say. Each section is published here with her and his written consent to do so.

Michael Parker

Jane: My time in the Women's Therapeutic Community

I thought I'd get a Drug Treatment Order but I felt my sentence was too harsh at five-and-a-half years. Although I knew deep down that my crimes warranted a custodial sentence. I arrived at HMP Holloway a mere six-and-a-half stone. I was mentally and physically beaten by my unhappy life and addiction. For many years I'd had psychiatric problems and had committed different levels of crime from the age of 14, leading up to my last offence of drug supply, aggravated burglary and theft. I had been to prison before in 1983 for a mere three months, not long enough for me to sort myself out. I had a settled period from 1994 when I had my son but in 2000 my marriage deteriorated and my life went totally out of control. It was the lowest point in my life.

I was now on the De-tox Wing at Holloway and in three weeks I was clear but I had deep down issues I knew I still had to sort out. Being in prison gave me time for thought and think is what I did. In fact I nearly drove myself insane with my thoughts of what had become of me. I was quickly transferred to HMP Winchester and within two days I was told of the TC by my psychiatrist. He recommended that I should seriously think about doing it. I was very unbalanced and on a lot of medication for personality disorder. I'd been on this medication for what seemed like all my life. I went back to my cell to read up as much information as possible about the TC and decided that there was no harm in trying and that it would be wise to do something constructive with my sentence. I was interviewed by staff on the TC and within weeks I was on it. It was Friday afternoon and I would be starting groups on Monday morning so I had the whole weekend to think about it.

The TC had groups every day, 'group therapy', where we would open up about everything in our lives, whether it be abuse, violence, neglect, all sorts of issues that people had. For me I had loads of issues, I'd come from a middle class background. My mother was a single parent of four children. I had been abused by two of her partners. I lived a fantasy life where my dad was concerned; he had died when I was five and I found out about this when I was 14 and went to his grave for the first time when I was 17. I had my own fantasy dad who was in fact just a friend.

I'd done poorly at school and was made subject to a care order at 13-and-a-half and got married at 19; this didn't last very long. Along with this I'd been on serious antidepressants and tranquillizers since I was 15. I'd tried desperately several times to take my own life and had been repeatedly sectioned under the Mental Health Act. I had also attended a TC, which I was meant to stay in for a minimum of a year, but at 17 I was more interested in boys and partying. I only stayed for a few weeks and then ran away.

Now I was hoping that maybe this time I would learn something about myself. Monday morning came and I was a bit nervous, didn't know what to talk about. My group had two other girls in it, both were lifers, and together we began to trust each other. We were all on the same landing and we were encouraged to support each other through difficult times. I found the first few group sessions a bit awkward as no-one would open up and I hated the long silences. Eventually I started to talk and open up. I found it hard to break down my barriers but I took a risk and trusted that my group would appreciate the confidentiality policy of the TC that anything said in the group would stay there. I got good support from my peers and the staff and in turn we all opened up slowly. It did become intense and very challenging and I got challenged about my lifestyle and behaviour regularly. I found this very annoying and would often become aggressive. The truth hurts.

I can only say that in my time on the TC the staff and my peers helped me deal with my pain and the torment of my life. They made me realize that such an unhappy childhood had consequences, which was my behaviour. My ongoing angry behaviour towards society and people stemmed from my abuse and I slowly realized where I was going wrong. I became a lot more tolerant but also assertive. I cried more tears than I can remember on those group sessions and I ran out of groups many times too because I found it hard to face up to facts, but I stayed with it. No pain, no gain. My time was in the very early stages of the TC and it hadn't quite established itself but I stuck with it and I can honestly say TC gave me an insight into how I could change my life around. We moved to another prison, HMP Send, and there were many problems with staff shortages and rooms for our groups, but slowly they were sorted out.

I'd been on the TC for five months. My medication had been reduced greatly for the first time in 24 years and I'd now decided to come off it all. After all, TC is an alternative to medication. In the five months I'd opened up to just about everything in my life, I felt depressed and sorry for myself at times, and lonely and scared but I stuck with it. Before TC I had huge resentments towards almost everyone. I hated men as I had been abused. I hated my mum because I was born illegitimate. I couldn't form any sort of healthy relationship. I needed to do something with these problems. TC helped me overcome my grief, my anger and most of all my behaviour.

I'd one last hurdle to overcome, my addiction to drugs, not only pre-scribed drugs but class A heroin and crack. After five months on the TC I decided I needed to deal with this and opted to come off the TC and do Rehabilitation of Addicted Prisoners Trust (RAPt), which was also in Send. TC gave me support in this and I was adamant. TC gave me the confidence to open up about my past and with the contribution of the two, TC and RAPt, I worked hard on my behaviour and my addiction and have since graduated from RAPt. I've been off my medication now for nine months and go out into the community three days a week, working in a charity shop. I do com-munity work in the nearby schools talking to 14- and 15-year-olds, hoping to give them an insight into how life can turn out and maybe act as a kind of deterrent, someone from prison who knows what it's like there. I hope I give a little inspiration to our younger generation and also to my peers who are still struggling with life. I am a peer supporter for RAPt helping others in their recovery and I'm extremely happy now even though this is odd since I'm in prison. I also have a more loving relationship with my family, my son and go out on town visits once a month. Today I live life on life's terms and I feel better about myself as I know I have a better future. TC helped me through my torments; RAPt helped me through my addiction. They both helped me with my behaviour. I'm forever grateful for TC for giving me that stepping stone to a better future.

Anne: Joining the Women's Therapeutic Community

My life was on a downward spiral, my marriage of nine years had broken down in which I suffered a lot of mental abuse. I'd lost all my self-esteem, my confidence and my self-worth. I didn't know where I belonged, who I was and what I wanted out of life.

I started going out drinking a lot and meeting people, trying to fit in somewhere. Sadly, the friends I did make were all into drugs and then, being a person who was easily influenced, I fell into the trap and my life became out of control and I ended up coming to prison with a very long sentence to get through. Prison gave me a chance to reflect on my life, what I'd gone through as a child, my relationships, my behaviour and why I put myself in destruct mode. I knew I had to do something and I needed help to do it but where do I go and who can I talk to was the big question.

I enquired about one-to-one counselling but then the chance came along to join the first ever women's TC to be set up in a prison environment. I thought about it long and hard and decided that this was my one and only chance to find myself again, so I signed up. A few of the women I'd made friends with said that I must be mad and that the TC was for 'nuts' as they called them and turned it into a big joke but I put that down to them not understanding what the TC was about and also to a fear of it. I didn't listen to the things they were saying and for the first time I stuck to my decision and started going to meetings and I haven't looked back.

Being one of the first people in the group wasn't easy as it was new to all of us including the group therapist. It was a learning process for everyone, learning how to trust other group members, learning how to open up and talk and face our fears. At first I had big doubts as to whether the TC would actually help as I didn't appear to be getting anywhere but I stuck with it anyway. After several months I sat down and started thinking about the things I spoke about and what I had learned about them. Suddenly I realized I understood why certain things happened to me, I also recognized the patterns my life was following and I knew I had to change my way of thinking, how I felt about myself and that the choices I made in my life are my decisions not everyone else's.

Not all of it was that easy though and about six to seven months into my therapy I felt it was time to face the one thing I'd never spoken about even though I'd tried as a child and was ignored. This was when I nearly gave up the whole therapy thing as it was the hardest thing I had ever done; it brought back all the memories, the hurt, the hatred, the anger and the fear. It felt almost as if I were going through it all over again. This affected me so badly that I couldn't sleep, I couldn't speak to anyone and I even stopped going to therapy groups. The longer this went on the more angry I got, not only about what had happened to me but with myself for feeling the way I did and allowing it to take me over like it had before. So I decided that the TC was not the place for me to deal with this issue but I knew I had to deal with it. I went back to the group and continued my therapy but concentrated on all the other problems in my life.

When I finished my therapy I went to one-to-one counselling to deal with the one thing I ran away from. This did help as I have now let go of the anger and fear and the control it had over my life but the one thing I am still unable to let go of is the hatred. I don't know if I ever will be able to but I know it doesn't rule my life as it did before.

There were a lot of ups and downs in the TC and disruption with it being a new venture and trying to establish itself but the worst part of all was when, ten months into it, the prison we were in was closed as a women's prison and we all had to move to another prison and practically start all over again. This caused a lot of anxiety and stress and this affected a lot of the women, me included. On reaching the new prison it was apparent that nothing was ready for us and we had to start things up all over again. This situation, along with other things, made some of the women leave the Community but I continued as I was so close to completing my therapy.

It is now 18 months since I completed the TC therapy and I have never regretted it. A lot of the things I learned about my life in the groups I can't put into practice until I leave prison but my confidence and self-worth just keeps growing and now I can say I like myself.

Stanley: Therapy in Grendon

I am 50 years old. Prison is familiar. So far in my life I've been sentenced to 21 years and served 12, almost four on this sentence.

I rape women. Five years ago I followed a young woman into an alley and terrified her with a knife. When she was willing to do anything to live I raped her. The next morning I ate breakfast with my wife and children. They may have thought I looked a bit uptight but almost nothing showed.

I'm intelligent. When I offended I lived in a world of intellect and did not acknowledge the mass of difficult feelings inside me. I used my intellect to distance myself from my reality.

There had been two strong and very twisted influences in my life as I grew up. The first was racism. I was brought up as a privileged white in South Africa and Zimbabwe. I was brought up to believe that anyone who was not white was almost not human. It may have felt like a strong position to be in, especially as my race had the power to enforce that 'reality', but what we did not see was how we, and I, became dehumanized by the racist system. The second influence was an overwhelmingly powerful father. He rose to great heights commercially and financially but the reality at home was a very different matter.

One of the first revelations I got in therapy was realizing that as a six-year-old I had witnessed him raping my then 12-year-old sister. In fact my father was a long-term paedophile offender, a man who battered his wife, my mother, who bullied and beat me and seemed to abuse everyone he came into contact with. He damaged us all deeply and I now see we were all affected in different ways. My particular type of damage was he would attack me physically along with verbal tirades for some 'wrong doing' of mine, say leaving my geography book on the lawn. The purpose of these attacks was to get me to leave the house, to upset my mother so she would retire into the gin bottle and so to be able to rape my sister without hindrance. I have learnt this in therapy. I have also learnt how this impacted on me, leading to a self-belief that I was 'bad', the cause of things, and many other confusions about myself. I arrived here with some knowledge of who I was but with a very sketchy idea of how I got to be that person. My sister did not survive our upbringing, she committed suicide. I survived by taking much of my father into me.

In here I have had to face myself, my terror of being vulnerable, and how hard I had become, how difficult I was with others, and how many of my reactions were automatic and really not in my control. This showed in my negative reactions to people and things I did not like, or could not control. In the past I would have accepted these reactions and seen them as the faults of others, or the faults of the system. Here these reactions were immediately seen and questioned. Soon after my arrival on the Wing I found someone to focus all my negative emotions on, a fellow inmate, Joe. I saw him as a total hypocrite, arrogant, thoughtless and self-seeking. I seethed and created a lot of conflict with Joe, then a member of staff asked: 'Why do you give Joe so much power? Why do you let him dictate your feelings?' I had a choice, to look at Joe or to look at myself. When I did I found Joe deeply reminded me of my father's hypocrisy and I stopped hating Joe and began to see a pattern of how I found Joes all my life and focused parts of my anger on them and had never addressed the original cause, my father. I could then begin to unravel other patterns, seeing how I'd created victims because of my child-hood feelings. I have begun the process of facing my offences and of seeing how these came out of my anger at my mother and becoming like my father.

The structures here of small groups of eight people, and living in a linked community of 40 means many of my behaviours are challenged and each time I have the choice of looking at others or me. It's not perfect. Some-times I'm playing the role of Joe for others and so the challenges are more attack and not to do with me but it all has lessons. I have also learnt how powerless I have been over how I protected my vulnerability. I deeply wanted to 'tell' my story, to be believed as to how bad it had been, but was terrified I'd not be believed. The small groups and psychodrama gave me a place to tell, and to learn how to tell my story piecemeal and learn that I survived each journey into vulnerability.

There is also the feeling of shame I feel for the crimes I've committed and the selfish life I've lived. This had given me a black and white outlook. Either I was totally accepted (or loved) or totally rejected. Living as part of a com-munity of other difficult people I've learnt to accept differences. That I can argue, disagree with and even dislike individuals but maintain working rela-tions with them and learn from them, I've entered the world of shades of grey. This is totally reliant on this being a TC with a structure that encour-aged challenge and demands communication. I've lived as part of many prison communities, all normal wings are communities but they are structured to make it difficult to be vulnerable or share honestly.

The Community and prison are far from perfect. I think the massive overreaction in Grendon by security in the last few years has damaged therapy but I also see that therapy is in a constant state of flux, and there must be grist for the mill. When it gets chaotic, when others can't stand me and I them, that's when I find more pearls of wisdom about who I am and how I impact on others.

Changing my ways: Jeremy

I am a young man with a lot to learn. I still find maturity a difficult process but I am slowly learning.

I've spent nine years of my adulthood life in prison. My offending started when I was just 15. Since then I have committed numerous sexual offences, including attempted rape, buggery, indecent assault and numerous other offences that were not of a sexual nature.

I myself was brought up in a very abusive and dysfunctional household, with a father who treated me like his personal punch bag. I was the only one treated like this, even though I have two brothers and three sisters. I could only find love and care from my elder sister in the form of having a sexual relationship with her.

I have treated so many people distastefully, preying on vulnerable women, boys and very young children: girls as young as six. I've always been a predator and a parasite, getting what I want, at the cost of victims, no matter what, or matter who.

I've lost my own children, leaving them with some of the damage that I felt as a child, not knowing who their father is, or why he sexually abused children the same age as them. In my time in prison I have never taken full responsibility for what I have done, or even thought about the pain I caused. However, since I came to prison on this sentence, I have undertaken all avenues of addressing my offending behaviour and gaining victim empathy for the people I have hurt.

I came into a TC not knowing what it was about, or knowing if I really wanted to change. But since doing the work I've done in this TC I've changed in ways I never believed possible. Our Community on this TC wing is made up of 40 members, ranging from men in their early 20s through to men as old as late 60s. There are five small groups, each consisting of eight Community members and one facilitator. We have three small group sessions per week and two full Community meetings per week, where the whole Community get together to speak about any aspects of concern. Also we have an art therapy session once a week and a psycho drama session once a week.

The work we do here is very hard and covers a wide range of emotions and feelings. We start dealing with each difficulty by trying to gain an understanding of where it developed. In the case of my sexual offending, I've spoken about how I got love, care and attention as a child. Through this I've found that the links are a learnt response, like getting love, care and attention from being sexually abused, and not seeing sex for what it is, or what it really means, but abusing it to meet all my needs in day-to-day life.

Each of us challenges one another in the groups, about the way we feel, encouraging each other to feel the feelings, rather than acting on them. We challenge thought patterns and behaviours, finding ways to help each other put in place coping strategies to stop offending down to even telling jokes that can be deemed as inappropriate. We also challenge each other about how we interact with each other. Also our thoughts, feelings, beliefs, fantasies, addictions, behaviours, cognitive distortions, decision making and all aspects of our day-to-day lives and are open to challenge.

The group of men on my group have helped me talk about the difficulties in my life, and find different skills that help me respond to things with a different attitude, helping me come to terms with my own abuse, and understanding the impact that I have forced on others.

Being able to talk about the most horrible things I have done, and suffered from has given me the chance to change my views, feelings, thoughts and behaviours. I have talked about all my fantasies, including sexual, allowing me to gain knowledge of the feelings, leading to thoughts. I have found that in my life I was very insecure and lonely, not ever speaking out but always making a noise so as to be heard or hurting people to make them feel the way I did, to make me feel that I am no different, because if they feel the same way then it helped me believe that I was not alone. How wrong could I get?

I've found that understanding the process to my offending can start from a small insignificant thing I have made out to be worse. Not telling anyone and then blaming others for the way I feel, led on to me wanting to have sex as a way of feeling better, even if that meant offending. Now I understand this pattern and can change it. The group of men on my small group and the whole Community help and support me, giving me guidance and help me to find ways to change the process.

I strongly believe that the time I've been in a TC unit, I've become a better man, a man who feels real-life emotions and a sense of humanity. I have been able to develop new skills and I can now care for others. I can also get the care and support without sex or offending. This may seem normal for you. For myself, making the changes I have, it is a real achievement. For the first time in my life I like me. I am disgusted at my offending. But I now like who I am and what I am doing to change.

I have now been in a TC for over three years. I feel a better man knowing that I am changing my thoughts and beliefs, which in turn has helped me to change my behaviours. I strongly believe that TC units, such as this, have given me the chance to change. I feel that anything I can do to stop preying on children and young vulnerable adults, is the right thing. As hard as it can get, my desire to change is very high, and I will succeed.

I believe TC units help people like me to change, instead of being a predatory paedophile and risk to the public. TC units will help others to change, but only if they want to change their ways, as I have done.

Chapter 20

Auditing of Prison Service Accredited Interventions

Danny Clark and Jan Lees

Why audit?

The auditing of interventions in the Prison Service is inextricably linked with the accreditation of programmes, which was instigated in the mid 1990s. The process of accreditation was initially concerned with ensuring that programmes were designed in line with the findings from the body of international research known as 'What works', so that they had the best chance of reducing rates of reconviction. In order to achieve this, a panel of experts was established to define a series of accreditation criteria for programme design, which identified a number of key principles in working with offenders to reduce the likelihood of reconviction. The panel then judged a programme's fitness for purpose against these criteria. The accreditation process was later extended to Probation interventions and the expert panel eventually became the Correctional Services Accreditation Panel (CSAP).

From the beginning it was clear that 'effective delivery' was as important as effective design in ensuring that interventions work. There are many examples in the research literature of well-designed interventions not producing the expected gains because of implementation failure (Quay 1987; Lipsey 1992; Debidin and Lovbakke 2005). It was clear that the panel members would need to accredit delivery as well as design. At the first meeting of the joint prison/probation panel in 1999, a working party was established to look at how this might be done in relation to TCs. Most interventions accredited at that time consisted of structured cognitive-behavioural group work. Accreditation of programme delivery for this type of intervention had two stages. An audit inspection was made at each site to check whether the basic requirements to support the programmes were in place, for example, a sufficient number of trained tutors, who were properly supervised, and that the appropriate resources are available. Auditors checked the targeting and selection of offenders and through-care arrangements for programme graduates. Each programme was also audited by experienced staff through a process of video monitoring. This meant that all the group sessions were filmed using a strategically placed video camera focused on the tutors, and a random selection of these videos was assessed by the audit team. The criteria on which the video assessments were made varied depending on the nature of the programme, but basically the assessments were concerned with the concepts of 'treatment integrity' and 'responsivity'.

Treatment integrity here is defined simply as delivering the sessions in the way it was intended, not making drastic changes or missing parts out. Hollin (1996) points out that treatment integrity applies equally to all interventions whatever their theoretical base, method of working, or client base. He suggests that the best way to reduce the threats to treatment integrity is to devise a means of monitoring and measuring programmes' integrity so that one is aware of what is happening and able to take corrective action. This is one of the major elements of the prison audit.

Hollin (1996) describes three potential threats to programme integrity.

1.   *Programme drift,* which occurs where those involved lose sight of aims and objectives of the intervention and there is a gradual shift in emphasis over time. An example encountered by one of the authors was a prison programme that originally focused on reducing re-offending in violent offenders, but which subtly evolved into a cathartic means of resolving staff and prisoner conflict. The sessions probably still had value to participants but they were no longer focused on the original long-term goal.

2.   *Programme reversal* describes the managers, therapy staff or other groups acting in ways that undermine the agreed approach. An obvious example would be facilitators modelling inappropriate behaviour during sessions, for example, by manipulating or failing to respect clients.

3.   *Programme non-compliance* is when practitioners deliberately elect for reasons of their own to omit or change parts of the programme or make improvements and introduce new methods.

> This can result in something only faintly related to what was originally to be delivered, especially if the programme has been handed down through several generations.

Responsivity means delivering the material in a way that takes account of the learning styles and diversity of the participants. For example, offenders usually have an active learning style and a fairly short attention span, which is generally catered for in programme design. However, responsivity also means being aware of the individual characteristics of members of the group and providing an experience that is meaningful to them. Andrews and Bonta (2003) describe responsivity as an essential characteristic of effective interventions. These two concepts – integrity and responsivity – can be seen as antagonistic, and are sometimes considered the opposite end of the same dimension. But an alternative view is that they are orthogonal dimensions and the delivery of any intervention can be rated on both of these.

The problem in developing an audit process for TCs was how does one capture these elements with this type of intervention?

The Prison Service Audit applied to TCs within prison establishments

The Prison Service Audit is split into four sections. In order to reach accreditation standards a TC must score more than 60 per cent on each of the sections. The sections are:

1. Institutional support

2. Treatment management and integrity

3. Continuity and resettlement

4. Quality of delivery.

The four sections are the same for all programme audits whatever the theoretical model and mode of delivery.

The *Institutional support* section deals with the level of support for the treatment ethos within the prison establishment. It sets out what is required of the senior managers in order to fully implement the programme, for example, ensuring the necessary resources are available, providing sufficient staffing levels, and making sure staff are properly supported. It seeks evidence to gauge how well the Unit is led and supported by senior managers. It monitors the ways the prison supports the treatment through making prisoners available and how the competing demands of the organization, which might disrupt therapy, are resolved. Most of the criteria in this section are the same for any type of treatment. However, one area, which is more important for the management of a democratic TC than for other types of programmes, is the degree to which maintaining security and other prison rules and conventions impinge on the day-to-day life of the TC. An important part of the therapy is the way the TC manages itself. In prison, this self-management is bound to be compromised to some extent. Managers and institutions can be sympathetic to the TC ethos to a greater or lesser extent.

The *Treatment management* section deals with the way in which the Unit management ensures that the correct treatment is provided in a competent manner to the right offenders. It encompasses staff selection, competency, training and supervision procedures, and how well these are monitored. How offenders are selected for treatment, and how their progress is assessed and recorded during treatment, is audited. For example, the auditors will look for evidence that the six-monthly assessment reports are kept up to date, and that any psychometric measures, which are used as an intermediate measure of treatment outcome, are administered on a regular basis. Here the emphasis is on process rather than outcome: are the measures made and records kept rather than the level of improvement observed? The section is also concerned with the ways in which threats to treatment integrity are managed. Are there sanctions for excluding offenders who are disrupting the treatment of others and are these operated in a consistent way? For TCs, one specific topic covered in this section is whether Community staff and residents are aware of the types of manipulative, threatening and deceitful behaviour often expressed by prisoners suffering from psychopathic personality disorder. There is a growing body of evidence that psychopathic offenders are less likely to benefit from therapy (Harris *et al.* 1994; Hare *et al.* 2000; Hobson *et al.* 2000) and that they can be extremely disruptive to the culture of the TC. The audit asks specifically how, when individuals with high levels of psychopathic traits are accepted into the Community, staff members recognize them and what steps are put in place to ensure effective monitoring and management.

The third section, *Continuity and resettlement*, examines how offenders can best be supported during and after treatment, so that the treatment gains made are most likely to be reinforced and maintained. This might involve providing links to the community and assistance in making plans for release from prison, or arrangements for follow-up treatments in prison. For TCs, the latter is more likely than the former, given that few residents are likely to be released directly from prison TCs, which are mainly found in the more secure prisons. The TC milieu, though, is different to the more usual structured programme and does require different measures. Residents leaving a TC do so on an individual basis, having spent varying amounts of time in therapy. There is a longer period of withdrawal from therapy and the offender will probably be transferring to another prison as well as moving on in treatment. The whole process of leaving is much more complex and requires more planning, which is reflected in the audit. This section deals with the integration of treatments. It also considers the links between the TC and any complimentary activities available to residents, which may include additional offending behaviour programmes.

The final section of the audit document relates to the *Quality of delivery*. It is concerned with how the treatment is working in practice. For accredited interventions, this means first that the treatment is being delivered as intended – i.e. the TC is operating in ways that are consistent with standard TC principles and practice, and that this can be evidenced in clear, valid and reliable ways – this part of the audit has been addressed in a very specific way, and is described later in the section on the Community of Communities audit process.

Secondly, the treatment means that there is evidence from a range of intermediate measures that offenders are benefiting from it in a way that will reduce their risk of re-offending (i.e. there are significant improvements in specific skills such as problem solving, emotional management and assertiveness). Applying this section of the audit to TCs was the most problematic because democratic TCs do not work on the basis that one identifies specific criminogenic needs and then designs a series of learning experiences to address them. Many of what might be said to be traditional TC 'treatment aims', such as increased self-esteem and social awareness, are not seen as criminogenic needs, in terms of the widely accepted definition that there is a clear link between the need and re-offending, and evidence that reducing the need impacts directly on the likelihood of recidivism (Andrews and Bonta 2003). Certainly, TCs do reduce risk and address criminogenic needs, but this is usually achieved as part of a wider process of change. Nor can one reasonably video, monitor or sample a treatment process that continues 24 hours a day in many different settings.

In order to develop this element of the audit, it was necessary to go back to the model of change proposed to the accreditation panel when TCs were first accredited and, working from this, define what one would expect to observe in a prison-based democratic TC that was successfully addressing risk factors associated with re-offending. The model of change, as described by Shine and Morris (1999), confirms that the key criminogenic targets addressed are personality disorder and antisocial personality. They state that

> the TC specifically challenges antisocial attitudes, values and beliefs; it specifically sets up an anticriminal culture in which residents associate; it explores and challenges the antisocial history; and explores in detail the

> problems of the family of origin … at the same time at another level, the internalization of new appropriate social models and experiences lead to the structural change of personality, diminishing the temperamental and personality factors that are conducive to criminal behaviour.

Shine and Morris (1999, p.17) add that in a TC 'pathological behaviour is a constant subject for discussion. Antisocial behaviour is repeatedly raised. Conscious management of behaviour is encouraged. Destructive behaviour is challenged by social sanctions. Creative and positive social and interpersonal behaviour is reinforced'. Genders and Player (1995) noted that the Grendon TC regime incorporates a strong behavioural element whereby an individual's actions are examined with surgical precision and commented on by the whole Community. It entails the detailed and comprehensive assessment and analysis of behavioural patterns, which bring a greater level of self-awareness.

From the above it can be deduced that one would wish to seek evidence at a number of levels, in order to confirm the model was impacting on recidivism. For a start, it should be apparent that staff members fully understand and are committed to the model of change. Residents should also be aware of how things work. It should be possible to ascertain that residents have engaged in exploration and review of their own offending behaviour from documented evidence that demonstrates they provide expanded accounts of their development history and offence cycle as time goes on. Progress in therapy should be marked by a discernible qualitative difference in insight and understanding of offending and risk factors.

The concept of offence-paralleling behaviours is particularly relevant to examining offending behaviour in the TC. Jones (1997) describes how factors that were present in the build-up and execution of the original offence may well have counterparts in the behaviour expressed in the Community. Residents can display more freely in the TC the characteristic behaviour and attitudes that underlie their offending behaviour. Jones describes the model of establishing links between the relapsing behaviour and patterns of relapse when at liberty as offence-paralleling behaviour. Once identified, the behaviour pattern is explored by the group and alternative strategies for dealing with the behaviour chain collectively identified. The model involves developing links between one's personal history, offending behaviour and current behaviour in the TC.

This implies that staff and residents should have a joint perception of the risk factors for each long-stay resident and be able to make connections with examples of their current behaviour. Auditors would wish to see examples demonstrating that behaviour in different arenas was laterally linked, fed back and explored in different groups. There should be evidence of single-issue tracking across different activities and meetings within the TC.

The quality of delivery audit methodology

Quality of delivery of therapeutic community treatment

As described earlier, the Prison Service began accrediting treatment programmes within the Prison Service, and auditing treatment interventions in the 1990s. As part of this process, and because TCs are a very specialist and complex treatment intervention, in 1999, the HM Prison Service Offending Behaviour Programmes Unit commissioned the national Association of Therapeutic Communities to develop a method of auditing democratic TCs in prisons, as part of their accreditation process; this task was delegated to two members of the Association of Therapeutic Communities who were seen as having some expertise in this field – David Kennard and Jan Lees, one of the authors of this chapter.

TCs are different from cognitive behavioural programmes, which follow a planned or manualized programme, and Kennard and Lees were asked to develop a checklist of standards that could be used to audit prison-based TCs – initially at HMP Grendon (Kennard and Lees 2001). This checklist had to be concrete enough to be objectively assessed, and to be used by a range of independent TC auditors, while at the same time reflecting the working of democratic-analytic TCs, of which the main tenets are:

- The TC environment is the central feature of the therapy, and treatment takes place in large and small groups

- A culture of enquiry, where members – clients or staff – can question any aspect of TC life, and an individual's behaviours and relationships with both staff and other clients are challenged, explored and discussed in order to develop insight and new ways of dealing with challenging situations

- Living and learning – where everything that happens between Community members (clients and staff members), in the course of living and working together is used as a learning opportunity

- Reduction of barriers between staff and client members of the TC, shared decision making and peer participation in each other's treatment and the daily running of the community

- Continual reflexive practice.

It also had to include an aspect specific to prison-based TCs – that the TC makes space for offence-paralleling behaviour and its exploration to occur.

While the authors of the Kennard-Lees Audit Checklist (KLAC) developed an initial checklist of 42 items, in accordance with democratic TC principles, these items were circulated for comments and further suggestions from the national TC field, which resulted in a 60-item version of the KLAC. This was piloted at HMP Grendon in January 2001, to check the items in the checklist, and their scoring – from the standard not being met, to being fully met – were appropriate, and that evidence could be found to validate and corroborate the items and the scoring. As a result of this pilot, the KLAC was reduced to 58 refined items, and instructions for use developed, particularly in relation to the collecting of evidence. This evidence was to be drawn from:

- Written documentation
- Direct observation of community meetings, therapeutic groups, group activities and informal interactions
- Semi-structured group discussions with staff members
- Semi-structured group discussions with client members of the TC.

Guidelines for auditors, on the types of evidence and methods of collection, were drawn up. All of this evidence was to validate the scoring of the items in the checklist, so written documentation evidence included the minutes of meetings, brochures for prospective clients and referrers, the Community rules etc. Direct observation of Community meetings and therapy groups was included to verify the scope and content of issues discussed, how problems are solved, and decisions taken; do discussions take place that encourage client members to learn from everyday living, including informal interactions with staff, etc.? Semi-structured discussions with staff members included questions about management structures and decision making; the handling of conflicts within the staff team, and the staff members' understanding of these; whether staff members can challenge each other and how staff members deal with difficult or challenging client members, etc. Semi-structured discussion with client members included questions about the clients' understanding of the TC, particularly how it helped them address their offence-paralleling behaviour; giving and receiving feedback about their behaviour and problems from other client members; their involvement in the selection of new members of their TC; and how they see their involvement in the management of risk, etc.

It was also hoped that TC principles would inform and influence all aspects of the audit process as well. This is discussed in more detail in the section below on the *Community of Communities*.

Community of Communities

Subsequent to this, and as a development of the KLAC, the Association of Therapeutic Communities, in partnership with the Royal College of

Psychiatrists Research Unit established the Community of Communities quality assurance peer-review audit network, in 2002, with the help of a three-year grant from the Community Fund. This was intended to expand and develop the prison audit process so that it could become generalizable to other types of TCs in other sectors, such as the NHS, and social care. Membership of the network is voluntary and, since the end of the Community Fund grant in January 2005, the main funding source has been subscriptions from members.

This quality network brings together TCs in the UK and abroad, in an annual cycle of systematic, standards-based quality improvement that incorporates both self-review and external peer review. The methods and values underpinning the project mirror the central philosophy of TCs, that is, the belief that responsibility is best promoted through interdependence, but also the notion of empowerment and democratic participation, with all TC members – staff members and clients – being involved in both their own self-review process but also being able to be involved in the peer-review process for other TCs. The review process is conducted in groups, and with the whole community, wherever possible, and there is feedback from the review team at the end of the day, with the possibility of further input from the staff and client members of the TC being audited, so the process is as inclusive as possible.

The explicit service standards, now in their 4th edition (http://www. rcpsych.ac.uk/cru/Ccstandards4thEd.pdf), provide a platform for staff and clients to participate in the evaluation of services, develop external links, share best practice and improve knowledge and skills. These standards are the basis for the self-reviews and external peer reviews. Most standards represent ideal practice and no TC is expected to meet every standard. Evidence of performance and year-on-year change is published annually in local and national reports. Although the process is rigorous and honest, it aims to engage TCs and their staff members and clients in the quality improvement activities, rather than to impose and inspect.

Some of the more prison-specific items in the KLAC were transferred to other parts of the Prison Service Standards for Therapeutic Communities audit document, and the remaining items combined into, initially, the first edition of the Community of Communities Standards and Audit Workbook in 2001 (these standards are revised every year and these revisions are made in consultation with the whole TC field.) The KLAC was also used to inform the development of the Democratic Therapeutic Community Core Model for the Prison Service.

Joint review

In 2004, following the first full audit of the HMP Grendon democratic TCs, the Correctional Services Accreditation Panel accredited a core model for the delivery and management of prison-based democratic TCs, bringing these communities into line with other offender behaviour programmes. In 2004–2005, the What Works in Prisons Unit of HM Prison Service, in partnership with the Royal College of Psychiatrists Research Unit, funded the Community of Communities to integrate the *Service Standards for Therapeutic Communities* (2004) with the Prison Service Audit Guidance Document for Democratic Therapeutic Communities. It also commissioned the development of a joint process of audit and review that would include full membership of the Community of Communities, and engagement in the annual cycle. The joint standards and review methods provide the data for measuring the performance of TCs within the Prison Service against the accredited model and links prison-based democratic TCs with the wider TC world. It engages them in a network of communities in different settings, while recognizing and incorporating the specific requirements of democratic TCs within the prison.

The joint review takes place over two days and is co-ordinated and facilitated by a lead reviewer. Prior to this, each TC will have completed their self-review, involving all client and staff members. The TC then participates in a peer review of a non-prison TC, and a two-day review of their own TC. The peer-review team draws its membership from four sources:

1. non-prison therapeutic communities which are members of the Community of Communities

2. TC specialist

3. prison service representative

4. a psychologist (located within the prison system but not involved in a participating prison-based democratic TC).

The Community of Communities peer review, consisting of the staff and clients from a non-prison TC and a lead reviewer, is the first day of the 2-day audit, and is a dedicated day to explore and discuss elements of Part 1 of the review – those relating to the service standards for the TC itself, and its functioning. The rest of the Prison Service audit team also participate in this day, and observe and/or review records in relation to Part I – the TC specialist, and to Part II – the service standards for the Prison Service democratic TCs – the Prison Service representative and the psychologist. The second day is intended for the Prison Service audit team only, to observe the TC's normal functioning and to meet with staff and clients both individually and in small groups.

The joint reviews must combine the supportive and inclusive Community of Communities process, which necessitates a high degree of openness and self-criticism, with one of inspection and accreditation. The scores and comments are recorded to enable the community to highlight areas of achievement and to identify areas for further development and improvement. In addition, it is important that reports demonstrate improvements year on year. The process requires that the mass of data collected is transformed into numerical ratings of performance. Each community must score 60 per cent or more to be compliant with the model. These scores are published within HM Prison Service and are included in the prisons' key performance targets. Local reports, which contain both numerical data and the free-text opinions of reviewers, are also aggregated across the whole of the prison service and published, as comparisons and overall recommendations, in a national audit report.

This process was then to be rolled out to all prison-based democratic TCs, and this is on-going. In the first year (2004–2005), 13 prison TCs were involved in the process: eleven Communities achieved full accreditation and two were piloting the standards and review methods in preparation for 2005–2006. 2006–2007 should see the first full accreditation of all 15 of the prison democratic TCs within the Prison Service, including HMP Dovegate (four TCs and one assessment unit), HMP Grendon (five TCs and one assessment unit); HMP Gartree Therapeutic Community; HMP Blundeston Therapeutic Community; HMP YOI Aylesbury Therapeutic Community; and the first democratic TC for women, at HMP Send (13 this year (2005–2006), as the assessment units will be piloting the standards and review methods in preparation for full assessment in the 2006–2007 audit).

Performance of the therapeutic community in addressing criminogenic factors and reducing risk of re-offending

In order to audit a TC's performance in addressing criminogenic factors and reducing risk, and thereby have some measure of effectiveness of delivery, a multi-layered approach was adopted. The unifying element of the audit is a case note study of selected residents. It would be impossible to examine the progress made by all members of the Community, so auditors concentrate on a small number of cases. Research suggests that offenders need to spend at least 18 months in a Community before they gain real benefits (Marshall 1997); only those Community members with at least this long in residence are eligible for selection. A number of names from this group are selected at random. It was agreed that this part of the audit should normally be under-taken by an experienced forensic psychologist.

The auditor and the TC are given the names of those residents whose notes will be examined. The task for the auditor is clearly defined as using the case study to review the work of the Community, not to comment on the individual residents' progress – Community confidentiality and anonymity are ensured. Therapy files, probation files and custody files should be assembled for the reviewer to study.

The first stage involves reviewing the case notes and searching for evidence of:

- expansion of the account of offending behaviour as treatment progresses

- expansion of the account of developmental history as treatment progresses

- recognition of offence re-enactment in daily activity

- the identification of criminogenic issues as treatment targets in the assessment/review cycle.

The TC prepares for this part of the audit by spending some time prior to audit highlighting evidence of issues tracked through case notes relating to the cases under review. This is done by marking relevant documents (e.g. individual case files, minutes of reviews, meetings, observation books, staff meeting minutes etc.) If cases are not prepared, the auditor may be unable to complete the review, as they will only have a limited amount of time to gather the evidence that they need to score the standards. A reviewer on behalf of the Community will formulate two main issues of criminogenic and personality pathology that in their judgement has influenced the offending history. Two specific incidents that have taken place during the resident's stay, which in the reviewer's judgement were sufficiently serious or sufficiently congruent with the core criminogenic need as to cause concern and require further exploration, are identified. The aim is to establish whether the incidents identified in the case note study can be tracked across different group settings. The role of the auditor is to examine the cases and assure that appropriate issues have been identified, and that tracking has taken place.

The second stage consists of individual interviews with the residents subject to the review, the purpose being to:

- establish how an individual has experienced the TC regime

- consider how the individual has benefited from being at the TC

- gather evidence as proof that the interviewee understands the main issues to be addressed during therapy in his case

- provide an opportunity for the interviewee to describe the links made between their behaviour in different settings (i.e. does the interviewee recognize the links between offending, developmental history, background and family circumstances in their particular case).

Residents have of course to agree to be interviewed and may refuse to take part in this part of the audit, without recrimination. The process usually takes around 45 minutes and is semi-structured, in that the auditor has a number of topics to cover but can vary or conceptualize the questions in response to the resident.

In the third stage, the auditor interviews a volunteer group of residents, which will include the residents whose case notes have been reviewed. The aim of this stage is to:

- discover how residents believe therapy works

- (for the reviewed cases) establish what the Community residents think are the main issues for that individual

- ascertain how often these issues are manifest in different settings and whether they are taken up in different groups, review meetings and so on

- ask how these issues are related to offending and developmental history, background and family circumstances.

Again, interviews are semi-structured and the auditor/interviewer is allowed to explore specific areas that he or she judges as relevant.

The final stage of the procedure is a staff group interview. A representative multidisciplinary staff group is selected, which should include the facilitators of the groups of the residents identified in the case studies. The auditor's task is to:

- discover how members of the team understand the therapy to work

- examine the cases under review, enquire about core issues and identify familiarity with criminogenic factors for individuals

- consider examples of offence-paralleling behaviour in residents' current behaviour

- enquire how behaviours are exhibited in different activity settings and being taken up and explored in different treatment settings

- ask about how this behaviour is understood in relation to offending history and in relation to developmental history and accounts

- assess the level of knowledge regarding psychopathic behaviour and how this is managed, with reference to tangible examples

- ask about the contribution of the complementary therapies and how these are integrated.

Following these four stages, the auditors then have the task of integrating all the information gathered from all these procedures. They are assisted in this exercise by a checklist, which is scored against defined criteria. But it is vitally important that auditors provide evidence for their ratings from the various sources accessed during the audit. So, for example, in assessing how offence-related risk behaviours are addressed, one would wish to see evidence that both offender and staff groups recognized these, that the individuals themselves were aware of them and that such behaviours were clearly monitored in the case notes and records. Only if all these were in place would the TC fully achieve this criteria.

Auditing in practice

The audit procedures have developed over a number of trials at HMP Grendon. Slight changes were made to the audit criteria during these pilots. The first full audit only occurred in 2003 at Grendon. The CSAP reviewed the audit report and concluded that HMP Grendon was operating broadly as intended. However, record keeping, information sharing, staff training and supervision were highlighted as areas for improvement.

There are undoubtedly still limitations and difficulties with aspects of the Prison Service audit, for example, the need to fully establish inter-rater reliability between the different auditors for all parts of the audit process. The limited sampling of individual cases means the relevant criteria could be erroneously scored, and the resource requirement placed on TCs to produce the paperwork to evidence their work is problematic. There are also issues around making the prison audit feel more positive to the prisons rather than a threatening exercise and producing a better fit between the prison audit requirements and those of the peer review by the *Community of Communities*. Issues were raised about the number of items in the *Quality of programme delivery* section, particularly and their weightings, which is substantially different from that for other programmes. (For more general qualitative feedback about how TC members experience the Community of Communities audit process, see Moffat 2005.)

Future developments

The CSAP annual report for 2002–2003 provided an account of the panel's thinking on the future of audit. This was primarily concerned with structured programmes, but of relevance to the auditing of TCs. One of the issues that concerned members was the apparent absence of any clear association between audit scores and the effectiveness of programmes in terms of reduced reconviction – however, there is a problem here, because of the large time lag between audit and post-treatment outcome. Many prisons were scoring highly on audit, but this was not reflected in follow-up outcome studies. The CASP indicated it was time to review again what the key factors of success were in order to produce an effectiveness audit procedure that looked at the critical variables. It would be important for this to be linked to research. It was vital that audit made it possible to distinguish between theory and implementation failure. It was noted that there was anxiety within the Prison Service about the burden of audit and there were also issues about the feedback of the audit to establishments and practitioners.

These issues, especially the link between audit and reduced recidivism, and the burden of audit very much apply to the TC process and will lead to further refinements in the future. Discussions are already taking place between Community of Communities and the Prison Service to try and reduce the number of items in the standards for TC delivery, and to try and reduce the current 2-day audit process to 1 day, which will combine all aspects of the audit.

Conclusion

There has been considerable progress in the development of the audit process for prison democratic TCs, and much refinement of the Prison Service and Community of Communities standards, and much better integration of the two processes. It has been important that the Community of Communities process has managed to maintain and implement the audits of these prison TCs in line with TC principles and practice. More work remains to be done in:

- integrating both processes
- reducing the burden of work placed on prison democratic TCs by the review process

- Reducing the amount of time taken to actually implement the joint review process

- Integrating better the methods and practices of the two parts of the audit – the Prison Service audit and the Community of Communities peer review audit process.

This work is already in hand, and we are confident it will produce a less onerous process that TCs will enjoy and feel they are active participants in the audit process.

References

Andrews, D.A. and Bonta, J. (2003) *The Psychology of Criminal Conduct*, 3rd edn. Cincinnati: Anderson Publishing Co.

Community of Communities (2004) *Service Standards for Therapeutic Communities.* 3rd edition. London: The Royal College of Psychiatrists' Research Unit. www.rcpsy.ac.uk/crtu/crtu/centreforqualityimprovement/communityofcommunities.aspx

Community of Communities (2006) *Service Standards for Therapeutic Communities.* 5th edition. London: The Royal College of Psychiatrists' Research Unit. www.rcpsy.ac.uk/crtu/crtu/centreforqualityimprovement/communityofcommunities.aspx

Debidin, M. and Lovbakke, J. (2005) Offending behaviour programmes in prison and probation. In G. Harper and C. Chitty (eds) *The Impact of Corrections on Re-offending: a Review of 'What Works'.* London: Home Office Research, Development and Statistics Directorate HORS 291.

Genders, E. and Player, E. (1995) Grendon: a Study of a Therapuetic Prison. London: Clarendon Press.

Hare, R.D., Clark, D., Grann, M., and Thornton, D. (2000) Psychopathy and the predictive validity of the PCL-R: An international perspective. *Behavioral Sciences and the Law, 18,* 623–645.

Harris, G.T., Rice, M.E. and Cornier, C.A. (1994) The effectiveness of therapeutic communities for psychopaths: Therapeutic communities. *International Journal for Therapeutic and Supportive Organizations, 16,* 147–149.

Hobson, J., Shine, J. and Roberts, R. (2000) How do psychopaths behave in a prison therapeutic community? *Psychology, Crime and Law, 6,* 139–154.

Hollin, C. R. (1996) The meaning and implications of ' Programme Integrity'. In J. McGuire. *What Works: Reducing Re-offending.* Chichester: John Wiley and Sons.

Jones, L. (1997) Developing models for managing treatment integrity and efficacy in a prison based TC: The Max Glatt Centre. In E. Cullen, L. Jones, and R. Woodward (eds) *Therapeutic Communities for Offenders.* Chichester: John Wiley & Sons.

Kennard, D. and Lees, J. (2001) A checklist of standards for democratic therapeutic communities. *Therapeutic Communities, 22,* 143–151.

Lipsey, M. (1992) Juvenile delinquency treatment. A meta-analytic into variability effects. In T. Cook, H. Cooper, D. Corday *et al.* (eds) *Meta-analysis for explanation: A Casebook.* New York: Russell Sage Foundation.

Marshall, P. (1997) *A Reconviction Study for HMP Grendon.* London: Home Office.

Moffat, J. (2005), Experiencing the Community of Communities review process: Views of therapeutic community. *Therapeutic Communities, 26,* 4.

Quay, H. C. (1987) Institutional treatment. In H. C. Quay (ed.) *Handbook of Juvenile Delinquency.* New York: John Wiley & Sons.

Shine, J. and Morris, M. (1999) *Regulating Chaos: The Grendon Programme. Grendon Underwood.* Bucks: Springhill Press.

Conclusion

The reforms initiated for a period of four years by Captain McConochie, who changed Norfolk Island Penal Colony from a barbarous regime with severe physical punishment into a regime where men could earn the right, in return for good behaviour, to join a small group and farm small areas of land from 1840–1844 illustrated that it was possible for men to alter their behaviour if the environment allowed it and consciously tried to facilitate change.

More recently, in March 2004, the Correctional Services Accreditation Panel granted Democratic Therapeutic Communities status as accredited regimes to help reduce re-offending in the prison service. Grendon is no longer an 'experimental prison' as described in the East and Hubert report of 1939 but a regime that has a clear research base on the strength of which Dovegate Therapeutic Community was established and is now flourishing and others at Aylesbury, Gartree, Blundeston and Send have been set up to include women and young offenders.

The concept *dynamic security* does not originate in the world of therapy or therapeutic communities (TCs) but was drawn together by Ian Dunbar, based on his exploration of the American and Swedish Prison Services in the 1980s. It points to what is a timeless value: being close enough to and talking with the prisoner population that prison staff members know what prisoners are thinking and what their concerns are within the establishment. It encompasses the concept, 'duty of care', but serves two purposes: that of ensuring the circumstances of men, women and young offender prisoners are properly understood and also as a means of developing accurate security within the establishment to ensure an underlying bedrock of personal safety for those within it. Prisons are only ever really governed with the consent of the prisoners governed and the balance between order and disorder is a 'continually re-negotiated state' (Sparks *et al.* 1996). This continual re-negotiation, dialogue and debate should very much be the state of play in a typical prison TC, but there are arguments that it should be the case more widely. To ignore this dynamic aspect of security in prison runs the risk of a slide into psychological splitting and the creation of a division between staff and prisoners with all the potential for the projection of irritation, hostility, blame and at worst brutalization to generate within the divide created and for dehumanization that splits readily promote to develop into conflict-ridden reality.

Democratic TCs in prison appear to be useful for a wide range of men, women and young offenders who want to change their behaviour and understand what makes them behave in the way they do and grasp the effect they in their turn have had on others. These Communities also seem able to help some who enter them cynically or without an idea of why they do so. Some of the recent success in TC work may lie in the efforts made to work with all departments more closely: security, education, work and programmes, rather than as an isolated regime delivered separately from the rest of the service.

There are concerns about as well as praise for what TCs do, namely, that some prisoners, the more fragile or psychopathic, appear to run the risk of being made worse by exposure to the challenge required in the process of therapy. Some degree of selection is necessary on ethical grounds to try to prevent harm to those we know might suffer from the process of therapy themselves or because of the harm they may do to others. The issues raised in Chapter 20 concerning the fact that some TCs may score highly on audit but not have a correspondingly high success rate in reducing re-conviction need attention and this must be work to attend to in the future.

TCs do appear to have become a microcosm within which aspects of life previously neglected can be improved and in which degrees of pro-social modelling can replace disturbed or abusive earlier life experience: this is certainly their intention. They are part idealistic, part rigorous regimes of challenge and change; part places of support, understanding and containment and part places in which to reflect and think about the distress that may have shaped women's or men's lives. What characterizes prison TCs is a level of tolerance of conflict and lively, sometimes intense or at times uncomfortable debate. Challenges to staff and their attitudes and behaviour can be difficult but are a core part of the process, if warranted, and if staff behave in a way that warrants challenge this is not always easy. When we think of the traumatic disorder many prisoners have faced in their own lives it is no surprise that it tends to reproduce itself within the prison environment but it may not necessarily be what is actually wanted. In the words of one man to me on A-Wing at Grendon in 2001:

> We all do it, we all keep up a hard man front, we have to, because if we don't we'll get crushed. We don't want to, though, not always. There's hundreds of us out there [in the Prison System] who are dying to find some peace and security for once in their lives but we're never going to be the first to say so, it's too dangerous, our fellow cons'll think we're soft and then we'll get hammered. (Personal Communication)

We might like to hope that in the Prison Service in general it is possible to bear this wish, possibly hidden behind so many hard fronts, seriously in mind and be able to think and see beyond the front as often as possible both in the TC world and in the daily life of prison.

Reference

Sparks, R., Bottoms, A. and Hay, W. (1996) *Prisons and the Problem of Order.* Oxford: Clarendon Press.

The Contributors

Peter Bennett is Governor of HMP Grendon and holds a PhD in Social Anthropology. He has had a long interest in Grendon as a therapeutic community and what makes it work. His recent work at Grendon has focussed on joining security with therapy in order to ensure a safe environment in which therapy can take place.

Dennie Briggs is a Clinical Psychologist and worked with Maxwell Jones at Dingleton Hospital, retaining a personal friendship with him for most of his working life. He developed a therapeutic community for offenders at Chino in California in the 1970s which ran for five years and has spent time chronicling the ideas and thinking of Maxwell Jones in several publications in the Planned Environment Therapy Trust archives.

Leonidas Cheliotis holds an MPhil and is currently studying for a PhD in criminology at the Institute of Criminology, University of Cambridge. In 2007, he begins a Lectureship in Criminology at the University of Kent at Canterbury.

Danny Clark is a Forensic Psychologist who worked for many years in the Prison Service. He is currently Head of Offending Behaviour Programmes at the Home Office, National Probation Directorate. Danny was formerly a member of the Correctional Services Accreditation Panel and was instrumental in creating the Audit procedure for democratic therapeutic communities in the UK together with members of the Community of Communities.

Jo Day is a Principal Forensic Psychologist who has worked at HMP Grendon and is currently working in the National Probation Directorate involved in projects to develop quality assurance and evaluation of offending behaviour group work programmes delivered in the community.

Ronald Doctor is a Consultant Psychiatrist, Consultant Psychotherapist and a Psychoanalyst and worked in the Max Glatt Therapeutic Community in HMP Wormwood Scrubbs when it was open.

John Gunn is Emeritus Professor of Forensic Psychiatry at Kings College, London. He is immediate Past Chairman of the Faculty of Forensic Psychiatry in the Royal College of Psychiatrists and conducted research into the effect the therapeutic community work undertaken at Grendon had on men in treatment in the 1970s.

Brian Hirons is Governor of Security at Grendon Prison and has previously worked at HMPYOI Aylesbury. He has an interest in security and how this aspect of prison service work can be combined with prison craft and therapeutic community work.

David Jones is Consultant Adult Psychotherapist in Forensic Psychiatry, East London and City NHS Trust, and has worked with police staff and with traumatized refugees. He formerly led the Assessment Unit at the therapeutic prison, HMP Grendon. He has edited two books, *Working With Dangerous People* and *The Psychotherapy of Violence and Humane Prisons*.

Jan Lees is a Therapeutic Community Therapist and Researcher at Francis Dixon Lodge Therapeutic Community in Leicester. She is also a Therapeutic Community Consultant to the Community of Communities peer-review quality assurance project, with special responsibility for prison-based democratic therapeutic communities; a member of the Editorial Collective of the Therapeutic Communities journal; and co-editor with Rex Haigh of the Community, Culture and Change (formerly Therapeutic Communities) series with Jessica Kingsley.

Kevin Leggett is Governor at HMYOI Huntercombe and prior to this was Deputy Governor at Grendon Prison for five years. He holds the Cambridge University Masters in Applied Criminology and Management and has an interest in combining security in an integrated way with prison and therapeutic work.

Alan Miller is a Forensic Psychologist and is currently Therapy Manager of the Assessment and Resettlement Unit at HMP Dovegate Therapeutic Community. He has worked at HMP Dovegate since 2001.

Mark Morris is a Consultant Psychiatrist, Consultant Psychotherapist and a Psychoanalyst. He worked at HMP Grendon as Director of Therapy between 1998 and 2003 and has worked as a Consultant at the Portman Clinic, London. He is currently Consultant Psychiatrist at Kneesworth House, Hertfordshire.

Liz McLure is a Group Analyst and works independently. She has been a group therapist at Grendon for a number of years and has an interest in writing about therapy work and its impact on the therapist.

Judy Mackenzie is a Psychiatrist and Psychotherapist. She has specialized in Therapeutic Communities in prisons for over 25 years, initiating two for young offenders. She is currently therapy manager for Gartree TC and psychiatrist to the TC at Dovegate.

Shadd Maruna is Reader in Criminology at Belfast University and in 2001 won the American Society of Criminology's Award for most outstanding contribution to criminology. He has contributed to criminology in exploring offenders' narratives: stories about their own lives linked closely with the work undertaken in therapy of making sense of offenders' lives from their subjective experience explored in therapy.

Joseph Murray is a British Academy Postdoctoral Fellow at the Institute of Criminology, University of Cambridge, where he received his PhD.

Tim Newell OBE was Governor of Grendon prison for ten years. He has written about therapeutic community work and retains an active interest in work with offenders, with Lifers and with Restorative Justice Projects in the Thames Valley Region.

Jim Ormsby is a Consultant Psychiatrist and works in the Regional Forensic Psychiatry Unit at Fareham in Hampshire. He provided invaluable help to the staff team of the emerging women's therapeutic community at HMP West Hill and supported its development there.

Michael Parker is Director of Therapy in HMP Send, the first women's democratic therapeutic community in prison in the UK. He is a Group Analyst and Clinical Supervisor at the Institute of Group Analysis, London and holds the Cambridge University Masters in Applied Criminology and Management.

Richard Shuker is a Forensic Psychologist and has worked as a Wing Forensic Psychologist at Grendon. He currently works as head of Research and Development at Grendon.

Caroline Stewart is a Clinical Psychologist and Head of Research and Development in the Women's Team at Prison Service Headquarters. She has actively promoted the establishment of the first women's therapeutic community in prison from its early days.

Teresa Wood is Therapy Manager of the male Young Offenders Therapeutic Community in HMP Aylesbury. She is a Forensic Psychologist and has an active interest in combined psychotherapy and cognitive psychology approaches to her work with young offenders.

Roland Woodward is Director of Therapy at Dovegate democratic therapeutic community, the first privately run prison therapeutic community in the UK. He is a Forensic Psychologist and has worked at HMP Grendon and was subsequently responsible for starting the first therapeutic community for lifers at HMP Gartree.

The men and women prisoners in therapy have made vital contributions to this book but wish to retain their anonymity and this will be respected here by making no reference to names that might identify them or identify them to potential victims.

Subject Index

Author Index

Adshead, G. 106
Agnew, R. 31
Allen, J. 100
Andrews, D. 104, 120, 121, 142, 257, 259
Applebaum, P. 40
Arlow, J. 173, 174
Arseneault, L. 40

Baker, A. 190, 191
Bandura, A. 50, 142
Bateman, A. 106, 116, 120, 153–4, 175
Bentovim, A. 196
Berk, R.A. 32
Bion, W.R. 151, 154, 174
Birtles, J. 224
Blud, L. 100
Blum, H. 174, 175
Bonta, J. 120, 121, 142, 257, 259
Bottoms, A. 24n, 124
Bowlby, J. 26
Box, S. 32
Briggs, D. 90, 92
Brofenbrenner, U. 23
Buber, M. 185
Bursik, R.J. 31
Butler, T. 190

Campbell Le Fevre, D. 173, 174
Campbell, D. 196
Campling, P. 78, 225
Casement, P. 128
Caspi, A. 32
Chasseguet Smirgel, J. 177
Cheliotis, L.K. 33
Chiricos, T.G. 31
Clark, D. 100, 101–2
Clarke, R.V.G. 52
Cohen, D. 175
Coid, J. 39, 41
Cordess, C. 13, 115
Cornish, D.B. 52
Cox, M. 13, 115
Crighton, D.A. 100
Cullen, E. 41, 65, 103, 116–17

Debidin, M. 255
Derzon, J.H. 27
Dodge, K.A. 27
Doehrman, M. 129
Driver, C. 123–4
Dunbar, I. 233–4, 271
Duncan, S. 190, 191
Dutton, D. 191

East, W.N. 62–5, 189
Eliot, T.S. 186
Etchegoyen, R.H. 162, 165
Eysenck, H.J. 53–4, 100
Eysenck, S.B.G. 100

Fabiano, E.A. 51
Farrell, M. 38
Farrington, D.P. 25, 26, 27, 28, 30, 32, 158
Felson, M. 30
Fergusson, D.M. 26, 29
Fliess, W. 162
Fonagy, P. 116, 120
Foulkes, S.H. 64, 120
Freud, S. 106, 162, 164
Freudenberger, H.J. 155
Fuller, G. 130–1

Gabbard, G.O. 154
Galsworthy, John, 145
Gandhi, M. 183
Ganzarain, R. 174
Garcia-Buñuel, Leonardo 86, 87
Gartner, R.B. 174
Gebhard, P. 191
Genders, E. 67, 102, 204, 223, 260
Giordano, P.C. 31
Glueck, E. 27, 48
Glueck, S. 48
Gluecks, S. 27
Golding, W. 110
Goldman, J. 192
Grace, C. 100
Gramsick, H.G. 31
Grinberg, L. 130, 197–8
Grubin, D. 189

Haigh, R. 102
Hanson, R.K. 99
Hare, R.D. 258
Harris, J. 100
Hart, S. 191

Hawkins, P. 116
Heimer, K. 31
Hemmings, M. 224
Her Majesty's Inspectorate of Prisons 42
Her Majesty's Prison Service 119, 138
Herbert, M. 156
Hinshelwood, R.D. 106, 225
Hirschi, T. 26, 29
HM Prison Service & NHS Executive 41
Hobson, J. 258
Hodgins, S. 40
Hollin, C. 49, 54, 72, 81
Hollin, C.R. 256
Holmes, J. 154
Home Office 142
Hopkins, S. 173
Horney, J. 29, 30
Horvath, A.O. 156
Hubert, de B. 189

Inciardi, J.A. 33

Jeffery, C.R. 49
Johnson, Spencer 224
Jones, L. 101–2, 117, 191, 260
Juby, H. 26

Kemshall, H. 142
Kennard, D. 261–2
Kennedy, H. 70
Kernberg, O. 175
Klein, M. 106, 154, 168
Kohlberg, L. 157

Land, K.C. 32
Laub, J.H. 26, 29, 30, 31, 32, 33, 34
Lee, H. 31
Lees, J. 261–2
Lewin, K. 174
Lewis, P. 115
Lipsey, M. 99, 255
Lipsey, M.W. 27
Livesey, W.J. 153
Lloyd, C. 100
Loeber, R. 25, 158
Losel, F. 99
Lovbakke, J. 255
Lundin, S. 224